I Am . . .

I am...

Biblical Women Tell Their Own Stories

Athalya Brenner

Fortress Press
Minneapolis

not A/F
free

I AM . . .
Biblical Women Tell Their Own Stories

Unless otherwise stated, all Bible translations are the author's own.
   Scripture marked NJPS are from the TANAKH: The New Jewish Publication Society Translation according to the Traditional Hebrew Text copyright © 1985 by the Jewish Publication Society. Used by permission.
   Scripture marked RSV is from the Revised Standard Version of the Bible, copyright © 1946, 1952, 1971 by the Division of Christian Education of the National Council of the Churches of Christ in the USA. Used by permission.
   Scripture marked NRSV are from the New Revised Standard Version Bible, copyright © 1989 by the Division of Christian Education of the National Council of the Churches of Christ in the USA and used by permission.

Cover and book design: Zan Ceeley
Cover art: *Nightswimming* by Graham Dean. ©Graham Dean/CORBIS. Used by permission.

         Library of Congress Cataloging-in-Publication Data
Brenner, Athalya.
   I am . . . : biblical women tell their own stories / Athalya Brenner.
      p. cm.
   Includes index.
   ISBN 0-8006-3665-1
   1. Women in the Bible—Fiction. 2. Autobiographical fiction. 3. Bible. O.T.—History of Biblical events—Fiction. I. Title.
   PR9510.9.B74I52 2004
   221.9'22—dc22
                                         2004014294

The paper used in this publication meets the minimum requirements of American National Standard for Information Sciences — Permanence of Paper for Printed Library Materials, ANSI Z329.48-1984.

Manufactured in the U.S.A.
09   08   07   06   05   1   2   3   4   5   6   7   8   9   10

For a Magnificent Seven,

in this or any other order:

Toni Craven	*(Fort Worth)*
Charlotte Faber	*(Amstelveen)*
Neel Korteweg	*(Amsterdam)*
Edna Krause	*(Bat Shlomo)*
Miri Kubovy	*(Boston/Jerusalem)*
Naomi Leeran	*(Tel Aviv)*
Ruth Stadler	*(Haifa)*

אֶת הַמַּנְגִּינָה הַזֹּאת...
אִי אֶפְשָׁר לְהַפְסִיק,
אֶת הַמַּנְגִּינָה הַזֹּאת
אִי אֶפְשָׁר לְהַפְסִיק,
מֻכְרָחִים לְהַמְשִׁיךְ לְנַגֵּן
מֻכְרָחִים לְהַמְשִׁיךְ לְנַגֵּן,
מִפְּנֵי שֶׁאֶת הַמַּנְגִּינָה הַזֹּאת
אִי אֶפְשָׁר לְהַפְסִיק...
כְּמוֹ נֵבֶל גָּדוֹל בְּעַל אֶלֶף מֵיתָרִים
שֶׁמְּנַגֵּן וּמְנַגֵּן וּמְנַגֵּן,
וּכְפַעַם בְּפַעַם פּוֹקֵעַ מֵיתָר
וּמַמְשִׁיכִים לְנַגֵּן עַל מֵיתָר אֶחָד פָּחוֹת,
וְעוֹד מֵיתָר אֶחָד פָּחוֹת
וּמֵיתָרִים פָּקְעוּ וְלֹא חָזְרוּ
חֶלְקָם חָזְרוּ וְיַמְשִׁיכוּ לְנַגֵּן
מִפְּנֵי שֶׁאֶת הַמַּנְגִּינָה הַזֹּאת
אִי אֶפְשָׁר לְהַפְסִיק,
מֻכְרָחִים לְהַמְשִׁיךְ לְנַגֵּן...

This tune, it can't be stopped
This tune, it can't be stopped
Must continue playing,
Must continue playing,
Because
This tune, it can't be stopped . . .
And every so often, a string snaps;
And you continue playing, less one string,
And less one more string;
And strings snap and don't come back,
and some came back, and will continue playing,
because . . .

From "Must Continue Playing," lyrics by Oded Feldman, and tune by
Yair Rosenblum (Text © Oded Feldman)

Contents

Preface

*T*his book grew out of some discontents that emerged over several years of regular academic work in biblical studies—more specifically, in feminist critique as applied to biblical studies. In this preface I'd like to trace these discontents and the concerns that promoted this project, together with some other relevant issues.

As is usual for me, the idea was initiated by conversations with friends. To begin with, I tried my discontents on out-of-guild patient and supportive woman friends in disciplines other than biblical studies. I was hoping that distance would make them understand my concerns better, perhaps, than dedicated bible scholars would.

[Re]reading the Bible

I complained to my friends that I was suffering from a malaise: an increasing mistrust of the many critics, and readers, who are devoted to the engrossing task of understanding the bible "as it was." This is a highly regarded scholarly pastime. Scholars who do so get prizes, as did James Kugel with his book *The Bible as It Was*. Paradoxically, scholars and other readers invest much energy in reconstructing an implied audience, an implied milieu, an implied culture, an implied religion, an implied theology, an implied author with which to understand biblical texts—not only for the past but especially for their own time and place and creed. This has been and to an extent still is considered true scholarship and a worthwhile if mostly unrewarding pursuit. Its results are the academic rewritings and updating of the biblical texts, which are laudable. What is not so great is the claim for authenticity—about the past on the way to the contemporaneous present—that is the name of the exercise.

Au contraire, I often think to myself, hardly daring to whisper my doubts to my guild colleagues. What if we disregarded such a pursuit by somewhat suspending this kind of inevitable curiosity about the past, if we temporarily suspended our desire for history (to acquire certainty, identity, roots imagined or otherwise, as well as to differentiate between our own "superior" culture to more "primitive" or "strange" earlier ones)? What would biblical narratives look like if reread confessedly and unashamedly with modern and postmodern concerns in mind, openly emphasizing concerns voiced by contemporary bible and literature scholars instead of guesses about "original" intentions and conditions? Such contemporary concerns might include issues of readership as well as authorship, but a different kind of authorship than looked for by "classical" bible scholarship, for instance. Or concerns of literary theory, such as narratology, which seeks to place characters and action in fiction (the bible is fiction, is it not?) in a way that will enhance our understanding and enjoyment of it as well as the world outside fiction? Or a focus on gaps and gap filling, which excavates what is *not* in a text in order to point out how readers construct and reconstruct what they read according to their needs, requirements, and personal imagination? Or the links between nationalism on the one hand, and group and individual identity on the other hand? Or the connections linking religion, sex, and war in light of recent world events? Or ethnicity and its ambiguities? Or history and historiography, and how we look at the past in order to comprehend the present and to create the future? And, ultimately, feminism and liberation from oppression—or, more specifically, "Third World"-inspired liberation theology. What would happen, in short, if we turned the tables and retold a biblical story, using our own intellectual and scholarly tools while openly voicing our own concerns rather than desperately alleging exposure of the implied biblical author's intentions in a less-than-distinctly-specified past?

[Re]writing the Bible

This cluster of questions concerning "the bible as it was" and academic *[re]reading* of biblical texts is one cluster I've been thinking about recently. Another one is the nature of academic *[re]writing* of biblical texts, or—in other words—the presentation of bible reading (fondly labeled "research"). In academic writing there are generally accepted ground rules that must be observed and obeyed, technicalities that must be adhered to if one's work is to be taken seriously by peers and students. Academic style in the humanities and social studies entails an intricate subtext of notes, appendixes, excursuses, bibliographies, and so on that contains documentation, that is, references to primary and secondary sources. The scholarly text itself is, thankfully, not required to pretend to be "objective" anymore, but a certain amount of detachment—reserve, really—is still expected and praised. Postmodern credos allow for viewpoints and personal situations up to a degree. And yet, and nevertheless, even postmodern scholarship is indecisive about too much undisguised involvement. At least a degree of impersonalization seems to be appropriate to academic writing. Therefore, let's face it: much academic writing tends to be dull to the point of dryness, often incomprehensible to those uninitiated into a given discipline, thus inaccessible to many.

Furthermore, academic writing is considered by most of its practitioners and consumers as not only distinct from but also privileged over narrative fiction writing. There's a mystique of accountability attached to the former, a mystique of imaginative creativity and artistic license attached to the latter. In truth, though, much academic discourse is as imaginative and intuitive as to raise conventional eyebrows, once respect is overcome; much fiction requires prior thorough research. But the claims made for both and for either, and the style, are supposed to differ. Nevertheless, as so many non-scholarly rewritings of biblical materials evidence—be they narrative or poetic fiction, visual art images, plays, films, and so on, not to even mention at this stage religious midrash*—they may contain interpretations that update the scriptures for their own authors in much the same fashions and for similar purposes used by bible scholars and theologians, past and present.

Midrash being originally a Hebrew term referring to the retelling and updating of biblical texts by ancient Jewish sages; more recently, it has acquired the more general meaning of "retelling," at times used pejoratively and at times used neutrally or consciously.

Accessibility and Personal Solutions

What to do, then, to sidestep the trap of imaging the past for its own sake and to overcome the oft-tiring nature of academic discourse, as well as to promote accessibility of one's rethinking on biblical texts and topics? Some years ago Gideon Bar Emun, an Israeli friend who lives in Amsterdam, said to me, "Your work and the work of other feminist critics in your field are hardly accessible to anyone outside your guild. Why don't you write something more popular, fiction maybe, so that the ideas you and your ilk are proposing would become better known? Write short stories, or a novel, do a bestseller," he said, "instead of splitting hairs in didactic manifestos for a limited elite." (Incidentally, he added, I may find myself making money out of my writing, for a change.)

In response, I produced a dismissive waiver. "My training," I said, "is academic. I can't write fiction." And of course, as this book amply shows, this is true. But this chance remark helped me clarify my discontent into a license to try to reach out, beyond the usual text/footnote-excursus-bibliography-subtext structure, into a median form, something a little different in style, a hybrid between academic content and non-academic—almost fictional, certainly bastard—style.

At this point I took an additional clue from the emerging trend of self-consciously biographical and autobiographical criticism—more precisely from autobiographical criticism as practiced by a few in the biblical guild in recent years. More specifically still, several years ago Philip Davies (of Sheffield Academic Press/Continuum) and the late Robert Carroll (of Glasgow University) had the idea of taking autobiographical criticism further in biblical studies by editing a volume of fictitious autobiographical essays. Each contributor to that volume was assigned a biblical figure whose story she or he would [re]tell in the first-person mode. The volume, edited by Davies, finally appeared after Carroll's untimely death under the title *First Person: Essays in Biblical Autobiographical Criticism* (2002). The invitation to write for that volume unleashed the exciting option of attempting an as-if, (hopefully) lighter-written academic discourse. Chapter 5 in this book (on Rahab) is a revised version of an article I wrote for *First Person*. That article, written five years ago, was one of the beginnings for the present volume. It was easier to experiment with other "autobiographies" after writing that one. And it seemed like an [un]natural extension of the project started over a decade ago, with the late Fokkelien van Dijk-Hemmes, in *On Gendering Texts: Female and Male Voices in the Hebrew Bible* (1993). In that book we tried to diagnose and to define gendered biblical "voices," that is, the abstracted notions of biblical texts' gender provenance. The questions we posed then were, with regard to specific texts: Whose text is it anyway? Could this or the other biblical text, especially one that deals with a woman figure, contain traces of female concerns, so that it can be (theoretically at least) gendered as a possible female "voice," or vice versa for male "voices"? Taking it one step further for female figures and female "voices," this volume literally—in both senses of the word—allows certain biblical female figures a first-person, autobiographical voice.

This exercise, this mode of bastard/hybrid but ultimately still an academic [re]writing of sorts, certainly involves taking liberties. It is licentious, lighter, and playful, also a gimmick, yes, but certainly not intended as frivolous and not lacking gravity. Scholarly conventions remain: an "autobiography" of a biblical character implies an attempt to imagine an implied author, albeit in transparent guise and in a brazenly different manner. Textual and other sources, primary and secondary, are still used and acknowledged, again differently. The literary device of an autobiography is clearly artificial and false, not to be taken too seriously; and yet, not everything goes. The fantasy reconstruction of biblical lives has to be informed, if not by a thorough knowledge of the past then at least by proper critical praxis. And the style, yes the style, has to be a little more entertaining.

No claims for "truth," or privileged information, are attempted here. I confess to not at all knowing "the bible as it was." The implied, cheeky claims of omniscient knowledge that underlie the autobiographical literary convention are, in the present case, an experimental device for enlivening presentation.

Framing the Subjects

To make this adoption of semi-fictive, fictitious [re]writing into the scholarly realm a little more palatable even to readers who self-consciously practice suspended disbelief, I've chosen to tell the partly known, yet rarely complete biographies of biblical female persons who do not die in the text—that is, no mention is made of their death and burial, hence they have been made immortal by the same text that doesn't pay them the tribute of decently and naturally disposing of them. Those persons are, in this book, female figures. This is an arbitrary personal choice made simply because, as a feminist critic, female figures intrigue me more than their male counterparts, about whom more is known or has been [re]written throughout the centuries, in scholarly discourse and in fiction. In order to make those "women" contemporaneous and accessible to each other, I bring them together, so to speak, into one location at one time (roughly the present), so that they can tell their stories—imagined yet deeply rooted in the biblical text as well as in selectively chosen chapters of canonical and reception history—to each other, as if they are delivering a paper at a quasi-academic conference (complete with a focused, round-table discussion at the end of the proceedings).

Choices, Modes, Methods

Each chapter (speech/"story") has at least one central methodological, theoretical, or ideological issue that is covertly explored in it. The chapters may differ with regard to the specific primary and secondary sources explored in each—once again, the choice of sources explored is personal and arbitrary—while some subtexts and sources are common to all.

A common dual-stranded subtext in my work is (1) my wish to establish panchronic intercultural connections in and beyond the bible and its immediate cultural environs in Judeo-Christian reception; and (2) as an Israeli, to foreground the [re]writing/ [re]reading of biblical materials in twentieth-century Zionist/ Hebrew/Israeli culture as a predominant cultural agent, a means for remembering the past in order to re-member the future and create icons of personal and collective identities, a process which was and is an integral if not always cherished part of my own life.

Some of the female figures/figurations that deliver autobiographical papers in this book are popular among bible readers to the point of being used as life models and cultural hero[in]es; others are seldom mentioned outside religious institutions or bible classes. While my choice of "speakers" was dictated by their textual non-death to begin with, particular choices were by and large motivated—again arbitrarily—by my personal dis/likes and scholarly subtexts, as well as by the wish to give voice to the more "silent" figures.

Two examples of the rationale for joining popular together with less popular female figures' stories will suffice here, one of a biblical narrative with well-known female figures and another of lesser-known ones. As an example of the first category, Ruth and Naomi are popular, and there have been many attempts, in scholarly discourse and in fiction, music, and other arts, to interpret their story and relationship with one another. However, much less attention has been paid to Naomi's other daughter-in-law, Orpah, who gets excised out of the biblical story—and of most readers' living memory—as soon as she leaves the other two women on the way to Bethlehem. In this book's first-person accounts, all three of them give their own versions, in their own "voices," Rashomon-style, even though and because Orpah has no personal voice in the biblical story beyond kissing Naomi goodbye. In this example, then, popular figures are heard together with a less popular one. In the second example, Lamech's wives, Adah and Zillah, are seldom studied as culture hero[in]es—even though they are presented as the literary prototype of the "two women married to one man," and they are mothers of culture-founding sons. Their tiny biblical story—nevertheless containing the genesis of bigamy and of art/culture—is intriguing and can be understood or imaged further by recourse to Jewish rabbinic midrash on the one hand, semantics and philology on the other hand, and, also, the cultural history of music and of birth control. Thus, a minimal and disused biblical story may be more productive for retelling than, say, a well-known story whose features have been ossified by repetition, representation, and convention. Moreover, the feminist convention of centering the marginalized or liminal at the expense of the already-centered is partial motivation for taking up Adah and Zillah's [non]story.

One of my intense personal pleasures in writing this book has been the drawing on and extensive rewritings of my previous research, done according to the regular academic rules, on some biblical female figures. Variations in approach or, conversely, the insistence on or the upholding of previous results—at times twenty years after the original publication—while transforming them into this book's style, represented an in-retrospect trajectory of personal growth and change. Extensively revised and transformed traces of previously published materials are to be found in the chapters voicing Madam Potiphar (chapter 3); Rahab, as already mentioned (chapter 5); Ruth, Orpah, and Naomi (chapter 6); Tamar and Tamar (chapter 8); Huldah (chapter 10); Shulammit (chapter 11); and The Convener (chapter 12).

Various sources of interpretation are taken up in individual chapters, such as media representations of literary renderings, and especially (in keeping with my overall second subtext), literature written in Hebrew during the twentieth century. Scholarly commentary, in particular feminist criticism of the Hebrew bible, is at the background throughout, as well as Jewish bible interpretation (such as Targum, midrash, Mishnah, talmud, medieval commentators). In the spirit of my wish for change in academic writing, and at a price for convenience, neither notes nor indices are offered. Rather, for the academically minded, a list of primary and secondary sources by chapter is presented at the book's end.

Midrash?

Toward the end of writing, I was asked to present this book at our monthly staff research seminar of Religious Studies at the University of Amsterdam. One of the questions raised at that meeting was, Do I and in what way might I consider my work different from the neo-midrash written by contemporary feminists, particularly by Jewish feminists? Jewish feminists, especially American ones, have espoused and expanded this ancient Jewish literary form, have in fact appropriated its techniques and updated it for their own needs of self-support, empowering, re-adoption, and consumption of scriptures in an edible manner.

On the one hand, and in keeping with my academic concerns as stated, in many instances I can detect no *fundamental* differences between the motivation for and process of feminist midrash on the one hand and scholarly writings on the other hand. But differences there are, of course: in the aspirations, be they conscious or otherwise, and in the results. Both processes use past materials in order to create new readings for interested parties. If more responsibility is often claimed for scholarly interpretations (that is, [re]writing), closer meta-investigation may prove such a claim suspect and in certain cases refutable. In that sense, once neo-midrash makes no claims for being anything else but what it is, in my view it may be scholarly, responsible, and beneficial. I hope this is what I've done here. But furthermore, I neither wish to psychologize biblical female figures' inner lives, nor have a claim on elaborating details of their physical environments, modes of dress, or similar details, which have turned out to be hallmarks of neo-midrash, undoubtedly re-imagining and re-creating biblical females in a manner more comprehensible to contemporary readers. Also, I do not wish to reclaim those figures as exemplary life models, nor is my approach confessional in any way—once again, widespread hallmarks of neo-midrash. On the contrary, my approach is utterly "secular." What I've tried to do is to ameliorate these biblical figures' obscurity and loneliness by providing them with continuous life and cultural connections—to semantic, etymological, semiotic, literary, visual, and other links—that are perhaps less usual in contemporary neo-midrash than in the present work. Let me re-emphasize the obvious, though: as a matter of course I do hark back to the same materials that neo-midrashists (and recently also biblical scholars) explore, and I similarly reappropriate Jewish and other midrash for my own purpose to, in E. M. Forster's famous motto from *Passage to India,* "Only connect." And then again, in a postmodern sense and much like neo-midrash, I try not to privilege any source of auxiliary material over others. In sum, therefore, I guess that bible scholars may look down their noses at this book and read it as a midrash, perhaps derisively, whereas neo-midrashists may read it as a failed midrash, shackled by the weight of too much academic training.

Reading This Book

How would I like *you* to read this book, then? Technically and preferably, with a bible in your other hand. I've tried to reproduce the relevant biblical story in each case, either by quoting in translation or by a "straight" retelling, before taking matters further.

However, consulting the original will perhaps remind the reader of the literary "facts"—and with pleasure, I hope, recognizing first and foremost the light seriousness of the exercise, of this tongue-in-cheek experiment, with or without the references to the sources and on any or every level of profundity. Let me stress once again that no claim for any "truth" is made here whatsoever. Let me duck under the usual cover: similarities to actual persons or events are just that. But claims for resizing, rethinking academic writing as well as retelling Hebrew bible female figures' stories are certainly attempted.

The device of fictitious autobiographical telling is my choice for this book. It is an admittedly artificial device. But hopefully, in order to make scholarship (and I'm well aware of the criticisms that may come my way for calling this exercise "scholarship") accessible beyond its limited designated audience, other devices may be enlisted. This is a postmodern prerogative. Let's pick it up.

Athalya Brenner
Haifa/Amsterdam

Introduction:
Prior to Touchdown

As we're approaching the helipad—we shall take off soon—I'm not at all at ease. Not at all. I feel as if I'm traveling in reverse. My confidence is ebbing instead of flowing forth, after all these months of preparations. The whole idea seems to lose its charm. I'm asking myself: What are you doing, and with this major dental job waiting to be tackled as soon as you get back? What in Yhwh's name are you doing?

In truth, I should be feeling excitement and anticipation. In the photographed brochure, which I peep into as it stares back at me from my satellite-connected notebook computer lying on my lap, the island we're heading to looks breathtaking, absolutely magnificent, wonderful (do excuse the Americanisms). A correct mixture of green and other vibrant colors. Pleasingly, remote enough, yet nevertheless inviting. Sun, sea, and sand, good surfing and other physical activities doable if you're so inclined. Lots of opportunities for sunbathing, passive self-pampering, and relaxation, otherwise. Vegetation in the right proportions, artificially planted for the most part to resemble "nature" but tasteful. The helicopter is stable, the pilot an experienced woman; flying is natural to her (and soon I'll explain this naturalness), therefore ostensibly nothing for me to worry about in the real as well as metaphorical fear-of-flying department. Takeoff and landing will be smooth, and even regular anxiety can breed no question about that.

1

The brochure once again: a hotel complex as many others, all rooms have balconies facing the sea or the grounds, a rounded oblong in form—not a bad choice given the alternatives. Expensive, yes—working through a conference bureau almost always adds 25 percent to the costs, but it is so much simpler. Three days of conference at the end of this helicopter ride, including creature comforts and—presumably—good company. Perhaps, even, excellent company. Good food and plenty to drink, certainly. How much of it I'll be able to sample, not to say consume, is a different matter: dental problems, as stated. But eating and drinking is not the object of the exercise, not in the very least—a bonus perhaps, part of the general setting only. The object of the exercise is different. And since I'm the initiator, the entrepreneur so to speak, of the proceedings, what will transpire does matter. So I worry about the success of this venture.

And yet, and yet. A feeling of elation, small but worth noting, is beginning to arise, hesitantly, from the knots in my anxious stomach. This is the first gathering—or what is it? Let me consult my computer's thesaurus: Assembly? Conference? Meeting? Congress? Convocation? Convention? Get-together? Jamboree? At any rate, it's the first of its kind ever. And an all-female, exclusively so, crowd to boot. Nothing new about an all-female gathering, on the threshold of the twenty-first century. Exclusively female gatherings have been organized before, again and again and with aplomb, during the second half of the twentieth century. But who are the female participants involved, or invited this time? This is precisely the point. But before proceeding, before landing—we've been airborne now for a while—let me introduce myself. On second thought, since we're flying now, and I'm the passenger, let me try to tell you about the pilot. In this way I can also introduce my scheme by an example.

She is a biblical woman. That is, a woman from the Hebrew bible. (You may know this canonical book as the Old Testament but since, no doubt of that, most of it was first written in Hebrew, not in Greek or Latin or any other language as you may imagine, I'll continue to refer to it as the Hebrew bible, at times HB for short.) Her name is Zipporah, pronounced *tsipporah* by contemporary Hebrew speakers, Zip (Tsip) for her many friends. Even I have forgotten how the name used to be pronounced, in the old days—probably with the initial consonant much as the hard Arabic /sa/ sound. Be that as it may and nevertheless, Zipporah still objects to the /z/ sound with which most English speakers endow the beginning of her name. English is now our hyper-language. This much I shall admit. And yes, Zipporah actually means "female bird" in the Hebrew. What's in a name? A lot, sometimes. And Zipporah flies naturally, like a bird.

The Hebrew bible tells a bitty story about her: in it, she's a fragmented woman, like many other biblical women, in more than one sense. She doesn't seem to have deserved a consistent biography, systematic or otherwise. What the good book has is that she is the daughter of a Midianite priest, variously named Jethro, Jether, Re'uel, Hobab. And wife of Moses. And sister-in-law of Miriam and Aaron. And mother of Moses' children. And there are a few other details, all linked to her wifehood and motherhood.

Wonderful, don't you think? Do you understand much of this, do you understand what Zip did and to whom? Or do you think, together with some scholars—past or present—that the quarrel of her in-laws, Miriam and Aaron, with their brother and her husband Moses was really on her behalf or partly so, since Moses has divorced her and taken another woman, a black woman? As it is written:

> Miriam and Aaron spoke against Moses because of the Cushite woman he had married: "He married a Cushite woman!" (Numbers 12:1)

Or, with others like Rashi and Ibn Ezra and some post-biblical Jewish midrashim, that she, she herself was that "black" woman? Do you know what she looked like? Or who her mother was (presumably she had one), or what were the names of her six sisters mentioned together with her upon meeting with Moses at the desert well (Exod. 2:16-22)? Or how she spent her early years? Or what age she was when she met Moses, and whether she did or did not love him? How was her sex life with him? Was she happy, or otherwise, in the company of the greatest Hebrew prophet and leader of them all? And did she get along with her in-laws and other members of the community into which she married? No, you don't know. She is "daughter of," "wife of," "mother of," always relational to certain named males, little data beyond that. And for all intents and purposes, she never dies, hence never ever buried either. Since no death, no burial of hers—unlike her husband's (Deuteronomy 34)—is reported in that holy book, she lives forever and ever and evermore. Meanwhile, I can't satisfy your curiosity. I can add no more about Zip at this time apart from these initial data and questions, and the information that she's a flier, a bird—in modern guise, a pilot.

To be fair, I must add two more clusters of information at this point. One, clearly, is this. As already indicated, Zip is not the only biblical woman to be so fragmented, to consist of gaps instead of a whole. Most biblical women, be they as important for narrated events as they are—think about her sister-in-law Miriam, or about Deborah, or about Jezebel—are badly gapped. Many are nameless. In passing, much can and hopefully will be said about names chosen for some female persons, when they are named—and don't tell me that the biblical authors had no choice, since those names were historical, were found in sources or traditions, and biblical authors couldn't change them. Naming, as well as name-lessing, has its own politics. At any rate, you find many more nameless women in the Hebrew bible than nameless men. Only in recent years has this phenomenon of name-lessing women been investigated, and the first ever encyclopedia defining nameless women as "entries" appeared recently, in 2000. So many women in the HB are known only as "daughter of [a male]," "wife of," "mother of [mostly a male]," or by another manner such as "a wise woman," "a medium," or "of [a place]." Interestingly, several contemporary feminist scholars have given such women names of their own invention, such as "Bath"—pronounced *bat*, meaning "daughter" in Hebrew—for the poor, willingly martyred daughter of Jephthah (in Judges 11; do you remember that horrible story?). Many women have no lineage at all. Some die peacefully, like Sarah (Genesis 23) and Rebekah and Leah (Gen. 49:31) and Deborah, Rebekah's nurse (Gen. 35:8); some die in childbirth like Rachel at Benjamin's birth (Gen. 35:19) and Eli's daughter-in-law, wife of his son Phinehas, at Ichabod's birth (1 Sam. 4:19-22). Yet others die violently, like Jephthah's daughter again, or Queen Athaliah (2 Kings 11 = 2 Chronicles 23), or the nameless woman gang-raped at Gibeah (Judges 19). There are even burial places recorded for some—note again the four matriarchs, or the burial of Queen Jezebel's remains (2 Kings 9:34-37).

However, many of us biblical women live on, an open-ended kind of existence not achieved by ordinary mortals, just like Zip, just like me: in and outside the biblical text that wasn't interested enough in us to record death and to bury, unless this served another aim of the story apart from genuine interest in our fate. I mean, for instance, the story about Sarah's burial in the cave Abraham buys from the locals (Genesis 23), designed more to glorify Abraham and establish the legal territorial status of the family tomb near Hebron than to pay homage to Sarah, who, after all, wasn't at all involved in the near sacrifice of her son Isaac only one chapter before (Genesis 22).

But this is highly fortunate for us, let me hasten to add. As literary female figures we live everlastingly, eternally, perpetually, as long as the canonical text is still alive, occupying various niches and fulfilling varied roles in the individual and collective cultural memory of Western and, to a lesser extent, Eastern and especially Islamic cultures.

Outside the biblical text as well? Yes. And this is my second point. The very long history of reception through which the HB has been dragged for millennia in the contexts of Judaisms, Christianities, and Islams, not to mention other persuasions and place variants, meant retellings as well as rewritings and reinterpreting. In the interest of social and religious boundaries, often parochially biased or at the very least confessionally inclined, communities rewrote the bible in their own interests and in their own images, in order to enhance their own dispositions and buttress their identities against Others from within and without. Such recycling projects require imaginative gap filling. This continuous interpretative reiteration started already in antiquity. There is a chain of gap filling from ancient Jewish midrash to pious exegeses to scholarly interpretations to present-day feminist midrash, sometimes with amusing parallel results—verbal, visual, plastic, you name it. (I'm talking now about Jewish interpretative traditions, but a similar process obtains with regard to Christian and Muslim interpretations.) We biblical women get to have a fuller biography, at times an imaginary virtual or physical presence, through such efforts. But, even in those and other retellings, few of those who didn't die in the biblical text finally attained the simple human destiny of dying (and being buried). Thus, a victory of sorts, we became doubly eternal. Ironic, really, wouldn't you agree?

So I thought to myself, let's have a meeting of such female survivors, the first of its kind ever. Let's have a conference; after all, what chance have I ever had to meet the female prophet Huldah, for instance? Or Rahab, that very interesting "whore"? Obviously, most of the biblical stories were written by men, interpreted by men, transmitted by men, copied by men, studied by men. The men seem less interested in us, or so they pretend to be, when it comes to compiling canonical literature. But then, life is comparable to fiction but distinct from it—dissimilar, too. So what would be the stories of eternalized biblical women as told by them themselves? Would they be different or the same as the men's? More interesting or less interesting? Subversive or compliant? This was the initial idea, borne out of curiosity.

Preparations for this occasion lasted for a couple of years. The format took some planning. I wanted a symposium in a relatively isolated location, paradoxically as little time- and place-bound as possible because of its well-defined but far-flung location. As similar to an academic conference as possible, yet intimate—no outside intervention by the press and popular media, for instance. Imagine the would-be furor if word got out—a frenzy of interest, paparazzi everywhere! Remember poor Princess Diana! I finally settled on this distant and almost inaccessible resort, an island. You won't get the location from me; my lips are sealed. The money was raised, but don't ask me how. I'm willing to admit to several corporate donations—one can't do without that nowadays— so I won't even claim all sources were kosher. Tracking down the participants, from wherever they put down their roots and created firm aliases, required mobilization of contacts and funds, a veritable process of espionage. Not all of those traced agreed to come: some for fear of blowing their covers, others for lack of appeal. And fewer of those who are coming actually wished to recount their stories. Understandable, although regrettable as well.

But let me reach into the appropriate file on my computer in order to produce the list of participants who have confirmed their arrival and agreed to talk. I'm not going to disclose where they come from at this point. It's up to them to do so if they wish, but don't entertain hopes that are too high.

Here's my list. I deliberated hard and long how to arrange the speakers, that is, in what order to schedule their appearances. By theme? By literary function? By original biblical family alliance? By family status? By age at the time of their biblical story's end? Finally I decided to take the easy way out and schedule the appearances in the chronological order the participants appear in the HB. Some speakers will appear singly, others as a small group of two or three speakers. Thus Adah and Zillah, Lamech's wives (Genesis 4), will speak first, then Dinah, Jacob's daughter raped then avenged by her brothers (Genesis 34), just before Madam Potiphar who tried to seduce Joseph and lives comfortably ever after in Muslim lands (Genesis 39). Zip will be next (Exodus and Numbers), followed by Rahab the whore (Joshua 2 and 6). Naomi and Ruth will come together; it will be the first time they meet Orpah after they parted company on the road from Moab to Bethlehem (Ruth 1). They will speak next, since their story is attributed by its very title to the pre-Israelite monarchy days of the judges (Ruth 1:1). Rizpah daughter of Ayah, wife of Saul and later Abner (2 Samuel 21), usually lives in seclusion but will come and speak before Tamar, daughter-in-law of Judah (Genesis 38), and Tamar, daughter of David (2 Samuel 13), to be followed by Zeruiah, sister of David (the books of Samuel and Chronicles), and Huldah the prophet (2 Kings 22 = 2 Chronicles 34). The anonymous woman from the Song of Songs, who is timeless, will come next. And last will be me, the convener, the conference organizer and director, since self-designated hosts should observe the proprieties of hospitality.

This is what I had in mind and what the participants have agreed to. We shall come together for some days, not too many. We shall socialize. We shall eat and drink. We shall undoubtedly gossip. We may dance or perform. We may quarrel and disagree; we may enjoy. Those of us who wish to will utilize the facilities—swimming, trekking, boating, fishing, fitness. Security will be tight. I'm not going to report on such activities: personal privacy is valued in perpetuity as well as in this life. I'm not going to report on arrangements, settings, workers in the resort, and so on. I'm also not going to comment on my colleagues' age, appearance, clothing, and past/present circumstances: let them do it themselves, if they so choose, to the extent they choose. I do assume, though, that each one of us will have remained where scriptures left her off, at least age-wise.

The main business of the event will be the telling: each one of us will tell her story, from her point of view. I hope the telling, or rather retelling (We can't forget the original, can we? We have to relate to it as to a vector!) will be done in a truly oral fashion, perhaps with notes but certainly not as papers read from written sheets, as people do in academic conferences. And I do hope for a final "round-table" session, with participants raising such questions as they find fit. The retellings will be audio-recorded but not videotaped (privacy again), without interpretation or substantial editing. I myself will then take the audio recordings home with me, will have them transcribed and prepare them for eventual publication. I promise to be a non-aggressive editor and to preserve the oral character of the proceedings, as befits women's oral literature (a fine contradiction in terms, that). I'd like all of us to listen to female voices directly, as they can and should be heard. And whether we decide to meet again, and when and where, remains to be seen. This is my plan.

And here we are. Zip is lowering the helicopter, expertly, as is her custom. We shall land in a minute. Don't ask me, once again, where I met her and how we've established contact. Like her, like me, our stories will be told independently.

And who am I, the initiator, the convener? In due course, my dears, in due course. I'm not telling you now. Later, after all the others have done their bit, I certainly will. A hint, though: I am one of the HB nameless female figures.

How we shall initially meet, how we shall settle into our respective rooms, is perhaps less intriguing than one may imagine. Besides, it's good to leave something to the imagination anyhow, wouldn't you agree? Let us then part company now, gentle readers. I shall go about my organizational duties. Until we meet again, therefore—and then we shall proceed directly to the retellings of the retellings, business-like. Let us now skip some time and go to the first scheduled session, as recorded—for obviously, when you read this, our conference has been over and done with for some time. Here we are, time to start.

ONE

∞

War, Culture, Wives-Mothers from A to Z:
We Are Adah and Zillah

*A*nd Lamech took unto him two wives; the name of one was
Adah, and the name of the other Zillah. And Adah bore Jabal;
he was the father of such as dwell in tents and have cattle. And
his brother's name was Jubal; he was the father of all such as
handle the harp and pipe. And Zillah, she also bore Tubal-cain,
the forger of every cutting instrument of brass and iron; and
the sister of Tubal-cain was Na'amah. And Lamech said unto
his wives:

> Adah and Zillah, hear my voice;
> ye wives of Lamech, hearken unto my speech;
> for I have slain a man for wounding me,
> and a young man for bruising me;
> If Cain shall be avenged sevenfold,
> truly Lamech seventy and sevenfold. (Genesis 4:19-24)

Preface: Adah Speaking

Let me be the first to speak on behalf of both of us, since I'm named
as the first wife, first in order I mean, and this often implies—in
biblical style—the senior member of a social entity as listed.

In English, our names may indicate a whole: you can draw a finite
line or a complete circle from *A* to *Z*. Had it been so also in the

original Semitic, or Hebrew, it would have caused me pleasure. I could have presented us as the alpha and the omega of—but wait, this will come later. But, how disappointing that this is not so in the original languages. There my own name is 'Adah, spelled with an initial *'ayin,* for which the exact pronunciation remains questionable but still extant in Middle Eastern languages. Why, Israeli women are still so named nowadays, or were until a few decades ago. And my colleague's name, Zillah, Lamech's other wife and my lifelong friend and ally, is spelled with an initial *ṣade,* a sound perhaps akin to a heavy /c/ and which seems to have been compounded from several similar sounds that still exist, for instance, in Arabic. Once again, this name is still given to little girls; I even know a Dutch girl of eleven years old who's a Zillah (and her brother's name is Boaz; Ruth, Orpah, and Naomi please note). These two initial letters, *'ayin* and *ṣade,* are located somewhere in the middle or the second half of the Semitic alphabet, not at its beginning or end. And yet, the possibility of a little fun/pun is too tempting to forgo.

If I dwell on a little game here, presenting myself and my colleague-in-marriage as equivalent to the proverbial alpha and omega of womankind in the biblical story containing our names, quoted above, there are several reasons for it. One, and as I've already noted, how can I resist this *A* to *Z* reference, although not original to the Hebrew story? Two, as you can see, the original pronunciation of our names was forgotten. It cannot even be recovered from the written biblical text or from oral traditions. This failure to reconstruct the pronunciation goes further: it has a bearing on understanding the meaning of our names too.

Moreover, in this little story we are mentioned and named but remain mindless and voiceless and devoid of appearance, having only the good graces to give birth to children and exercise our auditory faculty in our husband's service: we are his nonresponsive listeners. However, this little story is important beyond its significance for us since, in spite of its brevity, it is a foundational story of culture's coming into being. It attributes the institution of culture—tent dwelling and domestic animal husbandry, music, metal work—to our sons, and perhaps it also attributes the art of war—if art it may be called!—to our husband. In fact the sons' father, our husband, has real martial characteristic to define him apart

from his bad temper and his bragging, in poetry mind you, of his
military prowess past and present and future. So

> He is a poet
> And he knows it,

and uses his poetry destructively, encouraging—verbally at least—
revenge and physical violence and killing. But as for the rest, the
constructive cultural branches of knowledge attributed to our
sons—do you think that it could have come about without our own
wisdom and our own encouragement? Nevertheless, much like the
pronunciation of our names, and like information about Zillah's
daughter Na'amah, this part of our story was forgotten or—worse—
displaced or suppressed, depending on your viewpoint. So here are
our emendations to the biblical text concerning us, and they are
more than timely, none too soon, for even feminist readers of the
last generations neglected us. To begin with, let's take our clue from
linguistics and semantics, I say.

Excursus: Zillah Intervenes

But Adah, let me interrupt you at this point. In truth, you suffer
from linguistic amnesia and the resultant intellectual amnesia
concerning your name and other factors more than I do (although
both of us suffer from cultural amnesia to a large extent, as you
rightly state). By "you suffer" or "I suffer" I mean, of course, "you" or
"I" as presented in Genesis 4 and beyond in bible interpretation, not
the "you" and "I" as we really are. Some learned commentators have
surmised that my name derives from a Semitic root (*ṣll*, pronounced
something like *tsalal*) that refers to "shade, shadow" and by
extension "protection," "being in the shadow of," in the sense of
under shelter. Indeed, names containing that sequence of sounds
may occur in Hebrew and also in languages akin to Hebrew, such as
Akkadian and Amorite in that sense. But most commentators agree
that my name is actually derived from a similar homophonic (that
is, sounds-alike) term to the one that means "shadow" but with a
different meaning denoting some kind of "sound" (Hebrew צלל or
as in the word צלצל, which, in Hebrew, means "cymbal"). Thus, we

have the words "make a sound," "cymbal," and another word for an unidentified musical percussion instrument (*metsiltayim*) that was used in the Jerusalem temple worship, among others. This is my own preferred explanation and according to it my name is linked to making sounds; this is in fact my essence. This is also my excuse, built in and by definition, for allowing myself to interrupt you, Adah, who's my social superior and thus with right of precedence, as you justly claim. I'm destined to be a sound maker—if you wish, a noise maker—by name. Furthermore, as you've heard, my name is even linked distinctively to music and music making and musical instruments. Indeed, I was and am a musician. But this has been "disappeared" from the little story about us and about our family; it's been transferred onto your son Jubal, who's credited with being the father of flutes and string instruments at the very least, by metonymic extension of all music. Now, this would seem strange: in light of what I've just said, this foundational musical activity should have been attributed to a son of mine. So now, Adah, it's your turn to pick up this strand of thought.

More on the Politics of Naming and Remembrance: Adah Again

Thank you, Zillah. Now, I too intend to set history straight here, for me as well as for my later namesake, Adah daughter of Elon the Hittite, one of Esau's Canaanite wives (Genesis 36; although Esau's wives are called different names in Genesis 26 and 28.). Many dictionaries refer to the meaning of my name as "obscure." Theophoric, for some—that is, with an element of the Hebrew god's name in it. For others, it is derived from a Semitic and Hebrew term, a letter sequence that means "decorate, embellish," as in the Hebrew word *'ady* ("ornament"). In that sense, writes Umberto Cassuto, for instance, I and my colleague, Adah and Zillah together, would be "the-good-to-look-at" and "the-good-to-listen-to," a true pair of female perfection. Think for instance about a passage in the Song of Songs (fondly known as SoS by some; note the intentional meaning of that abbreviation as applied to love lyrics!), where a male lover addresses a female lover in these words:

O my dove, that art in the clefts of the rock,
in the covert of the cliff,
let me see thy countenance,
let me hear thy voice;
for sweet is thy voice,
and thy countenance is comely. (Song of Songs 2:14 AV)

Let me mark in passing that in this example from the SoS, appeal of both the visual and the audial kinds is attributed to one single female. Therefore, according to this understanding of my name together with Zillah's, does it mean that we are seen as one person or one female entity divided, literally, into two figures, each containing one attribute of pleasantness only? Such an understanding would solve a problem for the interpreters since, to begin with in the book of Genesis, bigamy isn't mentioned as a primary, or legitimate, human condition; we are the first such case, whose origin or justification is presented as factual albeit unexplained in the biblical story and is a headache for Jewish sages. But I'm digressing and we shall come back to this aspect later. Besides, let me point out, to explain my name as "sweet, good, comely" would fit in better with the name Na'amah, from a Semitic root *n'm* denoting precisely that, as also in the name Naomi. But look—once again and upon reflection, this doesn't fit: if so, and if we take biblical names seriously as a literary device (as we should, truly, more often than not), Na'amah should have been my daughter, the way Jubal should have been Zillah's son. But Na'amah is recorded as Zillah's daughter, the way Jubal is recorded as my son! So on we shall labor, attempting to uncover another meaning as a key for fleshing out our story.

Now, I hope to have established by now that the original meaning of my name (as well as Zillah's) has been forgotten. Once restored, it will introduce some order into our story, which in its present form is actually a non-story, so much has been either changed or not remembered or worse.

Consider the following. There is an Oriental musical instrument called in Arabic *'ûd*, with a pronunciation roughly equivalent in its letters (if not vowels) to my own name. You may know what an 'ûd is by the name "sitar," or "lauta," or "lute." It is a pear-shaped string instrument, guitar-like, made of wood, with a "neck" on which the strings are located. It was known in Mesopotamia as far back as the second millennium BCE; in other words, the 'ûd is one of the more ancient string instruments in human culture. From Mesopotamia its usage spread into Egypt, Persia, Greece, and Arabia. From these places it migrated farther into Europe via the western Mediterranean (Spain and France) and was widely played in Renaissance and baroque music and until the classical period, especially in the fourteenth to the seventeenth centuries. All this time, the 'ûd metamorphosed as far as shape and, especially, the number of strings are concerned—from eight strings the number went up to ten and even more. Thereafter it was displaced in popularity by the guitar, a well-known instrument with a wooden body and typically six strings. Indeed, the 'ûd is a close relative of the guitar: the term *guitar* comes from the Greek *kithara*; this same term is reflected in the biblical *kithros* or *kathros*, a loaned term from Greek in a list of musical instruments appearing in the biblical text of Daniel 3.

Do you remember the tale from the book of Daniel, told in Aramaic? Nebuchadnezzar the Babylonian king erects a golden idol and commands his subjects to worship it when they hear the sound of various musical instruments, and whoever refuses will be thrown into a fire. Three Jews, Daniel's friends, refuse on religious grounds. They are thrown into the fire. They are not burned. Nebuchadnezzar is converted to faith in the one and only Jewish god and makes the three Jews officials in his administration. A pious, exemplary legend, no doubt. Interesting for me, as a musician, are the musical instruments' names (a list that is repeated three times, in verses 5, 10, and 15), several of which seem to be Greek in origin. The instruments themselves seem to be a combination of wind, string, and percussion. As the translations show, there's no actual agreement about their identification. At any rate, the third item on the list, *kathrôs*, which appears to have a Greek ending and thus—without the /ôs/ ending— is akin to the word for quitar/guitar, is variably identified as harp, lute, or lyre. The translators' disagreement certainly shows that Western knowledge of ancient musical instruments was scarce. In addition, until quite recently Oriental/Arab music was considered inferior to European music and its musical instruments did not receive the scholarly attention they deserved. Therefore, there's a place for innovation in this field. So let me advance the notion that suits me, namely that this same kithros/kathros might be the 'ûd, which, as I claim, is also akin to my own name.

Please excuse the length of this mini-lecture. Nowadays you can find more information about the 'ûd in dictionaries and encyclopedias; it's widely available, if you follow either the Arabic name or its European equivalents. There are also many, many artistic representations of it; there are paintings showing 'ûd players in Oriental as well as European courts, especially but not only for music connected with love. But nobody, not one of the learned doctors—to the best of my knowledge—has ever raised the possibility that my name is linked with it, and this is why I've sailed into a long description of the 'ûd, to this day a popular and much decorated instrument in the Arab world.

The name of this instrument, as you can hear, is pronounced very similarly to my name—at least two of the consonants, the /'/ and the /d/, are almost the same. I'm no professional linguist, so cannot explain the changes in pronunciation that do exist between the term *'ûd* and the name *Adah* (properly transcribed, 'Adah, also with an *'ayin* as I've stated at the beginning of my talk). However, I've always known, from the time I was a little girl, that I was a musician and an 'ûd player. That was my destiny, as encapsulated in and by my name. I'm proud to be associated with such a musical instrument that, in one form or another, has been in existence for thousands of years, creating pleasure and expressing emotions across continents and cultures.

In light of my explanation, let's look again at the biblical "story" of our little family. The origin of instrumental music, pipe and string, is displaced from me onto my son Jubal—and his sister Na'amah, according to at least one feminist reading, is the ancestral singer, and this is neatly hidden in her name as well. As if it's fitting for a male only to be the originator of music—even the Hebrew bible acknowledges that women did play music and sang and wrote poetry; the examples of Miriam, and Deborah, and women singing victory songs to David and Jonathan, and lamenting women, may suffice here. However, there's a great distance, or so it seems, from such acknowledgments to attributing music as an original invention to females. Along this line, Zillah is of course correct in claiming that the music or voice contents of her name (and of Na'amah's) are half forgotten as well. Both of us co-wives are treated as a two-face pair, as by the scholar Cassuto. Furthermore, no details are given about Na'amah, "the sweet one"—is her sweetness visual or audial, or of taste?—perhaps there's a sexual overtone to her name, as in the adjective from the same Hebrew root in the SoS, when a male voice says to his female lover, with unmistakable innuendo—

> How beautiful, how *tasty* (or *pleasant*) you are, love and pleasure.
> (Song of Songs 7:7 HB)

That metaphorical "tasting" of love implied here is borne out by the references to food and drink as metaphors for lovemaking in the next verses (8-10). In short, our pioneering status as mothers of music culture is taken away, while our poor beloved daughter is reduced to an unexplained name and no cultural function. Also, look at this irony: if Zillah's name and mine (see further below) originally testify to our musical abilities, in the biblical text—lo and behold—all that's left for us to do is to listen to our husband's poetic creation, in verse but with no music, or did he compose the music for it as well!? But this is why we're here, to rectify the situation. It's your turn now, Zillah!

Zillah: On Initiating Civilization—New Customs, New Ways

It is our contention here, as you may have already guessed, that the two of us were involved in inventing human civilization as you know it. As you must have gathered from Adah's words so far, music was our special field, and we shall return to this topic once again as we must. But another, and perhaps related, issue was a mode of family life already alluded to, hitherto unknown and later widely practiced: bigamy. And we would like to tell you about that experience first, and about our other invention, that is, the beginning of birth control, before we come back to our contribution to art and culture.

You may as well know that we're close blood kin, Adah and I. And according to the Genesis narrative, Lamech is our not-so-distant relative—all three of us are the sixth generation after Adam and Eve, from the same family tree. We're cousins, and our children are the seventh generation, meaningful in terms of the stereotypical number chosen, as everyone knows. The seven-generation list in Genesis 4:17-22 (which contains our "story") has us all as descendants of Cain, the brother killer; but let's also note the other version in Genesis 5, a ten-generation list of humanity's beginnings, where Lamech is related to Adam through Seth—not Cain—and stands in the tenth generation. The list in "our" chapter 4 typically names only the son inheriting his father's line in each generation (apart from our story, embedded in it and intruding on the list proper). But the list in Genesis 5 mentions in passing and without naming the existence of additional progeny—sons and daughters—in each generation. The two of us are such daughters, joined to Lamech in endogamous matrimony, as not only the single choice available for the one human family on earth at the time but also the ideological choice exercised by the first humans and up to the times of Jacob's sons—at least as recounted in the book of Genesis. The preference for in-group marriage is widely attributed to Abraham, and Rebekah, and beyond.

The analogy to Jacob is important. Jacob married two of his cousins, two sisters, Lea and Rachel—which is closely similar to our and our husband's situation as close relatives. The bible insists Lea and Rachel were rivals, and the rivalry extended to their sons and to their sons of legal adoptive status, the children of their slaves Zilpah and Bilhah (Genesis 27–30). But Adah and I were not rivals. We were concerned with survival rather than with in-fighting, and our situation—two wives, one husband, for the first time in human history—dictated that we should devise a *modus vivendi*. Here, our husband's sexual desire came to our rescue. Lamech's choice to have two wives was irregular practice, when you think about Yhwh's decree that one woman is enough for one man, as when the woman and man were created (Gen. 1:27; 2:22-24). Listen to what the Jewish sages had to say about it:

> This is what the men of the Flood generation did: they would take two wives, one for breeding and one for sexual intercourse [תשמיש]. The one for breeding would sit like a widow throughout her [another version: his, i.e., Lamech's] life; and the one for sexual intercourse, he would make her drink a cup of sterility [כוס של עקרין] so that she doesn't

become pregnant, and she would sit by him adorned like a
prostitute . . . And an anonymous sage said, Adah was for
breeding, for she conceived [Aramaic: 'adah] from him
[Lamech] . . . and Zillah was for sexual intercourse, since she
would always sit in his [Lamech's] shadow [Hebrew tsel;
Genesis Rabbah].

Rashi, the authoritative medieval commentator on the bible and the
talmud, in his commentary on Genesis 4, copies this midrash
almost verbatim, but adds:

This is so in Genesis Rabbah, but is a thing of _Aggadah_
(rabinnic take).

Let's look again at this playful or, should I say, fanciful rendering
of our story, and try to differentiate between the true and the
imaginary. The Jewish sages did feel they ought to justify Lamech's
taking of two wives. So how did they do it? They exonerated him by
advancing several arguments:

1. He wasn't the only man to do so in his generation(s), that is, in
the seventh (according to the list in Genesis 4) or tenth (according
to the list in Genesis 5) generation from Adam to Noah.
2. Each wife was taken for a different purpose: one for business
(breeding), one for play (non-procreative sex).
3. According to some, the respective role attributed to the wives
was interchangeable.
4. When he wanted a wife to function as sexual plaything, he
practiced birth control, giving her a potion of sterilizing drink to
produce the desired effect.
5. According to another sage, the respective roles attributed to the
wives was permanent, not interchangeable. The first and presumably
eldest, Adah, was the one kept for procreation; the second and
presumably younger, Zillah (that's me), was kept as just a plaything.

May I point out the inconsistent, far-fetched, and whimsical
elements in this rendering, or multiple-purpose rendering? Let me
go through the above items one by one, in as scholarly a fashion as I
can muster.

1. We, the two wives, and the biblical scribes, have no confident knowledge of such a custom in our times, so long ago.

2. This argument is as rich as it is a fantasy. It allows a man progeny (a predominant social and religious duty in Judaism) as well as continual opportunity for sexual gratification. It doesn't take into account the women's desire, in this (maternity) or the other (having sex) direction.

3. We must agree this argument is reasonable: after all, both of us are recorded as mothers of children.

4. It is well known that women, not men, are the custodians of birth control. It is, first and foremost, women's self-interest (so many pregnancies, given the infant mortality in the ancient world, would deplete their bodies; note how many matriarchs were "sterile" until a ripe old age!). Women are known to be herbalists, and birth control in our milieu and in cognate cultures was primarily herbal. Midwives (women again) were as skilled in preventive medicine as in proactive medicine. Should we forget that women like to have their pleasure too? But true to form, the Jewish sages took away our invention of birth control—we cooperated, we helped each other to achieve a balance of fertility and sexual leisure—and gave it to Lamech. At any rate, it is worth noting that much, much later a residue of our ingenuity lingered, a twisted and wrongly attributed trace but nevertheless still there.

5. Finally, this opinion of a fixed role for each one of us doesn't hold water. The anonymous sage who expressed this opinion is probably influenced by the story of Leah and Rachel, referred to above. Leah and Rachel are sisters; Leah is the more fertile sister, Jacob loves the younger sister. This story was projected into our story, as is often done in bible exegesis, midrashic or otherwise. But it has nothing to do with our actual situation. It is flattering for me to be imaged as Lamech's favorite, but in the interest of veracity and sisterly (in the wider sense) love I have to reject this interpretation.

In fact, it seems to me that our husband is deconstructed by the sages, if only a little. They know full well that an elementary divine commandment specifies that one woman suffices for one man. They try to justify his bigamy, as recorded for posterity, but present him in their own image, as a sex-driven man. He's mindful of his social obligation of procreation, yes, but also as much by his desire to simply enjoy. And when they proceed to retell his motives for his poetic *oeuvre,* they say:

> And Lamech said to his wives, Adah and Zillah, "listen to my voice" [Gen. 4:23]: He demanded copulation from them. And they said to him, tomorrow the flood will come, and we shall be fruitful and multiply for the catastrophe? (Genesis Rabbah)

So the Jewish sages do admit, in a roundabout way, that Lamech's motive is sexual, that he's trying to attract us and seduce us by a dazzling verbal plume display as is customary in the animal world, and that he's attempting to gain our favors by showing us how violent and manly he is. We turn his demand into its result (thus negating his presumed expertise in birth control). Our response is, We know what's coming, we're not going to cooperate, we're *not* going to give birth to children who will perish in the flood (we can foresee the future), which implies that we're going to exercise *our* knowledge of birth control to prevent this even if we agree to his sexual advances, masked as poetic statement.

Adah Again

So there. Talking about our children, those we gave birth to after we prevented other pregnancies, we limited ourselves to four children between us. We were mindful of the sages' dictum: As long as a woman doesn't become pregnant she's a joy to her husband; when she does, she becomes ugly and unattractive to her husband. Let's go back to the Genesis verses, then:

> And Adah bore Jabal; he was the father of such as dwell in tents and have cattle. And his brother's name was Jubal; he was the father of all such as handle the harp and pipe. (4:20-21)

My—"our," if you wish—son Jabal took over from the shepherd Hebel, murdered by his brother Cain, to rediscover domestic animal husbandry and the nomad life. (My/our second son Jubal is accredited with inventing music, which should actually be accredited to me and to my "sister" Zillah, as explained). So there we are, textually exiled from the cultural invention or discovery picture. Let me return to the sisters, and co-wives, Rachel and Leah for a moment: "Rachel" means "ewe"; "Leah" means "cow." Rachel is a shepherdess when Jacob meets her. At least, in their names, some trace remains of their original occupation. The successful shepherd par excellence, however, is their husband, Jacob. Thus, the original occupation of the wives is displaced to the husband. Similarly, if not exactly, our crucial, innovative system of animal husbandry—much like our music—is displaced on to a male as well, this time to our son.

And Zillah, Once More

> And Zillah, she also bore Tubal-cain, the forger of every cutting instrument of brass and iron; and the sister of Tubal-cain was Na'amah. (Gen. 4:22)

And Tubal-cain, yes, he's [dis]credited with inventing metal works and therefore also weaponry, highly suitable for his father's violent tendencies, a further development of his forefather and namesake Cain's ways. We make no claim for his invention: on the contrary. War and weaponry isn't our thing. And soon you'll hear from Zeruiah, King David's sister and a mother of three generals, how she feels about war as well.

But let's talk about my/our daughter Na'amah instead—so much more rewarding. Yes, she is named but remains actionless in Genesis. Nevertheless, she gets her share of interpretive follow-up—she gets to be Noah's wife in the midrash, or perhaps the wife of one of his sons; hence she is saved from the flood, which occurs in the next generation. It appears that the mere mention of her name merits a discussion, since she's the only daughter of the pre-Noahite generations to be named. According to the midrash, the text remembers her by name because she "was righteous and gave birth to righteous persons." And why was she called "Na'amah"? Because her actions were pleasant and good. Bingo. And her beauty was legendary, as it is said in a legend about a learned man who had eyes only for Torah study, never for women. A Satan became jealous and transformed himself into a good-looking woman,

> The likeness of whom has never occurred since the days of Na'amah, sister to Tubal-cain. (Genesis Rabbah)

So far so good, you'd think; Na'amah's identity is accounted for and she's made properly respectable by being married (like Dinah, like Rahab, like many others: you'll soon hear about it from them). But what about the other side, what about male ambiguity toward even the best of biblical female figures? It is already present in the tying up of Na'amah's beauty with a Satan, a demon, and it continues—let us not forget the conscious or unconscious analogies to Na'amah the Ammonite, wife of King Solomon and mother of his royal heir Rehoboam (1 Kings 14:21, 31; 2 Chron. 12:13), who, together with Solomon's other wives, presumably gets her fair share of blame for paganism (1 Kings 11). So back to our own Na'amah. It's not enough to let her be beautiful and pleasant. A good-looking woman is dangerous to men. Therefore, probably, so write some Jewish medieval commentators for Genesis 4:22, following some midrashim:

> And another rabbinic midrash, that she [Na'amah] is the good-looking woman who caused the sons of god [or: of the gods] to deviate [from the right path], which is hinted in the verse, "And the sons of god [or: of the gods] saw the daughters of the Adam [that they were good, and took them for wives . . .]" (Gen. 6.2). And others say she was the wife of Shamdon, mother of Ashmedai, and the demons were born from her; and the text hints at but remains short about such things.

Or similarly and once again Na'amah is linked to Genesis 6, the fragmentary story about the sons of god/the gods who desired the good-looking human daughters.

> Uzza and Azza'el were angels of destruction who went down to the world in the days of Na'amah sister of Tubal-cain.

Or:

> Na'amah . . . she would make it pleasant for worshipping the
> heavenly bodies with a tambourine.

Wonderful! Despite themselves, here the sages and
commentators inadvertently admit that not only Jubal but also
Na'amah "invented" music—percussion instruments for her, string
instruments for him. She plays the tambourine like Miriam—but is
suspected of pagan worship! No real prophetic respect for her, I'm
afraid.

But let me assure you, let me stress, that I empathize with the
Jewish sages and commentators. They grapple with textual and
conceptual questions that are important to them and to their own
life and time, as usual. Questions abound even in our so-short
"story." For instance: Why is Na'amah identified as Tubal-Cain's
sister and not as a *daughter*, by her patrimony or at least maternal
descent? (My own answer: this sometimes happens. So Miriam is
identified as Aaron's sister [Exod. 15:20], and it happens to other
named biblical women—Zeruiah is among us and can enlighten us
further in this regard.) Or, Why is Na'amah named at all? (My
answer: she's important, if not in the way the sages present her.) Or,
Why is there no marital status given for her? (Their answer: she's
married, sure.) Or, Why is she given such a lovely name? (Their
answer: because of her beauty, or music-making; we concur.) We
understand that Na'amah herself didn't interest them much for her
own sake, but for their own. They couldn't and wouldn't let her go
until her beauty, and music, and marriageability—everything
condensed into that lovely name of hers—were accounted for
according to their own imagination.

In summary, please note. We're two women, co-wives, ostensibly
not too important. Foundational cultural factors are attributed to
our male sons and to our husband, certainly not to us personally,
and not to our daughter Na'amah. But we get to have names that
may function as clues for reconstructing the story behind the
biblical story. And we get to have stories imagined after our names.
And we have supplemented the story here—without dwelling too
much on our husband's history, since the sages do it extensively

without our aid. And besides, Lamech was not such a find, believe us—that bragging non-hero. In modern Hebrew, for instance, his name is a synonym for stupidity and cupidity: when you exclaim to somebody, "you're such a Lamech," it's a high insult. So Lamech is not important, and, moreover, he's been dead now for many thousands of years. Whereas we are not. So please take note.

TWO

∞

I Am the Twelfth Sheep:
Dinah

I'm Dinah, the one raped. Let us look at the biblical story about me. Briefly. In Genesis 30:21, after Leah is reported as having birthed six sons for Jacob, an afterthought is recorded: "And afterwards she [Leah] gave birth to a daughter, and she called her name Dinah." A little later, in Genesis 34, a terse account has me—specified as daughter of Leah, once more, not as Jacob's daughter—going out to gaze at the daughters of the land, the daughters of Canaan (Gen. 34:1). Never mind the fact that some later Jewish commentators cattily state that by "going out," like my mother when she went out to meet Jacob and tell him he should come to her because she "bought" him for the night from Rachel (Gen. 30:16), and by wishing to "gaze" or "see," I deserved that Shechem son of Hamor, of the town Shechem, "saw" me. A woman's place is of course within, not without in the public domain. This is a clear case of blaming the victim, so what else is new? At any rate, the story goes on, Shechem "saw her [me] and took her and lay with her and caused her to suffer." Some scholars agree that he raped me. Others stand on their learned head in order to prove, to their own satisfaction, that he in fact practiced pre-nuptial kidnapping, nothing more sinister than that, and that the terminology used—within the customs of the ancient Near East, as the sociologists will tell you—supports the notion that no rape was involved. Perhaps the politics of exogamy (marrying a member of a social out-group) are in evidence in my case,

unwished for by my clan; perhaps I consented, by way of escape? At
any rate, the biblical story (Genesis 34) continues, "and his
[Shechem's] being clung to Dinah daughter of Jacob and he loved her
and he spoke to her heart." Shechem and his father ask for me in
marriage from my father, and my brothers. They propose a political,
ethnic, and economic merger between the two groups, their
autochtonic group and our allochtonic group, including marriages
and all. My brothers seem to agree but ask the other group's males to
circumcise themselves, in order to accommodate to our habits. They
agree. They do. As they recuperate, my brothers Shimeon and Levi
come into the city Shechem, kill all the males, and plunder
everything including women and children. They then take me from
Shechem's house, where I'd been all this time, and depart. Jacob
protests; he feels insecure: he's afraid that the inhabitants of the land
would take revenge. His sons say this is a matter of revenge, of
upholding family honor, a principle well-known in Mediterranean
societies: he (Shechem) can't make our sister into a whore. Later, in
his so-called blessing or testament to his male descendants, Jacob
berates Shimeon and Levi for their bloody conduct in this affair
(Gen. 49:5-7), but, needless to say, I'm not mentioned.

Now, throughout the story I never get to open my mouth; not one
word do I utter. Nobody seems to be interested in my mind-set or
feelings, this way or the other. Do I hurt, physically or emotionally?
Or am I pleased by this event? How long do I sit in Shechem's house
and what do I do meanwhile? Do I welcome his amorous intentions?
How am I treated by his family? There's almost nothing concerning
me; gaps abound. So bear with me, ladies, if I claim that the biblical
story is *not* my story; it's not about *me*. This is really a men's affair, a
political story, as noted by several scholars and commentators. I am
but a pawn, an object.

Often in biblical narrative, violence in sex and violence in war are
analogous and intimately linked. A sexual union may symbolize the
politics of intergroup relations, and that union may or may not be a
matter of consent for the female involved. In my case, the union was
male-initiated and violent: don't believe for a minute that rape did
not occur here. It did. I was an innocent young girl who "went out"
unchaperoned (granted, perhaps I should have been more careful of
the wolves out there) because I was curious and looked for female

company. I'd been so lonely, with my mother, Leah, always busy competing with her sister Rachel for their husband Jacob's love, and in her spare time paying attention to her sons rather than to me. She plays no role in the story: in truth, as you'll hear at this conference several times, mother/daughter relationships in the Hebrew bible tend to be described as dysfunctional, if at all; contra several commentators, I really grew up as a motherless child. Anita Diamant, who in her book *The Red Tent* (1997) gave me such a glorious—albeit imaginary—voice, claims that I had four mothers: Rachel, Leah, Zilpah, and Bilhah. Well, she can claim her work is a midrash, not a work of fiction. I like Diamant's bestselling fiction about our family, told in my imagined voice, and read it with pleasure; also, she made me famous, which is gratifying. Nevertheless, I must confess that the book makes my life look so rich in female camaraderie as to, perhaps, reflect Diamant's reality or utopia. So stay with me, colleagues: I deny growing up with multiple mothers, in the Hebrew bible, at any rate.

And I was raped; I did not consent. The fact that my rapist decided to fall for me after the event and to ask my father—not me, of course—for my hand in marriage does not diminish his guilt. It can be worse, to be sure. A deflowered, nubile woman, raped or not, is damaged goods. Common opinion was that it was better for her, for me, to marry the assailant: in fact, there is a biblical law that states,

> If a man finds a virgin that is not betrothed, and he holds her, and lies with her, and they are found out, the man who lay with her will give the young woman's father fifty pieces of silver, and she shall be his wife, for he caused her to suffer. And he cannot send her away throughout his life. (Deuteronomy 22:28-29)

As you can see, the terminology used in this law is similar to the description in "my" story: if a man "holds" a young woman, in my case "takes"; if he lies with her, as in my case; if he causes her to suffer, as in my case. In both places, no account is given of the young woman's perspective. Would you fancy co-habiting with your assailant, with the person who raped you, as long as he, or you, or both, live? In order not to remain unmarried, that is, in order not to be considered a socially useless female? Is this a female perspective? Is it? And the woman's father is compensated, not the woman herself.

Do you reckon I got any support from my father, for that matter? But we shall return to this question, as well as to the political ramifications of "my" story, later.

Let me tell you this. At the time, millennia ago, the term "date rape" was certainly not known. Correction: a good girl was not even supposed to go out on her own, without a chaperone, not to mention on an actual date, or "assignation," as it was quaintly called centuries later. Now, after all this time, I'm prepared to concede that on meeting Shechem, by chance and not by design, I was intrigued. He was an "other," different, a diversion. I was drawn to him, at first. He was a welcome distraction, an object for my gaze: in that sense, the pious Jewish commentators may be a little right. I was curious about him, as curious as I was about "the daughters of the land," the young women of his community. I had seen him before, from a distance; he saw me. Looks can tell, even if my downcast glances were well practiced whereas his were bolder. We had eye contact, and a cautious mutual attraction was acknowledged without words. I gave no thought to his perspective; I was so innocent. But for me his appeal, like that of his female relatives, was that, like them, he was so much more sophisticated, so much more urbane than my good brothers, so much more cultured—or so I thought at first.

So we talked. And he invited me to his home. And I went there, unsuspecting. In hindsight, once again, perhaps I shouldn't have agreed to go. I thought there would be female relatives there, I was feeling safe because, in our culture, hospitality for strangers and protecting whoever comes under our roof was a sacred duty. Not for them, not for him, apparently—for he raped me and fell in love with me.

Does this qualify as date rape? I submit it does. Contemporary definitions of date rape characterize it as rape that occurs in a situation of trust, when the victim knows the rapist (or at least sort of), in a place assessed as safe, in a situation considered open for consent or rejection, when sexual intercourse is not the common target of both parties, when misunderstanding about the nature of the encounter and then violence practiced by one partner on the other occurs. According to contemporaneous statistics in the West, date rape is common, especially when the rapist is a male and the victim a female, and it is problematic for males to understand.

"When you say no, what do you mean?" "What do you expect, when you go out unaccompanied?" "If you wear provocative clothes, what do you expect?" "If you ask him for a drink, or go to his house, this is like bestowing license!" And so on. Once again, statistically, 50 percent of rapes are committed in situations when and where the victim knows the rapist, even if slightly, and feels initially safe. All rape-crisis centers are familiar with this basic factor.

This is what happened to me. I did not expect it, not in the slightest. This is why comments by scholars and sages to the contrary hurt so much. Feminist readers and scholars, as expected in this day and age, try to imagine my nonexistent point of view. And yet, even some of those miss the point and fall into the trap of arguing that no rape took place. I suffered greatly, but nobody voiced my suffering. Hamor kept me in his house. I stayed there, silent, in a state of shock.

There is, however, one man who is near the mark of understanding me, albeit not fully. His name is Shaul (Saul) Tchernichowsky. He was born in 1875 in Russia and died in the then-Palestine of the British mandate in 1943. A medical doctor, classical scholar, translator, and poet, he was a wizard with biblical language and rewrote, after his own fashion, several biblical passages. I do not agree with all that he says, as I shall explain. But first, this is what he wrote on my behalf, in two days, in Tel Aviv, in the summer of 1937; I shall explain the significance of the date later. The poem is titled "The Dinah Affair." Since—to the best of my knowledge—it's never been translated from the original Hebrew, I shall do it here for those of us whose life has been conducted for millennia in other languages, so that the mother tongue is a far-away memory. I translate it also for our eventual readers, since our esteemed convener is threatening publication of our deliberations. Please do not expect an artistic translation, although I'll do my very best. My own commentary will follow; meanwhile, please note that this *oeuvre's* structure proceeds from prose to poetry and then returns to prose. You can see that in the handout containing my translation, to which you can refer while I speak. So here we go.

And the two sons of Jacob, Shimeon and Levi, the brothers of Dinah, each one took his sword and came upon the city that defiled their sister. And they slew Hamor and his son Shechem

by the sword, and they took Dinah from Shechem's house, and
they went out. And the girl said, No, let me die, and refused to
be consoled. And Dinah conceived by Shechem son of Hamor,
and she knew that she was with child. And she said, May the
child live, for it did not sin. And she sat, desolate and
mourning, all the days of her pregnancy, with the sons of
Shimeon and Levi her brothers. And when her time came, she
gave birth to a daughter, and she called her name Asenath, for
she said, I gave her birth in my affliction (Hebrew '*ason*): "I did
not love, and I conceived a child my being hates to the father of
the fruit of my womb." And she was in arduous labour, and she
said, "I am dying. Send the girl to Egypt, so that her infamy is
not known. And carry up my bones to Egypt; do not bury me
here. Let my dust not touch his [Hamor's] dust, and let the sea
separate between me and him forever." And she sent and called
her brothers and said: "Gather and let me take my farewell, I,
your abject sister. I'm being gathered unto my people. Assemble
and listen to Dinah your sister.

Reuben, you are my older brother,
You have more versatility, more gentleness.
In front of kings you stand,
With princes you break bread.
You did not respond to me on my day of anguish,
You did not make me odious to the inhabitants of the land,
The Canaanites and the Perizzites.
For they went up to your sister's bed,
Then it was defiled, he went up my couch.
I would comfort myself for my blood!
Shimeon and Levi are brothers,
Instruments of nobility are their weapons.
Ionians from Crete crafted them,
Phoenicians in ships brought them,
Arabian traders to Harran.
Let my soul rejoice in their counsel,
In their assembly my honor is elevated.
For they slew a man in their anger
And according to their wish uprooted a garden.

Blessed be their anger, for it is fierce;
And their wrath, for it was hard.
Let there be many like them in Jacob,
In all of Israel's diasporas.
Bless, oh God, their might
And accept the deed of their hands.
Crush the necks of their foes
And their enemies—who shall stand up?"
And this to Judah.
"Judah, you, your brothers will praise you
Not your hand at the neck of your enemies;
your brothers will applaud you.
Judah stopped, still you were before the prey.
Stooped down like a lion in the valley,
Like a young lion in open country, in the south.
A sceptre was not seen in Judah,
Or a mortar between his arms.
He bound a spear to a boy,
And to war his tribe's sons.
He covered anger with his clothes,
His horse—cold blood.
[I am] red eyed with vengeance
Teeth-gnashing with shame.
Look, God, to Judah;
Bring him to his people."
And to Zebulun she said,
"Zebulun gets inebriated at the seashore,
He—to many ships,
Longing for Sidon.
Girls call for the mountain,
There they dance worldly dances.
For they suckle foreign money
And interest of market gains.
Rejoice, Zebulun, in your tents;
Son of Leah, in your dances."
And to Issachar she said,
"Issachar is a strong ass,
Trembling in the abattoir.

And as his neighbor saw that it was bad,
And that the land was confused,
He uncovered his pocket to pay,
And became a serving labor band."
And to Dan she said,
"Dan is a canine cub, escaping from the Bashan.
And say, Dan is a rider on the road,
Pointing the way
Who bites the horse's loins
And makes its owner plunge to the ground.
Salvation from you I couldn't hope for, oh brother!"
And to Gad she said,
"Gad, troops overcome him,
And he retreats.
Sassy, extending his mouth as a lion,
Leaping tearing devouring
Arm as well as skull.
And says, this is the beginning, it's coming,
Here is the uncovered portion, delivered—
But he didn't join the people's leaders.
He did the leaders' command,
But is the lowliest of Israel's people."
And to Asher she said,
"Asher, fat is his bread.
And he dwells in kings' courts.
He's more constrained than his brothers, Asher.
Let him be acceptable to his senders,
His leg is heavy in the stack.
Silver and gold are your jewels,
And like your speech, like your deeds."
And to Naphthali she said,
"Naphthali, a frightened gazelle,
giving forth fair words.
Satisfied with astuteness,
Full of godly wisdom,
Praised in west and south."
And to Joseph she said,
"Joseph is a fruitful bow, a fruitful bow by the well—

But the daughters will *not* sing for him.
His bow did *not* sit steadily,
Not were his arms as golden
As the hands of Jacob's God.
Not for him the name of avenger for Israel's vine.
Your father refused to help you—
and a lady's song will bless you
With the blessings of life from above,
The blessings of the ones going down under,
The blessing of old and young.
But he, his firstborn bull, is bald,
His horns are snails' horns.
Can he push peoples with them,
Together with all the land's demolishers?"

All these are Dinah's brothers, eleven in number, and this is
what their sister said to them and blessed them, each one
according to his blessing she blessed them.

And then Dinah rose from her sickbed and nurtured Asenath
her daughter. And she was training her, for she said, "Shaddai
has dealt her a bitter life portion, for he created her a woman. I
shall guard her footsteps in this life. A mountain cyclamen a
girl is: whoever passes by would connive to pluck her." And in
the fullness of time Asenath, daughter of Dinah, became the
woman of one of her people, and she had sons and daughters.
And Dinah found consolation in her daughter's sons.
And Dinah did not know a man, and she was shut up, a living
widow, all her life. And Dinah said, "I shall not go to a man's
house, and a man shall not come onto my couch. How can I
look at him, and I can't give him my youthful love? Defiled I
was, defiled; a boar robbed [my virginity] by brute force. If a
man made me drunk by the kisses of his mouth, I would
remember the love I was sated with despite myself. Polluted,
polluted is my flesh, for there's no spot in it where the son of
Hamor hasn't kissed. Angst became the first kiss a male kissed
me. My youthful dream turned into terror, the drunkenness of
my love into a curse. My night of nights, my calamity, when my

flesh was defiled, I shall not forget. A crushed bud, a trampled flower I am."

And the time drew near for Dinah to die, and she expired, and was gathered unto her people, and she died in Egypt, in the land of Goshen.

And her brothers fell upon the face of Dinah their sister, and they lamented her, and they kissed her. And they buried her in the cave, in the field of Baal Zaphon, between Migdol and the sea, overlooking the Philistine road to Canaan.

Let us now discuss what Tchernichowsky has done—once again, I truly believe, like nobody before him. He read the story of Genesis 34, not "my" story, as it is written. And he made it into my story, from the title he gave to it—"The Dinah Affair"—onwards. This is the first point worth noting. Second, he understood that I was cruelly raped and that I probably had/have certain feelings about it. He had no compunction about describing my hatred for the rapist Shechem: indeed, my initial attraction to him did turn into hatred after the event. Third, Tchernichowsky gave me a voice: remember, I don't get to say even one word in "my" story. In Tchernichowsky's poem, I get to pronounce a critical blessing for my brothers, assessing their past, present, and future from several viewpoints but also from the perspective of their behavior toward me at my time of need. Fourth, he lets me speak many lines in poetry. Fifth, as you may have noticed, he omits Benjamin from the count of Jacob/Israel's sons. (Benjamin is not reported as being born until Genesis 35; this is one chapter after "my" story, hence—in biblical terms—chronologically later.) Instead, Tchernichowsky made me Jacob's twelfth "son," the twelfth tribe of Israel. He acknowledged the fact that I became pregnant, that I gave birth to a daughter and named her Asenath, that she married or didn't marry the biblical Joseph (Gen. 41:45)—which means that this poet/scholar was well versed in the midrashim about me. Sixth, he allowed me to remain single out of choice, out of revulsion because of being raped, although he has me say that I feel defiled—as if agreeing with the conventional wisdom that Shechem's deflowering of my virginity is an uppermost consideration for *my* self-loathing. But, at the very least, the poet allows me fruitfulness out of this uncalled-for union, he allows me a daughter and male grandchildren, and he allows me history and genealogy for my pain.

Now, excuse me if I digress a little, I'd like to say something about the literary merit, and form, and sources, and the historical circumstances as they relate to the contents of Tchernichowsky's *oeuvre*, before we proceed to evaluate his contribution to understanding my own story, which is—I shall not tire from repeating it—actually absent from the biblical story.

Tchernichowsky constructed the story as a prose narrative beginning with a summary that foregrounds my brothers' attack on the people of Shechem, a city whose eponym my assailant was; then he embedded in his prose account a poem, which he puts in my mouth; and finally, he returned to a third-person prose narration that—much like the first part—has several short speeches attributed to me, in the first-person mode, once again embedded in the prose account. In so doing he imitated biblical style, in which prose and poetry interchange. Furthermore, the long poem he allowed me belongs to the genre of "blessing," or "last testament"; more specifically, a poetic last speech attributed to a patriarch, or a male leader, in biblical literature and beyond it. Jacob's speech to his sons—not to me, of course—before his death (Genesis 49) and Moses' last speech (Deuteronomy 33) are prime examples of this literary device, where tribal eponyms are depicted according to their character, or the past and present/future circumstances of their social group. Now, if you are versed in the bible, you'll recognize straightaway that Tchernichowsky used Jacob's testament to his sons as the basis for his own poem, supplementing it with references to Moses' last speech. And he also used, at times, with references to a similar but different genre, Deborah's victory song after the war with the Canaanites (Judges 5) and other biblical texts. While Deborah's song is special in its own right, the practice of females welcoming the returning warriors by dancing and singing in celebration of military victory is far from rare in the bible: think about Miriam's song after the crossing of the Sea of Reeds (Exodus 15—incidentally, Tchernichowsky used a passage from that song as well); or the women singing "Saul has smitten by the thousands, David by the myriads," after the skirmishes with the Philistines (1 Sam. 18:7;

21:12). But no biblical woman gets to have her own "testament" or expanded "blessing," such as the one he attributed to me, when I thought (according to him) that I would not survive the delivery of my daughter. By so doing, the poet elevated me with one stroke to the rank of Jacob, Moses, and the Twelve Patriarchs (their own literary "testaments" didn't make it into the Jewish bible itself but were preserved at first by Jewish circles then by Christians): higher than any so-called matriarch such as Sarah, Rebekah, Rachel, and Leah, who get to die and be buried in the family's burial ground, but never to deliver a last testament.

Moreover, those of you familiar with the original biblical materials, especially those of Jacob's testament in Genesis 49, will notice what Tchernichowsky did. Far was it from him to simply repeat the definitions/blessings/descriptions of his sons and to attribute them to me. On the contrary! Creatively, intuitively, he turned things around from the viewpoint he imagined to be mine, under the circumstances. For instance, and this is perhaps the most glaring modification he made, look at the biblical version of Jacob's words to his sons Shimeon and Levi, my full brothers (on my mother's as well as my father's side) who avenged my honor:

Shimeon and Levi are brothers,
Instruments of cruelty are their swords.
Let my being not enter their assembly,
Let my honor not be united with their gathering.
For in their anger they slew a man,
And willfully they uprooted a wall.
Cursed be their anger, for it was fierce;
And their wrath, for it was hard.
I shall divide them upon Jacob,
And shall disperse them in Israel. (Genesis 49:5-7)

Clearly, my father, Jacob, is displeased with his sons, my brothers', action on my behalf. As you may remember, in Genesis 34 he is worried about the political and military ramifications of his sons' ostensible reprisal, fearing that the security of his outsider group is compromised. He doesn't behave as a caring father for his raped daughter (me); rather, like King David when Tamar is raped by

Amnon (2 Samuel 13; and Tamar will undoubtedly tell us about this when her turn comes), he's more concerned with pragmatic considerations of group survival. But note how Tchernichowsky reworks these same words of Jacob/Israel in the testament he attributes to me, and let me repeat the reformulation here:

> Shimeon and Levi are brothers,
> Instruments of nobility are their weapons.
> Ionians from Crete crafted them,
> Phoenicians in ships brought them,
> Arabian traders to Harran.
> Let my soul rejoice in their counsel,
> In their assembly my honor is elevated.
> For they slew a man in their anger
> And according to their wish uprooted a garden.
> Blessed be their anger, for it is fierce;
> And their wrath, for it was hard.
> Let there be many like them in Jacob,
> In all of Israel's diasporas.
> Bless, oh God, their might
> And accept the deed of their hands.
> Crush the necks of their foes
> And their enemies—who shall stand up?

Do you see how the poet turned everything around? He endowed me with rightful and righteous anger. He allowed me to speak my mind as he sympathetically reflected it, in accordance with the imagined situation of rape or date rape: he leaves this question of rape or date rape open, since he starts his retelling from the fraternal retribution, but makes it clear that—from my viewpoint—rape did occur. He allows me to have presumed initial interest turn into hate instead, exactly the opposite of what happened in the Tamar and Amnon affair: there Amnon "hates" Tamar after raping her (2 Sam. 13:15; we shall listen to her story later); in "my" story, Shechem falls in love with me after raping me—but it is impossible for me to love him, practical considerations of diminished marriageable value notwithstanding. On the contrary, I came to hate him with the distinctive fervor of the victim.

Even better than that, the poet treated me with so much respect
that, in his work, he let me become a mother of a tribe not only *in
spite of* my tarnished image, but precisely *because of* it. In so doing, he
did away with conventional morality: that is, he let an unmarried
woman, a raped woman, a woman he knew full well was blamed by
readers for her own affliction (I "went out," did I not?), become an
honorable mother. I must, really and truly, applaud the poet. For
look, in truth, and if we go to the beginning of "my" story once again,
if we examine the information given about me as daughter, sister,
later sexual object, the account is full of irregularities. As Carol
Meyers, a famous female and feminist bible commentator notes,

> [Dinah] is the only female descendant mentioned in the Genesis
> account of Jacob and his twelve sons. But cf. Gen. 46:15, which
> mentions both Dinah and daughters [plural] of Jacob.

Indeed, there were other sisters of mine, but they remain unnamed
like so many other biblical woman—Meyers herself edited a
dictionary of named and unnamed biblical women not long ago
(2000), and you've listened to our sisters Adah and Zillah, and others
will refer to this sorry fact again and again. Further, Meyers writes,
and I'm paraphrasing now, the announcement of my birth in Genesis
30:21 stands out in the narrative both because it presents a female
child and because it lacks an explanation of my name, in contrast to
the explanations supplied to all Jacob's sons. And she decides, at this
point, that because of these features, the authenticity of my place
within a unit of Genesis (29:31–30:24) that lists the birth and names
of eleven of Jacob's sons has been called into question. Further she
writes,

> Dinah's birth to Leah follows the announcement that Leah had
> born six sons to Jacob. Her seventh child is thus a daughter; and,
> with a female, her childbearing comes to an end. The seventh
> position, considering the symbolic value of that number,
> represents the fulfillment of Leah's maternal role, one that
> includes at least one female child. Furthermore, the birth of
> Dinah occupies the pivotal spot in the transition between Leah's
> childbearing and that of the previously barren but favored wife,

Rachel. Once Leah's part of the Jacob family is complete, God "remembered" Rachel and opened her womb for the birth of Joseph. The lack of an etiology [explanation] for Dinah, a name that, like the name of her brother Dan, is from a Hebrew word meaning "to judge" must be seen in the context of the eponymous nature of the twelve sons of Jacob. All represent tribal groups, and the presence of name explanations contributes to the ancestor traditions surrounding the twelve sons. Because Dinah is not an eponymous ancestor, an elaboration of her birth announcement would be inappropriate.

I, Dinah, have no idea why Meyers, as I've said a respected feminist, arrives at these conclusions. She's very careful, perhaps because she's writing to a mainstream (read: malestream) publication here. But, look again. Most of the evidence points to the fact that, within the birth story of Jacob's descendants and later tribes, I am the twelfth descendant. This is why I have a name; this is why I appear in this story of Genesis 29–30. I'm special, I'm my mother's seventh offspring, and we all know that in the bible the number seven is special. One example will suffice: there are six days in a week; the seventh day, the Shabbat, is the climax of the bible's basic time unit. As the very short biblical report of my birth stands, it should be the climax rather than the addition to my mother's birthing achievements. Yes, this is how it should be read in this text instead of being viewed as an empty note.

However, already in Genesis 30, the discreditation of my position is expressed by omitting an overt explanation for my name, whereas some of my brothers get even two such explanations. In passing let me note that the first component of my name, *dîn*, in Hebrew means "law, precept," even "justice"; "Dinah" would be the feminine form of this term. There are other examples of such a word pair in Hebrew—a grammatically feminine and masculine doublet that means exactly the same, such as "justice" (*tsedeq* and *tsedaqah*). Benjamin, born later to my aunt Rachel, was an afterthought. Tchernichowsky, in his wisdom and poetic intuition, understood this perfectly. He reinstated me to my rightful position. It's nice to know that at least one male, not a postmodern feminist and not a woman, interprets the story's premise as it should be interpreted.

Perhaps now the rape story, or the "Dinah Affair," can be read differently and to better advantage. Meyers continues:

> Dinah's presence in the birth account of Jacob's family also anticipates her appearance in the unusual narrative of Genesis 34, which recounts the rape of Dinah by a local Canaanite named Shechem (son of Hamor), the attempt of Hamor to arrange a marriage between his son and the woman he has violated, the resistance of two of Dinah's brothers (Simeon and Levi) to the proposed arrangement, and the subsequent deceit and slaughter of the prospective bridegroom, and all the men in his city, by the vengeful brothers.

Do you see anything here about my own feelings, or stand, in this matter? Not at all. Attention is drawn, though, to the sociological aspects of what happened to me. In Meyers' analysis, I become a political as well as a sexual pawn in the power games of adult males:

> This story departs from the previous narratives in the way it moves from the stories of individuals to personalized history. . . . As such it deals with two interrelated and complicated aspects of proto-Israelite existence. Insofar as Shechem represents a Canaanite city and the two antagonistic brothers depict the ancestors of two Israelite tribes, the tale apparently reflects a proto-Israelite struggle and perhaps also the special position of Shechem as both a congenial and a troublesome place in pre-monarchic Israel. Unlike most of the Canaanite cities, it apparently became part of Israel without military conflict; it is the site of the great covenant gathering described in Joshua 24; it is the site of an early monarchic move by Abimelech that results in the destruction of the city (Judges 9).
>
> The second aspect of the story is related to the tension involved in Shechem's [the city] status as part of Israel, yet it is different. The personalized tale dealing with marital customs confronts the difficult problem of ingroup (endogamous) vs. outgroup (exogamous) marriage. Israel struggled with the advantages and disadvantages of limiting marriage possibilities to endogamy throughout most of its history. As

anthropologists . . . have pointed out, the shock value of the story draws attention to a sensitive issue. Marriage alliances are useful in territorial expansion or in compensation for demographic shortages; but they also involve the threat that divergent cultural values will be brought into the group and threaten the group's stability.

The story of Dinah is thus a reflection of both the political history of proto-Israel and early Israel and the social history of all Israel. This interweaving of themes is reflected in the long-recognized complexity of the literary sources and structure of Genesis 34.

We have here a wonderful example of the disparity between poetic imagination and scholarly criticism. Carol Meyers admits, readily, that in the biblical narrative I was raped. She has no problem with recognizing that. Nonetheless, she quickly moves on to view the rape as a metaphor for sociological issues, such as in-marriage and out-marriage. In so doing, she shifts the issue of rape into the public sphere and turns it into a symbolic issue. In so doing, ironically, she misses the point. She joins those who view me as a pawn in the male competition of adult males for power and supremacy over other male groups, competitions that are played and inscribed over women's bodies by violent means if necessary—which is true, I'd be the first to admit that, but it neglects the emotions of the female pawn. In so doing Meyers in effect complies with mainstream views, and she's not the only feminist or woman reader to do so. Tchernichowsky, on the other hand, apparently subscribes to another view. He allows me to feel, suffer, express my suffering, give birth, be a parent to a tribe, remain celibate out of choice after the rape—and still become an ancestor to a maternal tribe. In that sense, paradoxically and unexpectedly, I prefer the male poet's interpretation. It's closer to the grain.

However—and here's the rub—have you noticed how the poet, after making me into an inverted Joseph, has me ask to be buried in Egypt and, unlike Joseph, to specify that my bones be *not* carried to Canaan when the Exodus comes (Gen. 50:25-26; Exod. 13:19), actually killing me by his pen, or typewriter (we're talking a pre-computer age)? I do not die in the bible. What happened to him, to Tchernichowsky, at this juncture of the story he constructed for me? I can only guess. He wanted me to be a Joseph-like figure, sure enough, although it's not clear from his story whether my daughter, Asenath, is the same Asenath who married Joseph and produced two children for him in Egypt, children who became tribes in Israel (Ephraim and Mannasseh). Did he want me to have the dignity of being buried according to my own wishes, which is far better than what happened to the matriarchs Sarah, Rebekah, Leah, and Rachel, who were buried not according to their own wishes (these are never referred to) but according to their husbands' wishes? Did he want me to have the dignity of being a mortal, thus dying after enjoying the blessing of a third generation, wonderful grandchildren to console me? Perhaps all or some of the above. In addition, he certainly wanted to cling to my hatred of the rapist to the grave and beyond.

But listen, I'm not a woman. I'm a literary figure, like all of us here in this meeting. This issue, why the poet so sympathetic to my plight saw fit nevertheless to kill me by his writing is interesting. In that sense, let's wander off once again and have a look at what the American poet Edgar Allan Poe did to Sheherazade, the chief narrator and unparalleled heroine of the Persian/Arabian *A Thousand and One Nights,* in his "The Thousand and Second Tale of Sheherazade." Why don't you take a little time to read what Fatema Mernissi, a wise contemporary Moroccan sociologist-cum-author has to say about Poe in her recent book, *Scheherazade Goes West, or the European Harem* (2000)—a book, I believe, that will resurface in Zipporah's tale. Mernissi asks, mildly and with decorum but nevertheless insistently, why Poe has to kill Sheherazade as a literary afterthought to her indigenous story—nay, why he is compelled to have her be *willingly* executed—as an imaginary footnote to her contrasted story of literary ability and personal valor in the base story. Poe has Sheherazade tell her master one more story, about technologies of the nineteenth century, which he can't imagine to be true. Whereupon he decides she's a liar like all other women and deserves execution. Like Jephthah's daughter, Sheherazade complies. A range of interpretations is indeed possible here as well. Such as, for instance, that Sheherazade is so tired at this point of her project, that is, to stay alive, that she gives up. Or, she is so tired of her efforts to entertain the king; or, she admits defeat, for she'd never manage to restore his faith in womankind, and she gives up. Perhaps Poe was commenting on the impossibility for even such an accomplished and wise woman figure as Sheherazade to survive in a man's world. But, finally, there's also another interpretation, less complimentary to Poe. Perhaps Poe, consciously or otherwise, commenting on this impossibility, was also entertaining a modicum of wishful thinking: such a woman cannot be allowed to live even in fiction, not to mention in life (which, since Poe, is known to be stranger than fiction). She is, simply, an unfeasibility fated to be killed off by words, with her own consent.

Poe and Tchernichowsky were formidable literary geniuses, each in his own way and his own milieu. They did love and adore and appreciate women, after their own fashion, within the constraints of their own time and place. Drawing an analogy from Poe to Tchernichowsky, I will respond to both by stating my position. As a literary figure, I'm alive and relatively well, relatively because after all this time of literary this or the other afterlife, I submit that in Poe's literary killing of the famed Sheherazade, and in Tchernichowsky's literary killing of me, one may detect the possibility that—their male excellency and feminist leanings notwithstanding, their sympathy notwithstanding, other possibilities of interpretation notwithstanding—the suspicion that both could not, as a bottom line, let us live on in literature should be attributed to their (male) fear of an outstanding woman figure. Despite themselves, to be sure, despite their pronounced sympathy.

So what else is new? In the Hebrew bible, women are seldom allowed to be leaders. Hagar, you say? She is the mother of Yishmael, a real nation—not only a tribe—but she's expelled by Abraham (Genesis 21). Deborah, you say? Hang on, because she goes with Barak to battle and therefore he has to be known as the general whose war was decided by a mere woman, eventually Jael (Judges 4–5). Miriam, you say? Note how she's discredited in relation to her brothers Moses and Aaron, punished with a skin disorder, when she and Aaron compete for an equal prophetic status with Moses in the desert, while Aaron is not punished at all (Numbers 12). Jezebel, Athaliah—both queens, but known forever as idolatrous bitches and immoral usurpers of power (1 Kings 16–2 Kings 9; 2 Kings 11; and 2 Chronicles 22, respectively). What, indeed, shall be done with significant woman figures, with political potential, with social promise, with capabilities?

The answer, regrettably, in the bible as in much of the rest of Western culture, is: deny the extent of their contribution to public life as much as possible. Discredit them, so that the accepted social order, the shifting and insecure premises of male supremacy, can be upheld. The means for so doing are varied and nuanced. A woman figure can be trashed, that is, branded as sexually immodest: gossip will be valuable here, true or otherwise. She can be presented as damaged goods, that is, sexually molested: true or otherwise, her fault (very seldom) or otherwise, this can be exploited. Note the usage, in both cases, of sexual mores to discredit females: there's no symmetry with males in this dual-standard exercise. Let me note in passing that in the United States of the late twentieth century, political attempts to use sex scandals in order to discredit President Clinton and impeach him finally failed, although they caused much damage. Furthermore, a woman figure can be domesticated, that is, turned into a wife and mother who owes submission to her husband and has the *center* of her life in the domestic rather than the public sphere. Stress their foreign origin and, if this isn't the case, create a foreign connection for them. Finally, if all else fails, accuse them of being disgusting pagans and idol worshippers. Try to use all these propaganda tools together or just several of them, as the individual situation warrants. In any event, try not to state explicitly that their gender is what hinders them from becoming eminent leaders.

So Tchernichowsky, a better man than most, has me killed. And he does so after understanding my story perfectly. So let me reiterate that story, finally, taking into account what that poet understood and what he missed, and simultaneously with Carol Meyers' restrained but implicit help.

I've already mentioned that there are traces in the Hebrew bible that I, my mother Leah's seventh descendant, was destined to be a mother of a tribe, among the other male descendants of my mother, her sister and my aunt Rachel, and their handmaids Bilhah and Zilpah. My position as the seventh of my mother's children constitutes a pointer toward my destiny as leader, a stereotypic position more important than that of my full brother Judah (my mother's fourth son although so prominent later), my elder brothers

Shimeon and Levi (second and third to my mother), and my half-brother and cousin on my mother's side, Joseph (twelfth in Jacob's line, including me). Unfortunately, I was date raped. My father was at that time frightened and not supportive, bewildered, really, as fathers would be. My mother was dysfunctional as well, tired probably of her lifelong struggle with her sister Rachel over my father's love. My elder full brothers avenged my and their honor by killing the rapist and his community, thus serving our mutually inclusive agendas: my purpose (revenge) and their own (political aspirations vis-à-vis the indigenous inhabitants of the land). At a great cost to myself, I had a daughter and fulfilled my destiny. So far Tchernichowsky is absolutely correct.

And what did later scribes, authors, and interpreters do? They used my own tragedy for their own ends. They silenced me, taking away my voice. They made me into a barren non-entity, exploiting the fact that I was raped (discreditation by accusation of sexual immodesty, as well as becoming damaged goods). They took me off the list of Jacob's twelve descendants, parents of tribes, to be supplanted by Rachel's son Benjamin who was born later. Or, according to other lists, when Shimeon my brother is not reckoned as a "tribe" anymore, then Benjamin is in, and Joseph's sons Ephraim and Manasseh—my grandchildren from Asenath, perhaps—are reckoned each as a tribe in their own right.

I am Dinah, daughter of Leah and Jacob. My name is derived from a root meaning "to judge," as rightly stated by Carol Meyers, the same root my paternal half-brother Dan's name (from the handmaiden Bilhah) is derived from. Originally, in the bible, Dan is described as having settled in the Judaean plain, then as having migrated to the north (Judges 18–19). Big mistake, caused by the root similarity of his name and mine. Originally, his descendants settled in the north, next to his full brother Naphthali; my descendants settled in the south, next to my full brother Judah. Having obliterated my own tribe, the necessity arose for biblical authors to create a single Dan tribe that migrated from south to north, thus eradicating the memory of my own group while assimilating it into the group of Dan, of the similar name (Judges 17–18).

There were other ideological considerations for using the rape story to discredit me, however. I can't deny that. Over the years, over centuries, over millennia. For instance, as Meyers states, there is such ambiguity in the bible concerning in-group and out-group marriages—and, let me add, since no marriage finally took place in my case, over such sexual unions. The fear of losing group identity through outside sexual unions is great. Was it the fear of assimilation into the metaphorical Canaanites, the "Others"? Or, as Yairah Amit thinks, the more specific polemics against the Samaritans/ Shomronites, that pseudo-Israelite, non-Jewish, but related group that traces its holy center to Shechem and lives there until this day and age, from about the fifth century BCE onward? Or was it once again the fear of the "inhabitants of the land," the Arabs this time, during the unrest at the time of the British mandate, when Tchernichowsky wrote his sympathetic (my presumed death and burial notwithstanding) work in 1937?

Let me tell you a little about that node in history.* The rise of Nazism in Europe during the 1930s led to a great increase in Jewish immigration to Palestine/EI (Eretz Israel), the national home for Jews under British protection since the Balfour declaration of 1917. Whereas there were about five thousand Jewish immigrants authorized into the country in 1932, about 62,000 were authorized in 1935. The mid-1930s wave of Jewish immigration, named the "fifth *aliyah*" ("coming up"), was mainly from Germany and Eastern Europe and greatly enhanced the fledgling Jewish presence. As a result, the Arab unrest quickly acquired the dimension of a revolt. An Arab High Committee was formed to unite all Arab opposition to the Jews in Palestine. The Arabs called for a general strike, and rioting continued throughout Palestine. The general strike of 1936, organized by Haj Amin al-Husayni, the mufti of Jerusalem, lasted six months. Some Arabs acquired weapons and formed a guerrilla force. The unrest was such that the British appointed a Committee of Inquiry to investigate the situation and recommend a solution. The so-called Peel Commission (1937) found the British promises to both Zionists and Arabs irreconcilable and declared the British mandate unworkable. It therefore recommended the partition of Palestine/EI into a small Jewish state, a much larger Arab state united with Transjordan, and a small continuing British mandate presence in Jerusalem, Jaffa, and the road between the two cities. The Zionists reluctantly approved partition, but the Arabs rejected it, objecting

---

This section is with the aid of several Internet sources. I can give you the exact urls on request.

particularly to the proposal that the Arab population be forcibly transferred out of the proposed Jewish state. In 1936–39 there continued a concerted campaign by the Arab leadership to oppose these changes (despite the fact that many of the Arab leaders were involved in land sales to the Zionists). The British declared the Arab Higher Committee illegal in 1937—Haj Amin escaped to Syria and toured Arab capitals (and, later, went to Nazi Berlin) to mobilize support against the British and the Zionists.

With the possibility of a new world war looming, the British revised their political priorities in Palestine in the late 1930s and dropped the partition idea. The main aim now was to try to win support in the Middle East so that military forces there could be kept to a minimum. This meant trying to appease Arab opinion, and in May 1939 the British government published a so-called "White Paper" that proposed that an Arab government be established in Palestine, with strict limitations on future Jewish immigration (fifteen thousand Jewish immigrants per year for five years, later subject to Arab agreement—meaning, in effect, cessation). Jewish land purchases were to be restricted, and within ten years an independent, bi-national Palestine would be established. As a tactic, this was interesting but unsuccessful. The Zionists were shocked by what they considered a betrayal of the Balfour Declaration. The Arabs considered the plan not beneficial enough for them, demanding instead the immediate creation of an Arab Palestine, the prohibition of further Jewish immigration, and a review of the status of all incoming Jewish immigrants since 1918. Consequently, both Zionists and Arabs rejected the new plan, and the League of Nations (to which the British administration was answerable in theory) did not ratify the policy. As we all know, World War II broke out in 1939 and lasted until 1945. Everybody knows about the Holocaust, although some see fit to deny it. The British didn't allow Jewish immigration after the Holocaust: on the contrary, they tried to stop the illegal immigration. Finally the United Nations, the international organization to succeed the League of Nations after the war, voted for a partition and the establishment of a Jewish home in Eretz Israel in the form of a Jewish state. The British were driven out by both parties. The Israeli state was declared, and war between Arab and Jews immediately followed. It's depressing to see how now, fifty-odd years later, claims and counterclaims for land, historical right, just war, and so on resemble too uncannily those of 1937.

Why am I giving you this brief sketch of recent history? Tchernichowsky, do remember, wrote his "The Dinah Affair" in June 1937, in two days only, quickly and vehemently. It's difficult not to assume that his antipathy to the Arabs of Nablus (ancient Shechem) did play a part in his sympathy toward me. In fact, I suspect that his sympathy toward me was perhaps born out not only of his humanistic temperament, and his medical knowledge of what rape would mean for a woman, but also of cross-gender, *political* identification with me, as well as with my avenging brothers. I suspect he saw in me the young Jewish settlement forever "raped" by the Arab aggressors, whose behavior to Jews as well as to their own was far from humane. I suspect he saw in Shimeon and Levi's revenge just revenge, and in my reinstatement as the twelfth tribe a just reward for my metaphorical, contemporaneous counterpart. I feel I understand his motives—and perhaps also his literary killing of me at the end; perhaps, in addition to my earlier speculations, I should add another one: perhaps Tchernichowsky, the wise poet, was apprehensive about the fate of my mirrored image, the young Jewish homeland in Palestine/EI. At the time, he couldn't foresee the establishment of the Israeli state. But, perhaps, at this point I'm reading too much into his *oeuvre*.

Be that as it may, let me return to the main strand of my tale. I, a literary creation, was not spared much by way of being discredited. I was domesticated: in the Jewish midrash known as *Genesis Rabbah* I'm made into the wife of Job the sufferer, on the slimmest linguistic speculation. I referred to this domestication above as one of the practices used to diminish the stature of a distinctive female figure. Wrong, once again: how could I give birth to ten more offspring or more (Job 1, 42), how could I bear it, after Hamor's treatment of me?

To conclude, then. I'm Dinah, raped by Hamor as well as by the ongoing reception in commentaries on and interpretations of "my" story. Other accounts notwithstanding, I survived in the form of offspring descending from a daughter. As much as I hate the person who raped me, his daughter, conceived in pain, became my historical salvation—even if this salvation was distorted time and again later, even if the rape itself was doubted and made to appear *only* as a metaphor for political relations. At this time my personal abode is still in the city of Shechem, Tchernichowsky's poetical testimony about my death and burial notwithstanding. Shechem is troubled once more, Palestinians and Israelis fighting another *intifada* (uprising), battling once more issues of in-group and out-group problems, power politics, violence. As both a victim and a survivor, my lips are sealed: I'm waiting, once more, between Jacob/Israel and Hamor/Shechem. Both are inscribed on my body. Whether the hatred born out of violence will subside this time around, during this rape, and when, remains to be seen.

THREE

∽

Lust Is My Middle Name, I Have No Other: Madam Potiphar

*D*ear ladies. Before I start my little paper, let me give you two handouts. The first, as you shall see, contains the text of Proverbs 7, where a presumably immature man is warned against a foreign married woman in no uncertain terms: she's a temptress and will lead him to a certain early death. I'd like you to have it since it looks like a didactic warning, making a hysterical generalized manifesto against women like me, as I'm described in Genesis 39. And the text of Genesis 39 will be my second handout. Please don't worry if you haven't brought your reading glasses. Throughout my talk I shall project the two texts onto two overhead screens, so that we can have them in front of our eyes, and we can save time: I doubt whether many of you have bibles at hand, be it because of loathing for your treatment in it or just because of laziness. So here we are; let's read the texts. Please note, while you look at the handouts or at the screens: whenever the translation is uncertain since the original Hebrew is either ambiguous or else obscure, I've supplied alternatives in italics, in parentheses. So here's the first text.

My child (*son*), keep my words and store up my commandments with you; keep my commandments and live, keep my teachings . . . that they may keep you from the loose woman, from the adulteress with her smooth words. For at the window of my house I looked out through my lattice, and I saw among the simple ones, I observed among the youths, a young man without sense, passing along the street near her corner, taking the road to her house in the twilight, in the evening, at the time of night and darkness. Then a woman comes toward him, decked out like a prostitute, wily of heart. She is loud and wayward; her feet do not stay at home; now in the street, now in the squares, and at every corner she lies in wait. She seizes him and kisses him, and with impudent face she says to him: "I had to offer sacrifices, and today I have paid my vows; so now I have come out to meet you, to seek you eagerly, and I have found you! I have decked my couch with coverings, colored spreads of Egyptian linen; I have perfumed my bed with myrrh, aloes, and cinnamon. Come, let us take our fill of love until morning; let us delight ourselves with love. For my husband is not at home; he has gone on a long journey. He took a bag of money with him; he will not come home until full moon." With much seductive speech she persuades him; with her smooth talk she compels him. Right away he follows her, and goes like an ox to the slaughter, or bounds like a stag toward the trap until an arrow pierces its entrails. He is like a bird rushing into a snare, not knowing that it will cost him his life. And now, my children (*sons*), listen to me, and be attentive to the words of my mouth. Do not let your hearts turn aside to her ways; do not stray into her paths. For many are those she has laid low, and numerous are her victims. Her house is the way to Sheol, going down to the chambers of death. (Proverbs 7 NRSV)

Got it? I don't know whether the concerned speaker in this text is a male (as most readers imagine) or a female (as I do). The situation, though, is clear enough. From the speaker's perspective, a woman is trying to seduce a young man; the latter shouldn't succumb, although the temptation is real and the negative option offered extremely attractive, as is admitted. And here comes the story about me, although I'm made into a secondary figure by many literary devices by comparison with Joseph, the real hero (or so it seems at first reading).

Now Joseph was taken down to Egypt, and Potiphar, an officer (*eunuch?*) of Pharaoh, the captain of the guard (*chief cook? General?*), an Egyptian, bought him from the Ishmaelites who

had brought him down there. The LORD was with Joseph, and
he became a successful man; he was in the house of his
Egyptian master. His master saw that the LORD was with him,
and that the LORD caused all that he did to prosper in his
hands. So Joseph found favor in his sight and attended him; he
made him overseer of his house and put him in charge of all
that he had. From the time that he made him overseer in his
house and over all that he had, the LORD blessed the Egyptian's
house for Joseph's sake; the blessing of the LORD was on all
that he had, in house and field. So he left all that he had in
Joseph's charge; and, with him there, he had no concern for
anything but the food that he ate [*euphemism: his wife? See
further*]. Now Joseph was handsome and good looking. And
after a time his master's wife cast her eyes on Joseph and said,
"Lie with me." But he refused and said to his master's wife,
"Look, with me here, my master has no concern about anything
in the house, and he has put everything that he has in my hand.
He is not greater in this house than I am, nor has he kept back
anything from me except yourself, because you are his wife.
How then could I do this great wickedness, and sin against
God?" And [*although*] she spoke to Joseph day after day, he
would not consent (refused) to lie beside her or (and) to be with
her. One day, [*however,*] when he went into the house to do his
work (*business?*), and while no one else was in the house, she
caught hold of his garment, saying, "Lie with me!" But he left
his garment in her hand, and fled and ran outside. When she
saw that he had left his garment in her hand and had fled
outside, she called out to the members of her household and
said to them, "See, my husband has brought among us a
Hebrew to insult us! He came in to me to lie with me, and I
cried out with a loud voice; and when he heard me raise my
voice and cry out, he left his garment beside me, and fled
outside." Then she kept his garment by her until his master
came home, and she told him the same story, saying, "The
Hebrew servant, whom you have brought among us, came in to
me to insult (*play sexually with*) me; but as soon as I raised my
voice and cried out, he left his garment beside me, and fled
outside." When his master heard the words that his wife spoke

to him, saying, "This is the way your servant treated me," he became enraged. And Joseph's master took him and put him into the prison, the place where the king's prisoners were confined; he remained there in prison. (Genesis 39:1-20 NRSV, with possible modifications added in brackets)

Look at the two texts again. Got it? A woman shouldn't express lust, not even love, in relation to a man. She shouldn't make her feelings or desires known. Nay, she shouldn't have such feelings or desires to begin with, least of all when she's married and her affection turns on someone other than her husband (whether her marriage is functional or dysfunctional is of secondary consequence). If she nevertheless does have such illicit desires, physical or emotional or both, she should keep them to herself as a dirty secret. Most important, she shouldn't profess them to her chosen male sex object, or love object. She shouldn't make private or public claims. And she shouldn't, ultimately, propose any kind of liaison. And if the male sex object refuses her for any clear or self-righteous reasons, she should take immediate steps to protect herself, lest *he* tries to defend himself by blaming her. And if this requires a lie, so be it: she may save her skin if not her reputation. For the scales are loaded, always, against her. This gender issue, a cultural universal almost, is what I found out—to my cost.

Does it matter much whether my husband was a "eunuch," physically impotent, or an army official? Both translations are possible. If the first is adopted, then at least for some readers I may have had some justification for my feelings, but not for my alleged behavior. If the second, then no justification is possible at all; the familiar equation of "military" with "virile" would militate against me by association. But, whatever the choice, my attachment to the Hebrew slave my husband brought home was judged as inappropriate anyhow, be the case the one or the other.

Joseph, "Yahu will add," one of the explanations his mother Rachel gave to his name (Gen. 30:24), was indeed a welcome addition to our household. He was as good looking as he was talented. He was also aware of his appearance and his endowments. He was all things to everybody, to men and women alike: young, beautiful, flirtatious, clever, successful, friendly—a bi-sexual figure he was, a gender-bender genius, even at his tender age of seventeen or so.

And he grew up to be such an important economist, even though—mind you—he had no formal education in that field. Eventually he saved Egypt, and his original community, from extinction by famine. This, we're told, was the Hebrew god's original plan. But meanwhile there I was, a pawn in the divine game, hopelessly in love and desire with that slave.

So much literature has been written about Joseph. That he refused my advances, that he was so righteous as not even to consider my repeated offers. That I did try to seduce him with all the feminine wiles in any woman's possession, from fashionable clothes to tears to pulling rank to making threats. Joseph features as a hero of self-restraint in the bible itself, in the post-biblical Jewish literature as a man who adhered to the Ten Commandments (Do not Fornicate! Do not Covet!) and to Yhwh's words, in the Christian church fathers and the Qur'an and in subsequent Islamic literature as a saint. And in visual art, be it Jewish or Christian or Muslim, he fares well on the whole. Read Philo of Alexandria, Josephus Flavius, or most of *Genesis Rabbah* for our story if you wish. And at first, all through these afterlives of the Genesis story itself, I remain nameless, ageless, driven by lust, a sinner, a liar, a woman without honor, an ethnically foreign fornicator (as in the book of Proverbs), a source of shame and ridicule.

But then little chinks, cracks, crevices appear in various retellings of the story. In the *Testament of Joseph*, presumably Joseph's last will and testament, he devotes more space to an appetizing description of the mortal danger I represented for him (which he overcame, of course, and quite easily as told), than to all his other achievements altogether. Strange, wouldn't you say? In *Genesis Rabbah* some sages question Joseph's lack of interest in my advances, playfully; they claim he was interested but held back. I distrust this minority opinion, since I suspect those sages of wishing to glorify Joseph even further. You know their maxim: where a repentant man stands, the perfectly righteous can't stand; or, Who is a hero? Whoever squashes his desire (*Midrash Samuel* 5:16). So that tendency is of no consequence for my written plight.

But then, in some midrashic sources, suddenly—as it seems—some attention is being paid to *me*. A scene is added to the story, in which I make my passion public to other women, if not to the world at large: I invite them to a party and have Joseph serve some refreshments. Struck by his beauty, they cut themselves with the knives they have for slicing bread, or citrus fruit, or apples, or whatever—as the case may be in various Jewish and Islamic sources, dating from the sixth or seventh century CE onwards, from the Qur'an to other midrashic sources besides. And this scene also receives pictorial representations in Islamic art, up to and including the nineteenth century.

Furthermore, in some of these sources I acquire a name: Zulaika. And I become lovesick to the point of mortal danger. And the neighboring women, at least they become more worried about my well-being than about male shame/honor about their womenfolk's desire.

And all this time, Joseph's figure grows to be more ambivalent. Second thoughts are bestowed not only on secondary characters, such as me, but also on this primary character. When you look at Renaissance and later visual art re-presentations of the alleged and abortive temptation scene, when I lunge at Joseph and he leaves a piece of clothing (what clothing? Outer? Next-to-the-skin?) with me while escaping, some visual features recur regularly across individual artists, cultures, places, and periods as if, indeed, they are to be found in the original story. Almost all the visual re-presentations posit a bed in the middle of the scene. The bed is usually messy and jumbled, as if previously used. I am on the bed, in assorted states of disarray and part-nakedness. At times I look older, at times younger, than Joseph; at times I'm good looking, at others less so. A drape of some sort, usually red or crimson—symbolizing passion?—is prominent in the background. Ambiguity reigns: it's difficult to fathom whether this is a "before" or an "after" scene. Moreover, Joseph's body tells a twofold story: in most visual re-presentations he's caught as he leaves the room, granted. But not always is he in an apparent hurry. And even when he is, his eyes might tell a different story from his legs, or the lower part of his body. If his eyes linger on me, then his legs point to the outside. If his eyes are shady or already look outwards, then his lower body is still directed at me.

How did it happen, then, that Joseph got into my bedroom? According to Jewish law a woman and a man not married to each other shouldn't be alone in the same enclosed area, not to mention a room, not to mention a house. Why did Joseph come into the house, when he knew that I desired him and said so repeatedly and openly, when there was no one else around for some reason? Ladies, this is the crux of the matter. He may have been very, very loyal to his master, my husband, and to his god, as he claimed, in speech. But why did he come in, when he had to know that he shouldn't be in my company without any chaperon, and how and why did he get into my bedroom, as the painters visualize with their blessed artistic intuition?

Already the Aramaic translators understood that the biblical "and on a certain day he came in to do his work" (v. 11) was shady. They translated, "he came in to do his bookkeeping," and some other Jewish sources agree. Ah, I understand them: they wanted to show that he came in to do something he couldn't logically do outside the house itself. But this is a poor excuse and, moreover, doesn't explain Joseph's presence in my bedroom: no need to do bookkeeping there. Shall we therefore accept the Jewish sages' minority opinion, namely, that Joseph did desire me, and he did come in to accomplish his desire, only that, on the spot, his nerve—or call it what you will— failed him? As succinctly described, in one of these sources, which places Joseph firmly in my bed:

> The bow stretched and came back . . .
> His semen dispersed and came through his nails . . .
> He saw his father's icon and it cooled his blood . . .
> He saw his mother's icon and it cooled his blood.
> (*Genesis Rabbah* and *Midrash Samuel* for Genesis 49:24 and
> 1 Samuel 2:9)

Now, if you wish for my version of the events, here it is—for whatever it's worth. Joseph did desire me. Later Islamic tradition upholds this, as does Thomas Mann in his monumental book, where he names me as well ("mut-em-emet" he calls me, not "Zulaika" as in the Islamic or Islamic-influenced sources). But our love was tragic: it couldn't be fulfilled. And the world intervened, and the story was re-written. And I got the bad press, and Joseph escaped almost unharmed. Everything in order: the female side of the story suppressed, misunderstood, or condemned.

But, and this is the nature of things as well, such suppressions or changes or distortions return, sometimes with a vengeance. I do return in later versions beyond the Hebrew bible, as delineated above. My role grows considerably and retellers' attitudes toward me seem to become more sympathetic—people tend to feel for lovestruck women rather than for desire-driven brazen hussies, and I become more and more lovestruck as the centuries and millennia go by. I become stronger and weaker at the same time. I preoccupy male commentators' imagination, I grow, I become an obsession and a symbol, such as in Sufi mystical literature.

And Joseph? He's reduced to an eponym, a name signifying an affiliation to a patriarch or past leader. That's all. He's not even a tribe: his sons Ephraim and Manasseh become tribes, and his name remains an umbrella group name and no more. But I, who am I to take revenge; I shouldn't say so, but I still love him, although he died so many years ago after giving me so much trouble—the hypocrite, just look at what he wrote in his *Testament*—the stupid woman that I am.

We should perhaps go back to the beginning of my talk now. My life experience has shown me that a woman shouldn't express lust, not even love, in relation to a man. She shouldn't make her feelings or desires known. Nay, she shouldn't have such feelings or desires to begin with, least of all when she's married (whether her marriage is functional or dysfunctional is of secondary importance). If she does have such desires, nevertheless, she should keep them to herself as a dirty secret. And she shouldn't profess them to her chosen male sex object, or love object. She shouldn't make private or public claims. And she shouldn't, ultimately, propose any kind of liaison. And if she does become verbal nevertheless, and the sex object refuses her for any clear or self-righteous reasons, she should take immediate steps to protect herself, lest he try to defend himself by blaming her. And if this requires a lie, so be it: she may save her skin if not her reputation. For the scales are loaded, always, against her. This, a gender cultural universal almost, is what I found out—to my cost. But history, and storytelling, may subvert this. And those who understand, will understand.

FOUR

∞

I Am the Bird Woman:
Zipporah

Zipporah ... wife of Moses. The name of Zipporah's father is variously given as Reuel (Exod. 2:18, 21) and Jethro (18:2; cf. 3:1), priest of Midian. She was one of seven daughters (2:16). Zipporah bore Moses two sons, Gershom and Eliezer (2:22; 18:3-4). She appears to have accompanied her husband on his return to Egypt when, at a night encampment on the way, she averted his imminent death by circumcising her son with a flint (4:24-26). Zipporah seems to have returned with her children to her father's home in Midian, rejoining Moses at Mt. Sinai after the Exodus from Egypt (18:1-6). Nothing further is recorded of her.

This is the summary of my biblical life, a few liberties taken for the sake of clarity, as given by the Jewish-American scholar Nahum Sarna. The bare facts, if you will—but, like so many summaries, it misses the essence of my character entirely.

We can add to the verses cited by Sarna a single elliptical verse, which is sometimes understood as referring to me. A passage dealing with a personal and theological contest between Miriam and Aaron, Moses' siblings, on the one hand and Moses on the other, opens with:

While they [the Israelites wandering in the desert] were at Hazeroth, Miriam and Aaron spoke against Moses because of

the Cushite woman whom he had married (for he had indeed
married a Cushite woman). (Numbers 12:1 NRSV)

Whether this last verse does or doesn't belong to my life as
constructed in/by the biblical text will be discussed later. But so far I
have no biblical biography to speak of. I'm a typical biblical woman: a
female relational to father, husband, and son(s); a fragmented
woman, to borrow Cheryl Exum's phrase; not a speaking agent apart
from the twice-repeated obscure expression in Exodus 4
("bridegroom of blood you are to me!"), to follow Mieke Bal's
narratological principle. In short: not much is to be said about the
great man's wife even if the brief mythological allusion of Exodus 4 is
elaborated (see Ilana Pardes). Which, within the biblical framework
and frame-up (Alice Bach's phrase), is hardly surprising.

Perhaps more to the point at this moment is the summary of my
imagined life in the Midrash.

Zipporah is praised in the Midrash both for her piety and
virtue . . . and for her beauty. . . . Various explanations are given
of her name ("bird"): when questioned by her father about
Moses, she ran after him like a bird and returned with him; she
cleansed her father's house from every vestige of idolatry as a
bird collects the smallest crumbs from the ground. . . . She is
compared to the bird used in the purification rites of the leper.
(*Encyclopedia Judaica*)

Indeed, my name is indicative of my character, as is common in
the Hebrew bible. It means "female bird," or according to some
"small bird." Isn't it interesting that several prominent biblical
women have names that designate *domestic* animals' names—such as
Leah ("cow") and Rachel ("ewe")—or *small* animals, such as Deborah
("bee"), Jael ("mountain goat"), or Huldah ("rat")? It seems that,
name-wise, I should be classified firmly among those women. But
what does the given name indicate? Rachel and Leah indeed
represent the vocation of their husband, Jacob, a gifted shepherd (or
is their own vocation projected onto him?). And Deborah stings, a
little, by telling Barak that his insistence on his going with her, a
mere woman, for battle will take his victory away and place it in the

hands of a woman (Judges 4:8-9). Is Huldah a "rat" because she tells King Josiah's emissaries that the king and his kingdom will be toppled by god (2 Kings 22)? And Jael, does she behave as a mountain goat when she kills the Canaanite general Sisera? It's difficult to generalize a single meaning for this trend of giving females such animals' names, domestic or small. However, I'd like to think that in my case being named a bird, a winged creature, is both a measure and a decisive factor in my personal development—similar to the cases of Adah and Zillah, whose stories we've already heard.

Let me explain by seemingly taking a detour through a view from afar and into ostensibly altogether other literary cultures. Let me trace the literary trajectories of some famed female birds and interlace them with my own personal story. I feel justified in so doing since you do know, of course, what a "bird" may mean in American, actually, New York, slang of the early twentieth century.

My first stop will be with the mythological harpies. Harpies are Greco-Roman mythological creatures with the lower body, wings, and claws of a bird and the chest and head of a woman. They are often depicted as ugly, disgusting, fierce, ill-tempered. They are often associated with the winds, with ghosts, with the underworld. Their chief employer is Hades, but they also do vengeful errands for the other gods. In a famous Argonaut story they tormented a king named Phineus very badly, until he was finally rescued by two Argonauts. There were three harpy sisters, with various names attributed to them. The most noted is Podarge, who, despite her appearance, attracted Zephyr the West Wind (or his brother Boreas, the North Wind, according to another version). She bore Zephyr two beautiful colts, Xanthus and Balius, and these colts became Achilles' fabulous stallions. Besides being mentioned in the legend of Jason and the Argonauts, the harpies also appear in Virgil's *Aeneid* and in Homer's *Odyssey*. If you've never heard of them, go look for them on the Internet instead of in the tomes of Greek mythology!

I learn from the harpy image that mythological bird women (and note: the harpies seem to be females below the head and chest as well as above!) may be sexual partners/mothers but are negatively evaluated, much like sirens. (If one wishes, the many folkloristic images of the flying witch belong to this category as well, but more on that later.) Their size and freedom of movement, in this seemingly male phantasy, is associated with death, filth, danger to men and gods, and so on, but may be finally overcome by human male warriors. Hence, hermeneutics of suspicion are called for while remembering them. At any rate and without discussing them further, let me summarize their case by stating that I feel deep empathy with the harpies: they manage to retain their female sexuality *and* their mythological status and their ability to fly, even at that terrible price. A "harpy" in the English idiom is not much better than a "shrew," right? And I have a special weak spot for Podarge: both of us birds gave two important sons to a mythological, or near mythological, male.

So on we move to other birds. You must have heard about the collection of the deeply Islamic stories known as *The Arabian Nights* or *A Thousand and One Nights* (in Arabic: *Alf Laylah wa-Laylah*). In this collection, a frame story recounts how Sheherazade—a well-educated, clever, and attractive woman (in this or another order), but never described as beautiful!—volunteers to marry King Shahriar and tells her husband a series of stories every night for 1,001 nights. He has previously lost his faith in womankind because of his former wife's unfaithfulness. If Sheherazade succeeds in capturing his attention by her continuous chain narrative, he would stop killing all women he marries and has sex with (including her) after one night. This stoppage must entail a process of his soul's (and of the society he governs, therefore) healing through, well, oral bibliotherapy. As an example for socialized living, he must learn not to generalize from one woman (his first wife) to all women. Sheherazade is the would-be educative agent for effecting a change and mental health, at a grave risk to her person. It follows that narratives about women and gender relations and power and passion sexual and otherwise and the binary opposition love/death are the fictive texts of the subtextual therapeutic process. Sheherazade is ultimately successful in her tasks, by the way.

The collection has a long and complex history: as the personal names in the frame suggest, among other things, it harks back to Persian/Indian origins. Basically it is known from medieval times onwards (ninth century CE, or third century in the Islamic calendar) and has been subject to interpolations, additions, and a process of both Eastern and Western modification. Most of us would know of it through the modern media of children's books and Disney films: who hasn't heard about Ali Baba and the forty thieves or Aladdin's cave or Sindbad the sailor? These are colorful and are adapted in our contemporary Western culture for children. However, *Alf Layla wa-Layla* is certainly an *adult* collection, and there are other stories in this witty, poetical, and sexy collection, put into a young woman's mouth, that deserve attention although they are less known. Western adult readers may read it for exotica, for learning about social customs and Islamic norms, or for personal transformation through identification and engagement. The *Alf Layla wa-Layla* is mighty good entertainment—especially when suspension of disbelief is practiced to overcome matters of jinns, magic, and fictive inconsistencies—and when patience is exercised about repetitions of theme and subject matter.

Sheherazade stops telling her stories every morning at dawn and resumes the next night where she has stopped the night before: thus, tension and curiosity are maintained and she lives to continue the tale until the conflict in Shahriar's mind is resolved. Oops, let me add a footnote at this point. Some Western literary offshoots of this Arab tradition add a night to the proceedings, to make it into *A Thousand and Two Nights*. As Dinah has already told us in connection to her own literary killing by Shaul Tchenichowsky, this extra night bodes ill for Sheherazade. For some reason, some pre-modern Western men—artists! They should know better, perhaps, out of solidarity!—kill Sheherazade nevertheless in/by their text. Let me add my own thoughts to Dinah's. She mentions Fatema Mernissi's reflections on this matter. Indeed, Mernissi notes that both the American poet Edgar Allan Poe and the French poet Théophile Gautier, both of the nineteenth century, kill Sheherazade, but apparently for different reasons. Mernissi comments that Poe kills the storyteller for knowing too much—Gautier, for running out of inspiration. Pure jealousy perhaps? Let's stick to the original tale and uphold the image of the intelligent and inspired female storyteller who remains alive, shall we?

To go back to the stories, then. They are perforce, because of their literary frame, long and meandering. One of them begins on night 778 and continues through to night 831, that is, for more than fifty nights—roughly 5 percent of the frame's time duration (1,001 nights). It is called "Hassan of Basrah," and, for convenience, let me summarize it from Richard Burton's celebrated English translation.

A young and good-looking (as his name implies, from a word meaning "beautiful" in Arabic)—but naïve and lighthearted, charming but perhaps far from wise—man of Basrah (in the present Iraq; as I'm speaking there are discussions about the United States beginning its offensive on Iraq from this sea port on the Persian Gulf) managed to squander the fortune inherited from his merchant father, and to be tricked into captivity by a pagan (Zoroastrian) Persian. Hassan eventually freed himself with some sheikhs' assistance and arrived at an isolated palace, where seven (note the number!) king's daughters, especially the youngest, adopted him as a brother and became his devoted helpers. They were young, beautiful, and active amazons and hunters. One day they were summoned back to their father and left Hassan alone in the palace, with the keys to their apartments but also with instructions not to enter certain rooms.

True to human nature, he did enter the forbidden area to find a paradisaical garden within. And he encountered ten magnificent birds that came to drink and frolic in the garden. The birds deferred to their apparent leader; this continued when each and every one clawed her magical feathered costume off, and out stepped a beautiful maiden. The leader was the most wondrous maiden ever to bestride the earth, comparable in description to the maiden of the Song of Songs—but we shall hear *her* response to her biblical description from her own mouth. At any rate, by the time the maidens/birds depart, Hassan is so smitten that he can neither drink and eat nor sleep, and he wastes away. When his adoptive sisters return, the youngest tells him how to capture the Bird Woman, who is the eldest of the seven (note the number!) sisters and daughter of a demon king. When she comes again with her sisters and companions, he should steal her feathered costume by trickery. Her companions will eventually have to leave her; she can't perform without her magical wings, and she'll be at his mercy.

Hassan complies, and the adoptive sisters help Bird Woman reconcile to her fate. He marries her and takes her back home to his mother's house in Basrah, complete with the feathered costume in a locked chest. The family moves to Baghdad. She seems reconciled and bears him two sons (note the number again!). After a while, he becomes convinced of her genuine attachment to him. He departs, instructing his mother to watch his wife closely. This is the Bird

Woman's chance: she has a plan. She convinces her mother-in-law to let her go to the *hammam* (the public bathing house). Her beauty is such that it is reported to Zubayda, the Caliph Harun e-Rashid's chief wife. Bird Woman is summoned to Zubayda, convinces her to let her wear her feathered skin again, takes her sons and departs flying, leaving her mother-in-law desolate and a message to her husband to come and get her at the never-never land where she's bound to regain her freedom.

Upon his return Hassan is beyond himself with grief (it is worth noting that, throughout the story, men as well as women are equal in weeping and fainting copiously with emotion, as well as in bursting into poetic creativity). The legendary place where Bird Woman has gone is beyond the world, beyond geography, beyond humanity. But once again, after many tribulations and with the help of his adoptive sister and some other helpers, female and male, and magic, Hassan manages to overcome all evil powers that try to deter him and is able to reunite with his wife and sons; she, for her part, has regretted her departure bitterly and saves him from his foes more than once by her resourcefulness and courage. They return to Baghdad after visiting the adoptive sisters. Mother-in-law is ecstatic. The husband seems to have been educated into an adult male, while the mysterious and larger-than-life wife is domesticated: no need for flying anymore, it's been a mistake anyhow. They live happily ever after.

Before analyzing this story and stating how and why I chose to recount it as an introduction to my own story, Zipporah's story, an earlier Bird Woman's story, let me add one more detail. I've already mentioned Fatema Mernissi, the contemporary Moroccan Muslim sociologist. She has written *Sheherazade Goes West* (in English, 2001), or *Le Harem et l'Occident* (in French, 2001), or *De Europese Harem* (in Dutch), in which she reassesses Western views on female sexuality and femaleness in Arab Muslim culture, as symbolized in Western eyes and minds by an imagined harem tradition. In her book, Mernissi proceeds (in chapter 1) from this story, as told to her orally as a child by her illiterate, harem-dwelling grandmother. The grandmother, in a much abridged oral recounting, insists that Bird Woman was not rediscovered by the husband who had initially robbed her of her freedom to fly. He was doomed to an eternal search, whereas she managed to disappear back to where women are free(r) to fly, while raising their children nevertheless. The moral of the story, insisted the illiterate grandmother who never left the harem, was for women to be mobile, to travel, to fly, to become birds in order to be human.

Let us dwell on the story, complete with two opposed endings, for a little while. An unfortunate, socially maladjusted, and not-too-bright young man sees a Bird Woman. His gaze upon her changes his life: he needs to possess her. He can do that only by trickery, by robbing her of freedom of movement, by taking away part of what he admires—her non-human attributes. He does that, with female help. When she escapes her prison, together with her sons, he uses everyone and anybody and everything to take that freedom away again. In a voyage of self-discovery—for, indeed, it seems that by the end of his quest he retains not only his love object but also greater personal maturity through suffering and dedication—he remakes the other, his wife, in his own image. No more birding for her. If she has consented, love prevails as motivation for both genders (as in the literary version). If he could never find her, female freedom is valued above imprisoning male love, if not above maternal emotions (as in the oral version). The story is a phantasy; both endings are phantastic as well. But the question is: Whose phantasy, in which case? That the second ending is a female composition seems warranted by female performance, as presented by Mernissi. The first ending's provenance, like that of the story as a whole, is a bit more complex. It is told in a female voice, that of Sheherazade, and she is supposed to be the textual author as well as storyteller. Furthermore, as often in the *Alf Layla wa-Layla* collection, gender differentials are fluid, although, ostensibly, the characters operate within orthodox, rigid Islamic traditions of gender roles. Thus men may be beautiful and get by on their looks and charms; often, like Hassan, they are appealing and amiable but naïve and less than intelligent. By contrast, legendary (and isolated) females may be warriors and effective magicians, clever and learned and active and mobile and resourceful, like model men. Members of both genders may weep, faint, or fall madly in love to the exclusion of all other life pursuits. Gender stereotypes seem to become shifty when love is concerned; women seem to be the stronger somehow. Is Sheherazade's voice driven by male admiration and fear of the female principle, a phantastic being—or entity, if you will—that has to be contained in a real/metaphorical harem, although she is bound to escape from the futile imprisonment? This is Fatema Mernissi's opinion, and also that of many male readers who view the collection as male literature. Perhaps. But, equally possible is to view it as female literature, narrated in a firm and self-assured female voice. I prefer to leave the gendering of the *Alf Layla wa-Layla* authorship open, although its frame is well established as a female frame. As for reading it, yes, as Mernissi demonstrates, it can be read as a woman. And then, it does read differently. Or is differently retold, as done by Mernissi's grandmother.

Would you like another bird story yet, at this point? Bird Woman's story reminds me of Erica Jong's book, *Fear of Flying*. It was first published in 1973 and now, thirty years later, in 2003 with a retrospective author's afterword. Jong quickly became a culture hero. The book was celebrated for its subject matter—love and sex; for its perspective—female and feminist; for its tone and style—daring, outspoken, and cheeky stream-of-consciousness, back-and-forth framing monologue; for its narrative voice—autobiographical; for its central metaphors, the "zipless f--k" (which isn't our business here) and "flying" (in or out of an airplane) for emancipated, adult female sexuality. Upon rereading for plot (rather than for inspiration), it can be reorganized as follows. A young, educated, PhD student, Jewish, American, New York woman divorces a first, Christian, schizophrenic husband. On the rebound, she remarries a multiple Other—an American Chinese male psychoanalyst. During a Freudian conference in Vienna she meets an English psychoanalyst. They fall in love, go off together, anguish, and part when he explains that he has to meet his children and girlfriend. The flight for freedom was an illusion all the time and he knew it, although she didn't. The book ends with our heroine bathing in her husband's hotel room in London, where she returned in search of him, reflecting:

> I floated lightly in the deep tub, feeling that something was different, something was strange. . . . I hugged myself. It was the fear that was missing. The cold stone I had worn inside my chest for twenty-nine years was gone. . . . Whatever happened, I knew I would survive. (423–24)

And then her husband walks in. This is the book's end; but is this really an open end, if the flier has come home to roost? Does it really matter what the outcome is? They stay together, they split, they stay together and split later—the possibilities are not infinite. The fear as well as the flight have been male-relational and male-delineated—and will continue to be, or so it seems. A story that began with a fearful heroine in an airplane, flying nevertheless, ends with a wet bird in a tub, preening her wet feathers. How far can a wet bird fly? What kind of role model can she offer? Is she still truly a bird? I do remember the pioneering impact of the book's language and story when first read but am somewhat disappointed upon rereading.

Nevertheless, such stories can serve as prologue and corridor to my own story: the similarities are too many to be overlooked, although incidental they may be. And focalizing on my story through the prisms they offer may be helpful for understanding it. I am now a reader with four partly analogous and dialogical texts: my own as well as the harpies', Bird Woman's, and Erica Jong's. (By your leave, I shall add some more intertexts to my very own story later.) But let me leave Erica Jong aside and return to the bird who wasn't afraid to fly but was hindered: the Islamic Bird Woman.

Bird Woman has no name. I may extend Mernissi's approach in this regard and entertain the notion that the woman has no name since she's recognized as fabulous—although, in view of her ultimate full domestication, this may seem a little far-fetched. But I, do I have a name? As I shall be able to claim in light of Bird Woman's story, actually I have no name either. My figure has probably undergone a shift: from a super Bird Woman I became a Zipporah, the bearer of an empty "name"; from a female eponymous entity symbolizing female freedom I was demoted to a mere mortal female. In my case, decidedly, I recognize the hand of a male author or authors whose interest it was to downgrade me by comparison to my husband, Moses. And let me pursue this line of thought further, whenever appropriate. Here it is sufficient to note that an Arab/Persian story that has a phantastic female bird as one of its heroes, and so many other brave and unusual females without whom the male hero would come to nothing, is named precisely after this charming but idiotic hero; similarly, Moses couldn't have survived without all the females (the midwives, his mother, his sister, Pharoah's daughter, his wife . . .)

that made his salvation and growing to maturity possible (Exodus 1–2). And yet, my own minimal and cryptic story is but a comma adjoining my admittedly smart and historically significant husband.

Speaking of female helpers, have you noticed that groups of seven sisters appear at least twice in the *Alf Layla wa-Layla* story? So am I, one of seven sisters, and so is my father—like Bird Woman's father—an important man in a faraway land. Some Jewish rabbis designate my father a magician, like Bird Woman's father, before he's converted by Moses. And talking of Moses, like Hassan, he's a stranger encountering seven sisters when he's on the run from a foreign foe, in a hostile land (Exod. 2:15-16).

However, at this point my story is overturned and firmly positioned on its Islamic head. In the Exodus 2 story, Moses rescues *us* (the sisters) from the shepherds who, presumably, prevent us from watering our sheep. In this way, our meeting with him narrowly agrees with other biblical so-called "type scenes" of meeting at the water well as preliminary to marriage, as in the case of Rebekah and Abraham's servant (Genesis 24), or Rachel and Jacob (Genesis 29). But look here, in the other two biblical stories marriage has been a reason for the stranger's sojourn in the foreign land, and his meeting with the bride-to-be is presented as divinely ordained. Not in my case. In my case, the story is as follows:

> The priest of Midian had seven daughters. They came to draw water, and filled the troughs to water their father's flock. But some shepherds came and drove them away. Moses got up and came to their defense and watered their flock. When they returned to their father Reuel, he said, "How is it that you have come back so soon today?" They said, "An Egyptian helped us against the shepherds; he even drew water for us and watered the flock." He said to his daughters, "Where is he? Why did you leave the man? Invite him to break bread." Moses agreed to stay with the man, and he gave Moses his daughter Zipporah in marriage. (Exodus 2:16-21 NRSV)

Think about the situation. We belong to the desert and we are seven in number. Moses is a lone stranger. Clearly, without local assistance he couldn't have survived. And our father gives him the required assistance, he stays with us, he's given a wife. Let me note in passing that, strangely enough, both Bird Woman and I are presented as daughters of fathers, without any trace of a mother or reference to her lack; far be it from me to make any snide comment on this unnatural fact that has, apparently, gone unnoticed by commentators as if it's the usual thing. Furthermore, not only are we not allowed the consolation of a loving mother, but also—in my case—nothing is said about my own emotions; here, at least, the Islamic Bird Woman has the upper hand: at times her emotions are dwelt upon at length. At any rate, believe me, without our assistance and our balanced approach to our father—we let him make the invitation to Moses, we didn't even suggest it: a good example of female success in making a male think he makes the decisions—Moses wouldn't have, couldn't have, survived much longer. But the bible omits this common-sense consideration in its zeal to promote Moses and place him above everybody else. In that vein, the bible doesn't allow Moses any explicit love or sex interest in me, or in any other woman. And the Jewish sages follow, claiming that he was solely interested in his vocation, to the exclusion of everything else. Fortunately, other versions are more attentive. For example, three of the many twentieth-century feature films on the Hebrew exodus from Egypt tell a different story and promote *me* along in the process. Perhaps the makers of these films were motivated by the wish to supply the popular love interest to the story, thus making Moses a fuller man in modern terms. But no matter: my presentation benefits from this.

In Cecil B. deMille's famous cinema epic, *The Ten Commandments* (1956), all seven of us sisters fall for Charlton Heston's hunky Moses. We act flirtatious and bring about his invitation to our well-established household. He and I become a couple by mutual consent and enjoy a love relationship. When he departs from me to go back to Egypt, moreover when he sends me away later, he does so out of consideration for me and for his sons: he doesn't want us to come to any harm. Burt Lancaster's *Moses the Lawgiver* (1975) is loving and considerate as well, although preoccupied with his solemn task. Finally, the animated *Prince of Egypt* (1998) is the best of all, from my perspective: it has Moses meet me already in Egypt when he's still a royal prince, where I have been captured as prisoner because of my flighty ways and roaming wildness. I take this as covert recognition of my "birdy" status. Anyway, in this film I treat Moses contemptuously at first, even as I'm a prisoner and he a prince. Nevertheless, he discreetly helps me escape. I make it back safely to my father's house—how else, I ask you, if not by flying?—and this is the beginning of a love relationship resumed in the desert. Later I help him and take him home. So, at the very least, some later and different sources contain traces of my unusual nature, which is almost completely eradicated from the biblical text.

Almost, but not quite. Like Bird Woman and Hassan (and Podarge and the Wind, and unlike Erica Jong), Moses and I have two sons, named Gershom and Eliezer (Exod. 2:22; 18:3-4). But even before the second son is born, even as Gershom our eldest is our only child, we leave my father's homestead and go to Egypt to release the Hebrews from their forced labor. And here, in an anxious and edgy manner, the bible has a short and disjuncted passage, completely out of sync with what precedes and what follows:

> And it came to pass by the way in the inn, that the LORD met him [Moses], and sought to kill him. Then Zipporah took a sharp stone, and cut off the foreskin of her son, and cast [it] at his feet, and said, "Surely a bloody husband [art] thou to me." So he let him go: then she said, "A bloody husband [thou art], because of the circumcision." (Exodus 4:24-26 KJV)

The surface meaning or inner logic, or syntactic structure, of this passage is difficult to comprehend. It seems that the text has us on the way to Egypt, in continuation of verse 20—

> So Moses took his wife and his sons, put them on a donkey and went back to the land of Egypt; and Moses carried the staff of God in his hand.

Then we have to stop for the night. Then Moses' god, for an unspecified reason, attempts to kill him. Why that god would attempt to do that, when Moses is on his way to release his people from bondage, isn't specified. Some theologians who feel uncomfortable with this unpredictable divine attack would attribute the attack to a demon rather than to their beloved Hebrew god.

However, let me assure you this god indulges in this kind of wily behavior especially, if not only with his chosen ones, preferably on the road and at night, when women and children are presumably safe, and on the eve of the chosen's attaining an important transition in their life: the case of Jacob fighting an unknown being while attempting to cross the river Jabbok is a case in point (Gen. 32:23-33 in the Hebrew text; vv. 22-32 in the English text). A case of male rivalry? A case of an immature if well-meaning god, as Jack Miles claims in his celebrated book on the Hebrew god's biography? Or simply, as one would imagine, a single and therefore multisided god in his less friendly manifestation? Many male theologians think in binary fashion. It's difficult for them to imagine a god who is simultaneously or consecutively kind and cruel, merciful and avenging, loving and hateful, gentle and violent. Therefore, sometimes they split off what they view as demonic or satanic properties from him. This praxis may amount to a misunderstanding of the monotheistic, monogamous god they themselves create and recreate to their heart's content.

Please excuse this theological aside. The Hebrew god encounters Moses (so says the Hebrew biblical text) and wants or tries to kill him. But here he doesn't reckon with me. I—according to this text— swing into inexplicable action. I take a flint stone, I cut off my son's foreskin, thus performing primitive and risky circumcision, and then put the foreskin *at his feet*. Whose feet? The son's or the husband's? Another translation comes to our rescue:

> On the way, at a place where they spent the night, the LORD met him [Moses] and tried to kill him. But Zipporah took a flint and cut off her son's foreskin, and touched *Moses' feet* with it, and said, "Truly you are a bridegroom of blood to me!" So he let him alone. It was then she said, "A bridegroom of blood by circumcision." (Exodus 4:24-26 NRSV, italics mine)

But, truly, this doesn't help us much after all. How does an act of primitive circumcision performed on a son, and the foreskin put at the feet of the father, save the father? Is it a special case, unheard of, of substitution? How is the Hebrew god pacified so that he leaves Moses alone? How do I know what to do? How do I manage to

overcome the divine wrath, immediately and conclusively? Where do
I derive the power from, and how does the memory of my presumably
private and isolated act become so strong that it remains, textually
mangled but a brawny trace nonetheless, for a controversial event of
female victory over the male divine, a female saving her husband
from divine attack? Jacob should have been that lucky; perhaps this
would have spared him his crippling limp!

Moses is long dead and buried by his beloved god of mercy and
vengeance, place of burial unknown (Deut. 34:5-6), and he can't
corroborate my version of the events. Unfortunately: he was a fair
man; as far as he was concerned, justice was a supreme value. His
reputation in this regard is justified and well earned, even if—as he
grew older, and this happens to many people—he became obstinate
and opinionated in his interpretation of justice. Moses would have
been my witness. His god did attack him. Not losing my wits—love is
such resourceful motivation—I performed circumcision on Moses'
own body. As a wife I knew first hand, of course, that he hadn't been
circumcised in the Pharaonic court where he was raised. Common
female sense has always registered the awareness that in circumcision
the competitive god receives a symbolic, token acknowledgment of
his metaphorical son's castration and disempowerment. This is why
women, for ages immemorial, have performed circumcision on their
sons by way of initiating them into the Phallus of male social order.
But the Hebrew bible authors will have none of that; they attributed
the performance of circumcision to males, from Abraham to Joshua
onward, although, as in the case of Joshua, they retained the memory
of circumcision by flint stones (Josh. 5:2-8). So what could they do,
when they encountered a tale or a document stating that a woman
actually performed the rite, and on their most admired leader? What
could they do? They could have eliminated the information
altogether, sure; they'd done it many times. But somehow, they made
do with just, albeit inelegantly, falsifying it somewhat. Apparently it
was more acceptable to them for me to perform circumcision on an
infant, on my son. Hence the confusion, the lack of comprehension
how Gershom's foreskin could and did save his father Moses' life.

The truth of the matter was that Moses, trusting me implicitly
although fearful, was so frightened that he agreed to my quick plan.
He trusted me with his penis. And it worked. The Hebrew god's

attack was subverted. And the scribes, they couldn't stomach it. And they intruded, and "modified." But they couldn't change the fact that I, Zipporah the Bird Woman, like the Islamic Bird Woman, saved my husband yet again, even though—and this makes my own victory over the Hebrew god greater—unlike Hassan of Basrah/Baghdad, my husband was attacked by his personal god himself and not by a demon or jinn.

You may ask, How did I come to possess such understanding, such instant comprehension that allowed me to act instantaneously? My answer is consistent with the rest of my presentation. I was and am a priest's daughter, educated and versed in the art of living free in the desert. I inherited from my father, and received from him through education, powers to understand and to heal, powers that were extended by my female intuition. Like any proverbial Jewish wife and mother, I protect my own. And last but not least, I am and was a Bird Woman. That my husband's illustrious career overshadowed my own, that the Hebrew scribes wished to and largely succeeded in diminishing my role by comparison to my illustrious husband's function and character is regrettable but can be traced through tell-tale residues in the stories that remain, and through the partial analogy to the Islamic Bird Woman's story and its history, as well as through modern interpretations.

Consider, for instance, the interpretation offered by a contemporary Israeli feminist literary critic, Ilana Pardes. She reads this little garbled passage about me in Exodus 4 together with the Egyptian myth of Isis and Horus. Isis discovers Horus is dead; with the aid of her sister, a birded goddess, she reconstructs the dismembered Horus complete with rebuilding his penis. In Pardes' reading I'm a metaphorical (or residual) Isis, and Moses is Horus. I reconstruct him after his death because of divine wrath. Now, who knows whether Pardes is correct in assuming that "my" little story is a reflection of an Isis myth? I certainly don't. Nevertheless, claiming that a female god recreates a male god/leader through rebuilding his challenged body after a confrontation with another divine force by analogy to my case is refreshing. At the very least as refreshing and empowering as re-viewing me as a Bird Woman. It is indeed one more step back from domesticating me into a rather compliant daughter and wife with traces of idiosyncratically inexplicable and hardly

traceable independent action, as happens to me in the Hebrew bible
and to Bird Woman in the *Alf Layla wa-Layla*. Or, consider Marc
Chagall's rendering of the Islamic Bird Woman, and try to visualize
me as its twin—before the biblical authors looked into my case and
adjusted it to their own needs.

It's not my intention here to re-vision my case too much. My
father, the wise priest and legal expert (Exodus 18), taught me that
one shouldn't embark on a war whose chronicle of losing is a
foregone conclusion. I've been made transparent to the point of
disappearance by the mainstream traditions, hints to the contrary
notwithstanding. I don't wish to feed you here with too many details
about my husband (because of his prominence, I'm sure you'd have
welcomed some gossip!); or sons; or sister-in-law Miriam, the female
prophet; or brother-in-law Aaron, the priest. But let me add just a few
more pertinent details and reflections before I leave the stage for the
next worthy speaker.

I've referred previously to the controversy about my being "sent
away" or divorced—recall the "Cushite woman" mentioned in
Numbers 12:1. Here's a quote from the *Encyclopedia Judaica* relating to
later, post-biblical Jewish interpretation:

> The "sending away" of Zipporah after the Exodus [Exodus
> 18:2] is interpreted as meaning that Moses gave her a bill
> of divorce. . . . Identifying the "Cushite woman" (Ethiopian)
> in Numbers 12:1 with Zipporah whom he remarried, the
> rabbis explain that as a Cushite woman is distinguished by
> her skin, so was she [Zipporah] distinguished by her virtuous
> deeds. (CD-ROM version)

Take heed. The rabbis won't rest until they house-train and house-
break me totally, to the point of elevating me to a saintly status.
Mercifully, they don't transform me into a beauty (a fate from which
Sheherazade escapes as well, although this happens to both Bird
Woman and Erica Jong's heroine). I know full well that their making
me over into an esteemed upright woman is motivated by their
reverence for Moses; and their insistence that I'm in fact the "Cushite
woman" is, once again, stimulated by their need to exonerate Moses
from a second marriage (and, I suspect, they want to cleanse him

from a desire for a black— an even more foreign woman). Does it really or actually matter, after all this time has elapsed, whether he did or he didn't? Whether Miriam (a good friend of mine, according to midrash and film, who rebuked Moses for neglecting me sexually because he was too dedicated to his preordained task) in fact fought my battle with a neglectful husband or sought to further her own claims on prophetic knack, as in Numbers 12? She was punished severely; I disappeared from the scene. In hindsight, such squabbles leave a bitter taste. She lost. She died soon after and was buried in the desert (Num. 20:1). I don't wish to mourn for her, my friend, my empathizing if often reserved ally, at this point. Suffice it to say that the burden of being "sister of," for her, must have been perhaps greater than being "wife of" for me.

Indeed, that I was "sent away" was my salvation. The sons, my sons and Moses', joined their father and helped him erect (yes, I use this male word advisedly) the edifice of Israelite identity by extraction from diffuse characteristics of the Hebrew mob. The sons bonded with their father, and the mother remained in the shadows. In my case, this proved to be a blessing. Out of the limelight, having fulfilled my prescribed duties as wife and mother, being so thoroughly forgotten as not to be worth any more mention beyond my presumed high merit in post-biblical Jewish sources, I was left to my own devices. A female Icarus by birth and inclination, I was prevented by motherhood and wifehood from too wild experimentation as long as my menfolk needed my covert guidance. When I was set free by their growing preoccupation with religion and nationality, and finally by their respective deaths, I was left to my own devices. I could exercise my plumage in anonymity. That became harder and harder. Whereas not being killed in a canonized text does endow one with an immortality of sorts, age takes its toll nevertheless. So textual immortality has brought me further and further in time, but my physical strength waned, even though—paradoxically—I remained, like all of us here, ageless. Therefore it was such an alleviation of my personal burden when aviation was invented.

It didn't matter an iota that my own name didn't figure on the honor list of pioneer female aviators. What did matter was the fact that somebody had already paved the way for females to partake in that winged occupation. Now that "somebody" should be named.

She is Amelia Earhart, born in Atchison, Kansas, in 1897. Amelia
began flying in 1921, and, unlike me if I may modestly say so, flying
didn't come to her naturally. But by 1932, five years after Charles
Lindbergh had become the first human aviator to cross the Atlantic
Ocean from America, she matched his record. She was the first
woman to do so, no doubt driven by her own ambition but, at the
same time and as she repeatedly stated, by the wish to demonstrate
that women—because of their intelligence, coordination, speed, and
will power—could be aviators. Amelia disappeared—together with her
plane and co-pilot—in the Pacific Ocean in 1937, while she was trying
to set a world record for flying around the world. Neither the plane
wreckage nor the pilots' bodies were ever found, although rumors as
to their eventual fates abounded.

Amelia—take it from me so that you'll soon understand how and
why I feel so familiar with her that I refer to her by her first name—is
alive and well. She made a choice to forgo the world record and to
disappear until times for women were better and easier. She couldn't
just disappear before her true mission on earth was accomplished.
Indeed, her promotion of women's aviation was influential;
nowadays a minority of women fly passenger planes as well as
military and transport ones. But this is by no means easy: you have to
be extremely determined in order to achieve your aviatory wings. But
thanks to Amelia, I could finally fly, technically and in actuality, while
using wings other than my original feathered ones. I learned the art
avidly and easily. Flying helicopters is my favorite—short and sweet
and relatively supple to take off and to land.

Let me now introduce and reintroduce my closest mates, my
partners in the all-women aviation business that we run. Amelia is
the senior partner by virtue of her pioneering activities, although
she's younger than I and at least two other partners. She doesn't stop
marveling at the advances in aviation on the one hand, and *kvetching*
about women's still-limited opportunities in that field on the other
hand. The Islamic "woman with a feathered dress" from the Arabian
nights is my second partner. If you remember, there were two
versions of her story: the official and written one, in which her
husband finds her and they live together with their children till death
parts them; in this version Bird Woman eventually gives up her
ability to fly, and willingly so. But there's also the other, oral version

of which Fatema Mernissi speaks, in which the story is named after
the female protagonist (rather than her husband), abbreviated to
foreground that female protagonist, and in which she disappears
forever, preferring a life of winged nomadic liberty to domestication.
You may think that the latter version, the oral product of harem
women's imagination, is their phantasied antidote to their own
confined condition: if they can't travel, at least they invent the
possibility of brave escape for a fabled one of their own kind. But
imagine, just imagine, that this unconventional (in the sense of
marital societal norms) tale is the original tale. Then you'll
understand how and why I and my other mates—Podarge and Bird
Woman, who is second in my esteem only to Amelia—teamed up to
establish our own aviation company some years ago.

And we have a fifth partner, a youngster of whom all of us veterans
are extremely fond, and the time has come to introduce her. In 1964
the famous Dutch writer for children, Annie M. G. Schmidt, mother
of the *Jip en Janneke* series through which generations of Dutch
children have grown to respect the Other within and without, wrote a
modern fairy book for children and adults. One story in it is called
"Spikkeltje," "Little Speck" (or "fleck," from the Dutch in that
meaning). Here's the story in brief. Once upon a time a queen and
king were childless for many years. The queen consulted a witch—a
flying witch, mind you—with her husband's reluctant consent. The
witch gave the queen an egg to brood on. The queen complied and in
due course a beautiful little princess hatched out of the egg. Her
given name was Gloriandarina but, since she had three little specks
on her belly, she was nicknamed Spikkeltje and known exclusively as
such. The witch had warned the queen not to let Spikkeltje outdoors
during the thrushes' season for migrating southward. Inevitably,
Spikkeltje escaped monitoring and turned into a thrush, thus flying
away. The queen and king were distraught; in their kingdom and
because they did try to rediscover their beloved daughter, all thrushes
became honored and cherished. But Spikkeltje herself wasn't
rediscovered and metamorphosed back into a lovely princess until a
prince, following the witch's counsel, tempted her with pearls instead
of ordinary birdseed. Thus was Spikkeltje redomesticated and the
wedding was celebrated. The parents, the witch, and the loving pair
lived in domestic bliss thereafter. As for the thrushes, they remained

the main beneficiaries: they continued to be honored and cherished in that faraway land.

Here you are, then: yet another story of a female's domestication through love and marriage, necessitating a de-winging act by a male. In this world, the "happily-ever-after" is the domain advocated to daughters, albeit not necessarily what really happens. In the children's story, again a story—much like the *Alf Layla wa-Layla* tale— told by a woman, and even though it's a marvelous tongue-in-cheek story, Spikkeltje apparently trades her birdy magic and freedom of movement for the prince and his pearls and his love, even if she refuses to do it for her parents' love alone. In reality, also in children's reality as well as perhaps also in my own, divorce happens. And it did happen to Spikkeltje, beyond the horizon of Annie Schmidt's story but in keeping with contemporary Dutch social statistics. You can understand my affinity with her, and you may understand how, having lost—through love—her native ability to fly, she regained it by becoming a pilot whose preferred destination is southern lands.

So here we are, five female figments of popular or literary imagination (granted, Amelia stands out here; she's more than real, at least before her inexplicable disappearance), four out of diverse ancient literary sources and one of recent history: a figment of the bible from the ancient Near East, that's me. A figment of Greek mythology, that's Podarge. A figment out of Arabic/Persian oral literature, that's Bird Woman. A figment out of twentieth-century Dutch children's storytelling, that's Spikkeltje. And Amelia, of living aviation memory. A team of female figments of Jewish, Islamic, and Christian provenance. Together in an all-female aviation firm.

We did consider Erica Jong as a partner but decided to let her go for several reasons. To begin with, she has a perfectly good vocation she's fond of and successful in: she's a poet and a novelist. Also, she's always been afraid of airplanes—which is how her story begins. She insists it's not a metaphor only, and anyhow there's no such thing as a "metaphor only"; and, unlike what Amelia did, we're not convinced that Jong has ever conquered her real as well as metaphorical fear.

Recently we did consider another candidate, though, and again rejected her, this time with real sorrow. My friend Mary Hill has given me a book, a thriller, she thought would interest me. In that thriller, called *When the Wind Blows* and written by James Patterson in 1998 (and it has a sequel I didn't read, *The Lake House*), a chilling story is told of GenTech experimentation by ruthless scientists that produces new engineered mutations of human-animal children. The true heroine of the story, who manages to rescue some such "inmates" from their laboratory/prison and get rid of the scientists, is a girl bird called Tinkerbell, or Max (for Maximum). She—and some of the other children—is part human and part bird: she has beautiful wings and can and does fly. She has no human reproductive organs (unlike Podarge) but possesses human strength, intellect, emotion, courage, and speech together with bird instincts. And she's only eleven years old. Understandably, Podarge's imagination was fired. She sought Max out and adopted her, together with her similarly gifted brother Matthew. And indeed, Max is a beauty and a joy to all of us. But she's too young, too daring to be a responsible pilot. So she sometimes, discreetly, accompanies our short-distance, low-altitude assignments. And we all love her. And she may be the future, the way science is progressing. And perhaps she should be a scientist rather than a pilot, since she can fly so wonderfully on her own.

We're successful, financially. We cater for various tastes and needs, and we employ female pilots in our company: in fact, without much ado or advertisement, all our employees are female. This is company policy: it's conditioned as much by our life histories (please note my reluctance to insist too much on any "correct" version, for any of us; a postmodern malady perhaps). And, whenever possible, the five of us coordinate our individual timetables to share flights or stopovers in order to entertain ourselves with passionate theological discussions. After all, Podarge is a pagan; Bird Woman remains a devout Muslim; Amelia is private about her denominational status, silent unless moral issues are at stake; Spikkeltje, in the best Dutch fashion, belongs to the Dutch Reformed church; and I've evolved into a reform Jew.

I can hear a clamor in your midst. You dislike the fact that Bird Woman remains anonymous; particularly against the general biblical background of not naming women, this seems to you ideologically incorrect. Let me apologize, then. This is not a good time to name Muslims, especially Muslim pilots. For business as well as for political reasons, and in response to the post-9/11 spirit of indiscriminately naming Muslims of whatever gender and condemning them . . . Sorry.

Reign in your curiosity, good ladies. I, Zipporah, have vowed that Bird Woman shall remain nameless, even if by this—perish the thought— I reaffirm biblical practices that many of us suffer.

Talking of prejudice and past attitudes, let me add a postscript. Recently I've come across a scholarly book, written in Hebrew, called *Women and Masks from Lot's Wife to Cinderella: Representations of Female Images in Women's Hebrew Poetry.* I leafed absently to the contents page, where I was understandably intrigued by the title of chapter 5: "'And I shall be like a bird, like a bird': On the image of the bird, its roles and meanings in female Hebrew poetry." I started to read, discovered that the female poetry read and discussed was twentieth-century poetry (which I like), and immediately became shocked beyond measure.

You see, all this time the only female bird image that has occurred to me, in my internal dialogues and in my dialogue with you, was that of a wild bird, free, flying. My emphasis, as in my internal feeling, was on the divine or Icarus freedom from being earthbound, in the spatial as well as the social sense. The main issue for me—as for Fatema Mernissi—was and is the female ability to fly in the wild, to move freely, or to its (temporary, unsuccessful) disablement by socialization and domestication. To my great surprise, the woman poets of twentieth- and even late-twentieth-century Israel chose other bird images. Their lyrics focus on bird song, bird beauty, and, most often, the caged bird longing for freedom as indexical of the female poets' own female/feminine poetic self. Inasmuch as a liberated bird is depicted, she's mostly an object of unattainable yearning rather than a projection of the inner poetical self.

Now, to view a bird as a female singer is almost a convention of Romantic and also post-Romantic literature—unnatural, certainly, since in the wild the male bird sings to attract his female mate. (Incidentally, many male birds are smaller but, on the other hand, have more attractive plumage than their female counterparts, presumably once again in order to successfully draw females in the mating game; but logic be hanged when it comes to anthropomorphizing birds, or to romanticizing them—a gender-bender is immediately in evidence inasmuch as looks and singing are concerned.) Note, for instance, the singing birds of Hans Christian Andersen's "The Nightingale" (1844) and Oscar Wilde's "The

Nightingale and the Rose" (1888). Both authors feminize the birds
and minimize their size and physical appearance. However, in their
different ways, they leave the birds to make their own choices: in the
former case, to sing for the Chinese emperor but to retain its flying
freedom, and in the latter, to dye a rose red and to die uselessly in the
name of romance for an ungrateful and unknowing pair of humans.
Even the so-called father of Hebrew poetry, Chayim Nachman Bialik
(1873–1934), whose much-celebrated first published poem on the
threshold of the twentieth century is called "To the Bird" (Hebrew *'el
ha-zippôr*), addresses a poetic she-bird who freely migrates between
the "hot lands" to his cold Russian "window," bearing news from the
Holy Land and being the subject/object of almost erotic poetic
vicissitude. He addresses her as a generic "bird" by my own "name,"
Zipporah (although the poem's name is "To the [grammatically
male] Bird," as if to prove my point: in that literary milieu, a singing
bird is a female bird!). But even Bialik makes no attempt to jail the
flying bird. On the contrary, her nomadic facility, so different from
his earthbound condition, is what makes her valuable and attractive
to him as an object/subject for his romantic longing. Like Andersen
and Wilde, Bialik feminizes the bird and, once again, doesn't lyricize
a big, wild bird. His bird is a singer, a potential communicator who
partakes in humans' lives. However, she's not caged and, in the last
analysis and in spite of services rendered to humans (men), remains
free. In contradistinction, the female Hebrew poets cited in the
interesting book I've read opt for the singing-bird-in-the-cage icon:
this is how they see themselves reflected in the bird. They do not
identify with the primordial, divine, wild, soaring, nomadic, self-
willed birds—like the harpies, like Bird Woman, like Amelia, like
Spikkeltje, like me, certainly like Max (of whom they don't know)—
that escape metaphorical or real incarceration. They see themselves as
small, imprisoned, plaintive-sounding lyricists. In short, they choose
another bird model to mirror their existence, as they experience it. I
don't doubt the validity of their experience, as encoded in poetry.
However, this is such a disappointment: we, the flyers, are living
proof that birds can and should be otherwise. So I rest my case at this
point, with sorrow and frustration, but still hoping for a
fundamental change for all female birds, wherever they are.

FIVE

∞

I Am Rahab, the Broad

The following is an attempt to retell a biblical narrative, "my" narrative as it were, focused on me, the narratologically prominent figure in this story, from "my" viewpoint, by way of redressing the usual biblical balance. This will be the revis[it]ed story of Joshua 2 and 6—the story of yours truly, Rahab, and the Israelite spies.

You may remember the story, as it appears in the Holy Book. After Moses' death the Israelites, under Joshua's leadership, prepared to enter the Promised Land from the east. Joshua, who earlier in the wilderness had served as a spy together with Caleb, sent two spies to Jericho to gather information and, especially, to gauge the mood of the inhabitants. They came to my house. Word reached the king, and he demanded that I turn them in. Instead, I hid them and then sent them away safely, asking in return to save me and my family when they conquered our city. They agreed. Later, when they took the city, they fulfilled their promise and made me integrate into their society—but let me now give my own version of the events.

My real name is . . . it doesn't matter what it is. I *do* have a proper first name, although no lineage in "my" story. But even my first name has been forgotten, or perhaps suppressed by the biblical writers. I wouldn't bother to disclose it even to this unusual assembly. My nickname, the one that supplanted my real name until the real name had been deleted from all the official documentation is—as you all

know—"Rahab." Now this, in Hebrew, in case you ladies have
forgotten, means the "wide" or "broad" one. Please do not think for a
moment that this "wideness" refers to my being far from slim. No,
although that might be true as well: even in those far-off days I never
lacked for food in my childhood, being a member of the upper
mercantile, landholding class and later an enterprising professional
woman. There is a sexual pun here; those of you with a little bit of
remembered or recalled Hebrew and imagination are right.

From antiquity on, this is how I was known. Listen to this passage
from the Jewish Midrash known as *Sifre Zuta* (10):

> Rabbi Yehudah says, she had four names of disrepute. Her
> name, Rahab the whore, says it all. Another thing, Rahab the
> whore because she fornicated with the city people from within,
> and with the bandits from without, since it is said that "her
> house was in the wall" and "she sits in the wall" (Josh. 2:15).
> Another thing, Rahab the whore since she was a Canaanite, and
> there were no more evil and wicked people than the Canaanites.
> Another thing, Rahab the whore since she was from the people
> of Jericho, those about whom it is written that they should be
> demolished and banned (Deut. 20:17).

Don't you find it interesting? On the one hand, I save their people
and they acknowledge it, in writing. On the other hand, they play
with and expand on the sexual possibilities suggested by the text. Do
we forget that prostitution—in this case, female prostitution—exists
because of simple supply and demand processes? At any rate, the
Hebrew scribes who wrote down what they imagined as "my" story
preferred to introduce me by that nickname, The Broad.

Those scribes often suppressed women's names in their stories:
this praxis made the woman figures seem less real, less important. A
basic literary technique that suited the writers' and scribes' purposes,
as theologians Carol Meyers and Adele Reinhartz have pointed out.
The sages of that motley group, members of which wrote stories later
incorporated into their sacred writings, enjoyed the vulgar
connotations. This is how I am known, although later generations
elevated me to the status of matriarch. And I, from where I am, from

where I've been all this time (I refuse to divulge my exact age; female wiles, so what? Stereotypic, so what?), I can laugh and cry in equal proportions. But let me tell my story from my own perspective, even some of the suppressed parts, in the order of events I remember well. As they happened. From my viewpoint, rather than from theirs. And if I rewrite history here—who am I to deny that a little bit of that will occur, it always does—so be it.

I was, am (my afterlife in the canonized literatures of the belief systems that later came to be known as Judaisms and Christianities allows me the present tense; so does my standing here today), an ordinary upper-middle-class girl. My mother was a housewife and mother; my father was in the textile business. Really, let me be true to my origins: he was in the *shmate* business. Let me digress and elaborate a little on this. You must have noticed that, in my story, flax—call it linen if you will, if you're fashion-conscious—occupies an important place. Now, while it is certainly true that processing flax may have been a traditional woman's job in those days, it is perhaps surprising to find raw flax on a bordello's roof in quantities sufficient for hiding one or two persons (Josh. 2:6)—even when the flax is needed for the plot, even when a realistic picture should not be expected. We may therefore assume, by way of filling a gap, that I was somehow familiar with flax processing as a profession or trade. A similar echo underlies, perhaps, the insistence of some Jewish midrashic sources that a guild of white linen workers, mentioned in 1 Chronicles 4:21 as a family ("house of byssus work"), was descended from me (see *Sifre Zuta* 10; *Ruth Rabbah* 2; and more). But I have digressed here too much and will return to this as my story unfolds, below. This is just background.

I grew up with the smell of flax and expensive cloth, international trade, political gossip. We had lands and a town house inside the walled city. I had brothers and sisters; I was the eldest. I was born and raised in Jericho, an oasis, a very ancient city near the Dead Sea not far from Jerusalem. This town still exists today, a village really, but it has been in existence for thousands of years before and after the events I'm recounting here. Nowadays it is Palestinian; it used to be Israeli; before that it was Jordanian-Arab; in my time it was labeled Canaanite. I loved it and I still do. A person is but the format of her or his native landscape, as the poet says.

My childhood was uneventful. I was an obedient child, good looking, pleasant. I loved my siblings and honored my parents, as prescribed in our law tablets (and theirs; I mean the group that became know as "Hebrews" and evolved into "Israelites," later still "Jews"). I looked forward to a stable life like my mother's, with a husband and children, eventually grandchildren, under my own palm trees (neither the proverbial vine nor the fig trees grow well in our immediate geo-topographic neighborhood). When was that? Ah, about twelve to thirteen hundred years before the man Jesus, described as a descendant of mine, was born: for that, have a look at what is known as the New Testament (Matt. 1:5-6). Or perhaps I confuse the dates; certainly this happened all too long ago to remember exactly when. But dates apart, events are still vivid in my mind.

History—as it sometimes would—intervened into my modest, internalized vision of a future, conventional domestic bliss. Suddenly, it seemed, there were waves of invaders from the southeast and the northeast and the east. Hungry, unruly mobs of desert and margin shepherd-warriors would descend on our arable lands and unwalled towns, the desert-encircled agricultural hinterland of our marvelously cultured, ancient, walled city. They would demolish or capture everything in sight. They also, sometimes, had the nasty habit of killing all males, sparing women and children only, or killing all human beings in the name of their religion. On such occasions, taking captives and keeping them alive was not for them. They recorded the practice in the name of a jealous god, in their holy writs, much later (Deut. 20:10-18; Joshua 6-7). A much later doctor/ philosopher that they acronymed "Rambam," "Maimonides" for the rest of the world, further coded this practice of holy war by stating (in his *Kings* 6.4) conditions and targets for demolishing, killing, and banning enemies. If you want the witness of a modern critic, read Susan Niditch's work, *War in the Hebrew Bible: A Study in the Ethics of Violence* (1993). In that, their attitude was very similar to that of some contemporary Palestinians, although without the martyrdom halo attached to suicidal attacks on the "enemy." At any rate, the invaders did make an exception in the case of female virgins, though, especially the young and beautiful ones (Deuteronomy 21). But let's not dwell on the fate of those: too unpleasant to recall, although these virgins' lives were spared.

This process of slow infiltration, in waves, from the east happened over a few decades with monotonous regularity, usually in the spring and summer and during the abundant harvest time. The crops from the hinterland, the ones we depended on, were increasingly lost to us. Inflation and scarcity of food became commonplace. Gradually, the business that fed us all became paralyzed. My father lost most of his merchandise and property. Most of the younger, marriageable men were maimed or died in attempts to stop the seasonal attacks of the invaders from the eastern desert, or they were captured and killed. In addition, life became so boring and sad!

None of my brothers and sisters was ever taught how to earn a living outside the family firm, which, in fact, was so well established that while it lasted it nearly ran itself of its own accord, sustaining all of us in the extended household. In fact, our own models of urban, upper class, and otherwise household arrangements were taken up later by the Hebrews themselves, as they became "Israelites" and established themselves as conquistadors of their promised land. This gradual process of long duration, as you may imagine, entailed what they saw as contamination, the learning and internalization of our ways, while at the same time attempting to annihilate us physically. But I'm digressing and should go back to my story that—apart from unavoidable quasi-philosophical reflections—I'm attempting to retell chronologically.

At this stage of the terror, we began to feel helpless. Our family compound, usually so joyful, became silent—especially my mother, who had hitherto spent a lifetime of relative leisure.

Something about my mother and her influence in her children's lives, in passing, since the Hebrew bible seldom if ever discloses anything about daughter-mother relationships: it is as if mothers are dysfunctional with their daughters, if not necessarily with their sons. Where is Dinah's mother when Dinah was raped? Whatever happened to Jephthah's wife when her husband sacrifices his daughter to a god that doesn't prevent this monstrosity as he prevented Abraham from sacrificing Isaac to him—and for that matter, where is Sarah then? And where is Zelophehad's wife when his five daughters, named, praise be, ask for their paternal inheritance from Moses when there are no sons to inherit? Where indeed? You can find these mothers of daughters in later Jewish midrash perhaps, but not in the Hebrew bible. My mother was my father's only wife. Her name was Yarchit, derived from our word for "moon," a word that is evident in the name of our beloved city Jericho, properly pronounced *yericho*. Although the Hebrews often claimed that we Canaanites were morally inferior to them, sexually corrupt like our Ammonite and Moabite cousins, females and males alike great philanderers, bigamy and polygamy were very seldom practiced, even by the well-to-do. My mother, then, was my father's only love both emotionally and legally—at least as far as we children knew—which was a source of great comfort and stability for us. She was a lady of leisure, then, if you discount the fact that she was almost always pregnant. She gave birth to twelve babies, eight of whom survived beyond early childhood; this, given our usual infant mortality rates of two infants out of five reaching the age of ten years old, was pretty good. My mother loved us, and she was patient with her daughters as well as with her sons; she believed in education for all her children, regardless of gender. She didn't think that "whoever teaches her daughter Torah is as if s/he taught her nonsense." Bourgeois values can come in handy, for girls, I mean. My mother's bourgeois values dictated that girls should be proficient in math and rhetoric as well as fine, feminine arts and skills as were conventional, so that they could help in the family business. Literacy was considered a basic requirement for both genders in our household.

Things gradually became worse: a real *intifada* (uprising). Our country relatives left their homes and came to ours, since all their property had been vandalized or taken over, and they feared for their lives. It was rumored that the infiltrators/invaders were a cruel crowd; they took whatever they could: chattels, animals, food. They burned and destroyed whatever they couldn't take with them. They were, let's risk saying it aloud, barbarians by our refined, urban standards. They dressed unfashionably, poorly, with no taste and no care. Most of them were illiterate: in fact, the groups that attacked us, the groups that later forged a national identity labeled "Israelites," were largely illiterate until so much later, probably the eighth century BCE at the earliest, as agreed by many scholars. Their women and children were socially inferior to adult males, especially to the so-called elders—not always chronologically old or older than others, but certainly invested with an authority attributed to (metaphorical) aged wisdom. They had strange religious practices, such as pretending to worship one invisible male god while, at home, paying homage to symbolical statuettes of other male and female gods, whose business it was to care for the family's welfare. But they were invincible, they pressed forward, behaving as if our ancient and civilized land belonged to them. So great was their self-conviction that our own people became scared and ran. This is the power of religious and political propaganda: you hear it often enough, it's reiterated in and by the media, it acquires a life, sheer repetition convinces, you begin to believe in your own inferiority. Furthermore, we hadn't had war for decades, we had been so peacefully intent on our good life. We were civic and peaceful, rather gentle: we were nothing like our kin neighbors to the east of the Jordan, the Moabites who would sacrifice infants for the common good, as they did at times of military danger. Remember their king, Mesha, who sacrificed his own firstborn son on his city's wall in order to stop the Israelite invasion (2 Kings 3). This worked: even the bible half-admits that the Israelite invasion was checked. Or like the traders from the north, our sea-faring cousins the Phoenicians, who sacrificed infants regularly, in order to ensure the welfare of the community: archaeological traces of this practice are much in evidence. But we abhorred such practices. And we didn't know how to fight back and how to react—first to the Hebrew infiltration of our hinterland from the east, then to their continued presence and to their destructive behavior.

On the other hand, these people's physiognomy and language were undeniably close to ours. Had we been a racially prejudiced society (but as traders sitting on an important oasis in a route from east to southwest, we could not afford to be), we would have said that they must have shared some ethnic gene pool with us. We were wondering how we could exploit the similarities in order to contain or repel them. But meanwhile, food was becoming very scarce. Commodities, international trade, communication came to an almost complete halt. My father's house, our kinship unit, could no longer function, as it should have—this was its *raison d'être*; we're not talking emotions here—as an economic unit successfully for its various consanguineous and other members.

I was just coming of age. I was quite well educated, as I mentioned above. Our parents taught us at first, and then we had tutors: once again, this parental home education system, in which both father and mother functioned as teachers, was later copied by the Israelites, as evident in their sacred writings (Proverbs 1-9). The women too knew about textiles, helped in the family business. This wish for everyone to be involved in the family business dictated that everyone, female as well as male, would be well educated, at least enough to function as international traders. We were introduced in court; we had social connections. We still owned property, including real estate. But we had no food. And together with my sisters, older and younger, I could find nobody to marry: it became so bad that up to seven women would beseech a single man to marry them, for food and honor, as stated by the prophet Isaiah in a different context centuries later:

> And seven women would get hold
> of one man on that day
> saying, we shall eat our food
> and wear our dress
> just let your name be ours
> get rid of our shame. (Isaiah 4:1)

Gradually it dawned on me that the only way to gain some livelihood for myself and for my family would be to open a brothel: such institutions flourish, especially during hard times. With an eye to the changing situation, with the knowledge that ultimately the invaders would covet our walled city, with cold calculation, I asked my parents to have the lease of a house by the city wall. I was given a house from the family estate. I turned it into an organized, clean establishment. What can a woman do? Sell her body and the bodies of other women, when all else fails; there's always a demand for that. If you have to buy food and shelter, save to maintain children, support your family, pay your dues to the cult, repay vows, and there's no one to help you, you resort to the last commodity you have: your sexuality—and morality be hanged.

We had a nice byline in paid hospitality, food selling too. In fact, some of the later Jewish commentators insist I was just that, a food seller and an innkeeper: the word for "whore" in Hebrew, *zonah*, is

phonetically similar to words for "food" and "feeding." This is
nonsense, of course: prostitution, because of male cupidity, is a much
more stable and viable occupation than even food selling. That later
generations attempted to emphasize my choice, or obliterate it, is
beside the historical point. Listen to this. It gives me pleasure that
several later Jewish scholars, from the translators into Aramaic to
medieval Jewish commentators on the bible, insisted that I was an
innkeeper and food seller. Others felt a little offended on the one
hand, and yet stressed by the unnatural explanation of "whore" as
food seller. One commentator takes a middle position between the
two explanations, "innkeeper" and "whore." He states that (1) a
woman's modesty is ultimately affected by the things she sees, the
people she meets, etc., if and when she's an innkeeper; and (2) most
female innkeepers had been prostitutes before starting the inn
business. Josephus Flavius, that treacherous ex-military Jewish leader
who became a Roman dependent in the second century BCE, and a
scholar, in his rewriting of biblical history (*Antiquities* 5.1.2) forgoes
my profession (which he never mentions) and designates me an
innkeeper from beginning to end. It seems that designating me as an
innkeeper was motivated by the ideological attempt of exonerating a
future foremother from a shady past—I did get to become a glorious
figure later on, but we shall return to this. And also, as we shall see,
Flavius did this to whitewash the Hebrew spies somewhat. It must
have seemed better to present them, piously, as resting at an inn than
beginning their mission at a brothel. Once again, we're getting to
that in a few minutes. But, believe me, there's no shame in what I did,
under the circumstances. I did run a brothel. In addition, we—I and
my girls, good girls, from good homes, suffering the same hardships
that I did—processed flax regularly, to help father, since all better
textiles could not be sold by then.

Pretty soon men started to flock to my "house," Rahab's house,
The Broad's house, from Jericho as well as from outside it (as long as
the roads were open). In spite of my relatively young age, I was the
madam. I ran the show. I shall leave aside the question of whether or
not I supplied sexual services myself, although later generations of
scholars were convinced that I did. The Jewish sages said: "There was
no great man or high official in the land with whom Rahab did not
have intercourse." At any rate, my girls were clean and discreet.

Knowledge about abortifacients and birth control, officially denied but preserved as female oral traditions, was turned into praxis, thus preventing complications for girls and customers alike. Did you know that female traditions about birth control, mostly of organic and vegetal extraction, persist until this day and at times are scientifically mass-produced by big-name chemical laboratories, without acknowledgment to the traditional sources, of course!

In short, my business flourished. I now knew everybody, and everybody knew me. My family was now both shamed and ashamed. Surely you do know that, in the Orient, a woman's modesty is a man's honor; a woman's sexual immodesty, or what is construed as such, is a man's shame; a woman's shame is her exposure—to public gaze, to gossip, to allegations of misconduct. So my family, dominated by males, of course, at least as it seemed, was shamed but no longer hungry. Situated as I was by the city gate and meeting (so to speak) many travelers and politicians and other imminent males, as well as ordinary people (I ran an egalitarian establishment; modest rates, value for money, few if ever any questions), my political awareness grew by the day. Through listening to many conversations I came to realize that those invaders, those "Hebrews" as they called themselves, might prevail, might inherit the land. I began to realize this might indeed happen. Not so much because of their wit, neither because of their potent god (they only had one god, didn't admit to any goddess at all—hard to imagine at the time—or so they said; later evidence pointed to the existence of goddesses, on the level of household worship as well as public worship), but because of our complacency, our blindness, our fat and peaceful ways. A scandal about the reinforcement of the city wall, not done properly by the appointed contractor, and corruption in the matter of hand-thrown defense stones (communal warehouses found mysteriously half-empty), were unsettling. Stones were an important weapon. See Judges 9 for the (Canaanite) woman who kills Abimelek by throwing a grindstone at him from a city wall. For stones as weapons in general see also the book by Yigael Yadin, *The Art of Warfare in Biblical Lands* (1963, in Hebrew). Yadin should know; he was a general, son of an archaeologist and an archaeologist himself, once upon a time the army's chief-of-stuff of the renewed Israeli state, and a politician. Throwing stones are also mentioned in Ugaritic literature as "hand stones." So the scandal—actually finding out that the stones supposed to be stored in warehouses and ready for military usage of deterring enemies while in siege of our walled city, those same stones were sold to and by traders for building purposes and were not available for defense purposes—was really shocking. And I was uneasy in my heart.

Well, one day in the early summer two strangers came to my establishment. Their version of the story or, rather, the story as seen from the heavily ideological perspective of their source group, is written in the book called after their chieftain, Joshua (chapter 2), as I mentioned before. I knew they were strangers right away. Local dress codes couldn't be applied, they were so poorly and peculiarly dressed. Their language, though intelligible, sounded a bit quaint and archaic, kind of a bygone tongue, an odd dialect. They weren't particularly clean. Their skin was rough. One of the two pretended to be a traveling carpenter, the other a traveling potter. These were their cover stories. But their act was not convincing. They were watchful, observant, conversational. I had a hunch that they were spies for Joshua's small crowd: rumor had it anyway that Joshua's crowd, the Hebrews, were nearing the city. They had done their best to run a propaganda campaign, trying to convince the city's king and council that their army was a huge "national" army and that we should surrender to them without battle. Their sage Rambam (Maimonides) claimed centuries later that before he entered the land Joshua sent to the land's inhabitants, that is to us among others, three messages. The first, whoever wants to flee should flee. The second, whoever wants to make peace should make peace. The third, whoever wants to make war will do so at their own peril. The king and his council laughed. So here were the spies, I thought, here it comes.

But what kind of spies were they, in fact? Inadequate and comical, real jokers and fumbling idiots, I should say. They had no proper cover story: traveling artisans, indeed! They didn't look like traveling artisans, not at all: no tools, hardly any baggage, hands not rough enough. They did not speak the dialect of Gibeon, from where they claimed to originate and to have come. They referred to each other as "brother," as often portrayed in the Hebrew bible, pretending to be real blood kin but it was really just part of their ideological identity;

they displayed no blood kin resemblance. They didn't even step out for a walk, to inspect the city walls for instance: later historians, such as Josephus Flavius, make them do just that, once again in order to save their dubious honor. Please take my word: they never did that. In fact the heat was so unbearable that they didn't even take advantage of the early afternoon breeze to learn about their surroundings. They stayed put. They drank, a lot. They had their fun with the girls. They appreciated my food. They paid and tipped, rather lavishly I thought, using our local currency. Then they went to sleep, as if they were safe in their own territory. They seemed careless. And yet, and yet—there was something forceful about them, somewhat menacing and aggressive yet at the same time curious and selfish. So I spied on them and watched them. Discreetly, as is my habit.

The king's men came toward evening. "You're harboring Hebrew spies," they said, "hand them over." Now, I'll never fully understand why I denied any knowledge of them. The denial was instinctive: my motives, for whatever they were worth, could be analyzed later. At the time, they were of no consequence. I reminded the captain of the guard, briskly, that his wife could be told about his recent visits to my establishment. He turned away together with his men, not searching the premises properly. When notified of the king's men's arrival, I'd quickly arranged to hide the Hebrew "spies" on the roof, under some flax drying in preparation for its processing by my girls. The Hebrew men were lying there, frightened and silent. They were in my hands. I had to decide what to do.

By nightfall I'd made my decision. I'd help them escape—on condition that they promised me that, if they conquered the city, they would grant political asylum to me and to the rest of my family. Please understand: their stories present me as being full of faith in their eventual success, hanging on the power of their omnipotent, single god. They even make me present a speech to that effect (Josh. 2:9-13). The truth was different. Although at the time I doubted whether they'd ever manage to conquer the city, I decided to let them go—if they gave me their word—as insurance against such an eventuality. I can hear you think, But that's treason to your source community! I can answer, ideals aside, that I was beginning to suspect that nevertheless, in spite of my hopes and in the face of events "on the ground," in spite of the unevenness of force and strength, political and material survival were at stake. To all intents and purposes, I was by then acting as the head of my father's house: the responsibility hung heavily upon me. I was no convert to the new religion, although, in their *Meklilta*, they stated that I did convert to Judaism after forty years of harlotry during the wilderness period. After all, that new religion was a religion without goddesses, and this turned me off. Presentations of me as such a convert, for instance in the Christian text called "Letter to the Hebrews" (11:30-31), make me chuckle to myself. I acted rather than "believed" (James 2:25) because I could act, because my vanity rejoiced in the possibility that I could affect local history, because I too love to be childish and play spies, because I love to defy authority (my own king's authority, in this case). And the thrill of danger! And the sense of revenge! I remembered the gossip about my "house," the shaming—as in other Eastern societies, shaming in ours had a devastating effect, especially the shaming of women in the name of male honor, the shaming of my family. But, primarily, I did it because I wanted that extra insurance. What can a woman do?

So I extracted a promise from the so-called spies. That indeed was a richly humorous scene. I had them hanging on a rope, between heaven and earth, speaking at length and demanding an oath before letting them off on the external side of the city wall. Luckily I knew the schedule of the guards' patrols; luckily, I could give the spies directions for a temporary hideaway. Before I lowered them to the ground, on the other side of the wall, they did give me their promise to save me and my household and family from extinction if and when they conquered our city.

So, you may ask, how sure were you that they'd keep a promise thus extracted under duress? I wasn't, actually. An oath is an oath, though. According to Josephus again, the spies' oath was rectified by Joshua, Eleazar the high priest, and the elders' council, hence was absolutely valid and secure. Besides, the whole thing was a long shot, and I was enjoying myself, playing with males' life and death.

You know the rest of it, as told in Joshua 2 and 6. The two men managed to escape. They went back to their leader, Joshua, and reported to him. How they glossed over their behavior, their inadequacy as spies, I don't know. They managed to convince their leader that all inhabitants of the land were persuaded of the Hebrews' might. Later, actually, they managed to conquer Jericho—they say the walls were felled down by their god, after their priests circled it blowing their ritual trumpets. I was there, so can tell you how it really was. An earthquake, not big on the Richter scale, perhaps 4 or 5, but the walls hadn't been maintained properly for a long while. And it was easy for the Israelites—this is how they started to call themselves rather than "Hebrews," as soon as they began to annex territories here and there—to take it from there, in the panic that ensued. (If you press me I'd agree that the timing of earthquakes could have been divinely determined, at least in theory. This would make the event a miracle by definition, by timing, but I am and always have been a skeptic, you see.) So they came, they saw, they conquered. And demolished the city and its civilization. And looted: whether they used the loot or sacrificed it as burnt offering to their god (such uncivilized and commercial waste!) is immaterial. And they killed. And they saved me and my father's house, all gathered in my house that was marked by a red ribbon. And they wrote everything down for posterity, including the ideo-religious embellishments, and a very serious attempt at saving face for the spies/agents of victory.

So my life and my family's life were saved. But otherwise . . . The family business was lost. Everything was lost. My family dispersed: they were assimilated into the inferior culture of the conquistadors. It was easily done: similar origins, similar backgrounds, a language that was like a simplified version of ours—think about the relationship between German and Dutch, or Dutch and Afrikaans. There was the little matter of official religion, monotheism they called it. You weren't supposed to worship any of the old deities any more but only one, Yhwh. This was in fact no problem since many traits of the old religion were incorporated in "him"; besides, even the Hebrews/Israelites weren't as strict about worshipping only him for centuries to come, remonstrations by their spiritual leaders notwithstanding. Even the beloved goddesses could still be venerated, in this or the other guise.

And what happened to me? There's nothing about my eventual fate, beyond being saved, in the Israelites' first canon of holy writs. Later on, when they were already "Jewish" and their sages were compiling subsequent tomes, some of them commentaries on and updates of the original writings, they noticed my disappearance from the earlier text and speculated about me. They had me domesticated, of course, made me into a wife and mother rather than the whore they initially designated me. I was made foremother of a linen-making family guild by virtue of my flax drying on the roof, in which I hid the spies. I was made into a foremother of priests and prophets, including Jeremiah and Huldah the female prophet, who will tell her own story later in this conference. They even made me foremother of kings. They were prepared to forget and forgive my foreignness and my sexual past, my being a Broad. For them, the overriding consideration was that I acted out of faith, or so they fondly imagined. At times they even had me converted, as I mentioned earlier in my story. Baloney, as I've explained.

The Christians, to their credit, married me off to an even more prominent figure. They put me straight into the lineage of King David and, therefore, their own Messiah, in one of their first canonized testimonies. To quote:

> Salmon [was] the father of Boaz by Rahab, and Boaz the father of Obed by Ruth, and Obed the father of Jesse, and Jesse the father of King David. (Matthew 1:5-6 NRSV)

We shall have to hear Ruth about that as well. At any rate, they also made me into a model of faith in god (Heb. 11:30-31) and a model of positive religious action (James 2:25).

I'm not impressed, however, by all this good and—as the Hebrews turned Israelites turned Jews think in my case—posthumous publicity, in fact, religious propaganda. First they make fun of me by nicknaming me The Broad; then they have me believe in their superiority and their god; then they forget about me, only to domesticate me once more in the service of their ideologies. The Christians are no better than the Jews in this respect. And, throughout it all, I have the feeling that they have constructed me as an anonymous woman, a nicknamed whore, in order to emphasize my faith or whatever else they attribute to me in the service of something else than just that. You see, in their culture women are considered politically inferior to men. They reason that, if even a whore could realize the result of the Israelites' infiltration into Canaan, then her menfolk should have been that acute at the very

least. If a whore has faith, anybody else should. In short, they used
me. And then, after I've done my bit, pressed me back into the mold
all their women share, that of domesticated wifery and motherhood.
But the truth of the matter is that I did *not* become a wife and
mother. That is a much later fiction—attempts to honor me (in their
eyes) for what wasn't mine. Like other figures of fiction whose fate
isn't specified in their original stories, figures who don't get to die in
their own stories as they regularly should, I live forever. I am forever
young, forever attractive, I don't have to get married and bear
children, I don't have to talk, I can continue to be near my beloved
Jericho and observe. Observe it, and observe history and the way it is
retold and rewritten and constructed into ever-shifting-while-
remaining-the-same identities.

I was there, therefore, when my beloved city was rebuilt at a great
personal cost to the contractor (there was a divine curse to prevent
the reconstruction). In Joshua 6:26, a curse specifies that the man
who rebuilds Jericho will lose his firstborn upon laying the wall's
foundations, his youngest upon completion. The realization of the
curse is reported in 1 Kings 16:34, during King Ahab's reign. I saw
this personal tragedy. I also saw how Jericho redeveloped again,
slowly and over hundreds of years, from an oasis and watering place
for passing trade caravans and once again into a civilized city. Herod
the Great built a palace there. Men were again playing backgammon
under the palms in the city's main squares; elegant ladies were carried
about chaperoned while walking, parasols protecting their skin
against the desert sun. And so on. And then decline again—I lose
count of the years, and it doesn't really matter.

And of late, of course, things have been beginning to happen again
in Jericho. Recently it was given to a political body that calls itself a
Palestinian-state-to-be, or something like this. Most of these
"Palestinians" are Muslim, another religion yet. They claim to own
the place and other territories conquered by the Israelis a few years
back. Now, the Jews suffered greatly before they came back to the
land they took over, and not always gently, from us "Canaanites": this
is true. They are now back in their land, and they have a political
organization called a "state." Since they trace their lineage to the
Israelites/Hebrews who took the land from us, they lay claim to all of
it. The Palestinians, on the other hand, also claim that it's theirs.

(Their roots might be shorter than the Israelites', but they are long enough). People were sitting again in the town squares, playing backgammon. Traders traveled through it and across the Jordan bridges. For a short while, I looked at my beloved city. It even acquired a casino, where Palestinians were only too happy to grab the losses of Israeli gamblers (casino gambling is not allowed in Israel). Jericho is more of a village now. But I was hoping that soon it would grow again. I wished that those squabbling descendants of the Hebrew/Israelites—if they are that—and descendants of Yishma'el—if they are that—would remember that this city has been there for thousands of years. Jericho has outlived many rulers, many governments. It has outlived the "Canaanites," the "Israelites," the Jews, and the Romans, among others. I was hoping that it would outlive the conflict between Israelis and Palestinians. I was hoping that it would flourish once more. And yes, for the last year or so, yes, another Palestinian *intifada,* another uprising, and Jericho is once again isolated and poor, as predicted, as happened, as will happen. Woe is me, the matron saint of my beloved city. I sit here, I wait, I wish for my guilt of helping the Hebrew/Israelites to demolish it in order to save my own skin and my family, to be put to rest. Until then, until my city is finally rebuilt for posterity, I can't rest. I can't disappear. I can't die. I need absolution and vindication—in my own eyes, in my own conscience. Territoriality is, regrettably, so often linked to civilization and culture, not to mention to religion. Meanwhile, I sit at the deserted gambling casino, and there's yet another round of hostilities between Palestinians and Israelis, yet again. I look at the men rolling their prayer beads, the women in their black dresses, the young boys who throw stones and yearn to become *mujahideen,* that is, suicide martyrs who blow themselves up together with innocent Israelis. They use themselves as a military-political weapon of destruction. Is it time for me to despair?

I am Rahab, The Broad. Nobody knows my real name. I live, I see things: I'm in your holy texts. As long as these texts continue to serve as such, as long as my city is not reconstituted, I'm alive if not always well. And so is my city, the ancient Jericho of the Asian-African great rift, by the Dead Sea.

SIX

∽

The Three of Us:
Ruth, Orpah, Naomi

Ruth: Am I an Intellectual Worker Turned Do-Gooder? Think Again!

Yes, I am an intellectual member of the proletariat; this is how my life turned out to be, although this hardly gets substantive expression in the bible. But, please believe me, I'm a link in a very long chain of such women, remembered in history as dutiful daughters and wives rather than class-conscious, self-taught, developed personalities. And because I am a scholar, I do wish to introduce my story by referring to some academic practices. This is rather dry, but please bear with me.*

Scholarly discourse, especially *written* scholarly discourse, has a certain format. It is supposed to be factual and dry, "objective," or at least relatively clean of personal influence. It is supposed to contain extensive references to previous and current chains of learning. It is supposed to ignore political (in the wider sense of the term) realities. It is supposed to display the writer's knowledge to advantage. Notes are expected, and the more the better, so that a text and a subtext run

---

*Editor's note: This chapter is the transcript of the three short presentations delivered during one morning of the conference by Ruth, Orpah, and Naomi, in that order. This way the two most traditionally loved and significant figures (Ruth and Naomi) flank the traditionally less appreciated figure (Orpah). Since all three of them appear in the same compact biblical novella, and since their stories begin by being interwoven and only then diverge into different directions only to be linked again outside the bible, I've chosen to group them together.

concurrently. A certain degree of originality is demanded, even when it is the result of hair-splitting, but it should not come at the expense of "depth." Literary style, when too personal, is frowned upon. A clear distinction is made between "literary" discourse and academic or scholarly discourse. And thus, and increasingly so, academic/scholarly so-called research, in its written forms, is becoming more and more boring and less and less aesthetically pleasing.

In the last decades certain scholarly developments have occurred. Literary criticism has shifted to include in its practitioners' considerations not only authors and intentionality but also readers and their response. Feminism has infiltrated academe and brought with it a renewed appreciation of personal experience as a critical tool. The expansions of leisure time and search for fun, at least in the more affluent parts of the world, have had their impact as well. It is therefore perhaps a good time to try and revise scholarly discourse, to make it more fun and also more accessible. Serious fun, but fun nevertheless. So in that vein, here's my story.

Who Was/Am I?

You know that I too am still alive, at least in fiction if not in reality. The devoted scribes who wrote down my story, later to be included in their holy writs, actually describe only one year in my life, and of that only several months in detail. They focus on the weeks I spent walking with my mother-in-law, Naomi, across the Jordan to her hometown, Bethlehem, from my country, Moab (Ruth 1). Then they tell of my activities during the coming harvesting season in Bethlehem (Ruth 2). Then they go into a real, if polite, song-and-dance about the single illicit night I spent with Naomi's relative Boaz, later my husband, on the threshing floor (Ruth 3). Then they jump to the legal discussion concerning Boaz's planned marriage to me (Ruth 4). They never mention the wedding itself, but they do glorify its fruit, a son. The son is then assigned to Naomi (4:16-17), and I disappear from the story that carries my name. The genealogy of King David, beginning with my son Obed at the end of *my* story, is a male genealogy that never mentions any mothers, just fathers and their sons (vv. 18-22). It is as if Boaz gave birth to our son without my help. And this, of course, is nothing new in biblical terms. It happens

more often than its opposite: consider, for instance, the list of the ten
pre-flood great fathers of the world (Genesis 5), already mentioned by
Adah and Zillah:

> And Adam lived for 130 years and begot [a son] in his likeness
> and image and called his name Seth . . . and sons and daughters
> . . . and he died . . . And Seth lived for 105 years and begat
> Enosh . . . and sons and daughters . . . and he died.

And so on, for ten generations, from Adam to Noah, when only the
father and his firstborn son are named. Mothers are not even
mentioned, a kind of Adamic, virgin birth in reverse.

Fortunately, and to prove my point, another scribe—of the slightly
different Christian religion, so called—remembers to state in the
genealogy of his Messiah Jesus (Matt. 1:1-16) that Boaz was:

> The father of Obed by Ruth.

So I am remembered but, in both the Hebrew bible and the new
testament texts, I neither die nor get a burial. This, as we shall not
tire of mentioning in the present context, often happens to biblical
women—also to biblical men, to be sure, but more so to biblical
women, which is not a bad thing: it makes it possible for us to
convene here today. You can consider the gender significance of this
point at your leisure and to the satisfaction of your own personal
ideology; at any rate, I too am therefore able to retell the scribes' tale
and to supplement it with my own untold tale. We've heard this
"confession," in this or the other formulation, from previous
speakers and will undoubtedly hear it again.

According to the biblical scribes' tale, then, I was a Moabite, of a
people much maligned by the Israelites and Judahites, held in
contempt for our presumed lack of sexual mores and collectively
despised. According to the biblical authors, my community of origin
was pagan and idol-worshipping and hostile to the Israelites during
the Exodus (see the Balaam story in Numbers 22–23, where Balaam
the sage is called upon by the Moabite king to curse the Hebrews, but
blesses them instead)—and it was promiscuous, especially the

women. According to the written tradition, Lot's daughters (Gen.
19:30-37) made him lie with them and produced two incestuous
sons, Ben Ami and Moab, and the Moabite women in the desert
(Num. 25:1-4) supposedly seduced the innocent Israelite males to
perform idol-related sexual acts with them. Therefore, there are
warnings against allowing Moabite people to join god's people—as in
Deuteronomy (23:4), in Ezra (9:1), and in Nehemiah (13:1). Such
warnings are especially if not exclusively directed at liaisons forged
between Israelite men and Moabite (and other "Canaanite") women.
In other words, women like me. And, who knows, perhaps "my" story
was canonized precisely because it overturns this Israelite prejudice
against women of my kin and kind: Foreign women. Poor. Childless.
Widows. Single. Women who, at least for a limited period, voluntarily
set up house with other women (in my case, with my mother-in-law,
Naomi).

So you're undoubtedly familiar with my story. If you are Jewish,
you read it every year at the feast of *Shavu'oth* ("Weeks," seven weeks
after the Passover night), and you tend to look upon me as a model
of faith, the mother of all converts to Judaism. If you're Christian,
you remember me as a foremother of Jesus (Matthew 1). Therefore
you may assume, across centuries and geographic domains and
together with countless learned commentators, some things about
me: this is the nature of reading or listening to a story, particularly a
familiar one. You probably think that I *chose* to go with Naomi to her
own land mainly or only out of love and devotion to her, and chose
to follow her god out of knowledge or inclination. You may assume,
at least some of you may, that I was young and attractive while Boaz
was old[er], or that we had a love affair. You may assume that I was
good, but hardly think me intellectual, and that Boaz was the wise
one. Here, may I just state in short (modesty intervenes), that some
contemporary feminist readers have hit the mark by linking me to
the Torah (*halacha*), traditionally the intellectual domain of the
Jewish male.

And you may ask why I disappear from the story after my son is
born, when the son is called "Naomi's son" and she takes care of him
and I'm neither seen nor mentioned again after being praised for
loving her and being better to/for her than "seven sons" (Ruth 4:15).

So let me try to relate to these likely assumptions: we shall have to leave other gaps in my story for another occasion, or for Naomi and Orpah to discuss in their own presentations.

Choices
Why did I choose to go with Naomi to her land, to her people, to her god—oh, please notice that in my oath to adopt her religious beliefs (Ruth 1:16-17) I say,

> Your *elohim* is my *elohim*,

which, according to the Hebrew, can be read

> Your gods [in the plural!] are my gods,

not as you have been reading it for millennia, in the singular, that is,

> Your god is my god.

I am pointing out this alternative reading because you assume that I adopted Naomi's monotheistic beliefs in order to be with her; hence I am a model proselyte. This isn't necessarily so: at that time I was still a pagan. I thought in pagan concepts, and polytheism was indeed in my blood. Truly, unlike my sister-in-law Orpah I went with Naomi away from my country, my people, and I tied my fate to the unknown. I swore to Naomi a highly irregular oath to "cling to her" (Ruth 1:14-17) like a man to his woman: remember that in Genesis, when the woman is created, the man says:

> This time, this is a bone of my bones and flesh of my flesh.
> This will be named "wo-man," because she is taken from the man.
> Therefore, a man will leave his father and his mother and will
> cling to his woman and they will be one flesh.
> (Gen. 2:23-24)

The Hebrew word for "cling" is identical in the case of the first man's first behavioral response to his woman, as in Genesis, and in

my attitude and behavior toward Naomi my mother-in-law, as
recorded. And please don't let the erotic overtones of the word "cling"
escape you, in light of the quotation just read.

So why did I do that, why did I "cling" to Naomi and make those
sweeping statements? Have you considered that, like many other
single women with no men to protect them, I *had* to move away and
go with her? I was a widow, learned but untrained in any useful skills.
I had to work wherever I found work to support myself and Naomi.
Consider my plight, for a moment, in the light of what you
encounter in your own society even nowadays. Have you ever met
migrant workers, female or male? Often they are treated harshly;
seldom are they integrated into their host community, even when
marriage with a local spouse takes place. Being a foreigner, of a lowly
class and on charity or in a menial job, is difficult. Why do such
migrant workers stay in a more affluent place, then, even though
affluence is seldom shared with them? Why do they come back when
ordered to leave, as they sometimes do, instead of going back to their
source community? The answer is, obviously, that perhaps they do
not have much of a choice. Granted, home is home and roots are
roots. However, necessity might intervene; economic and financial
factors cannot be ignored. So please stop to consider that, in my case,
having been married to Naomi's son for several years and having
endured his untimely death, returning to my mother's house—as
Naomi graciously suggests in chapter 1 of my biblical story—was not
an option I felt I could exercise. In other words, my motivation for
accompanying Naomi on her return to Bethlehem was complex and
not devoid of personal motives. I did feel love and obligation toward
Naomi, yes—she'd never treated me insensitively while my husband
was alive. She could have; she could have reigned supreme, as
Bedouin mothers-in-law do until this day, as any Arabist or
Orientalist or Mediterranean scholar would tell you. Simply, or is it
really more complex than it bears explanation, after all this time I
had nothing to return to in my own mother's house, as Naomi
suggested for me to do. I was financially destitute and, in addition,
too far gone by then, too much in between the two cultures of
Moabites and Israelites, to return to my roots. Does this confession
change your opinion about my presumed selfless, sterling qualities,
those qualities that make it possible for you to accept me in spite of

my being a Moabite foreigner? Ultimately, on this point as on others, you should listen to Naomi's version of our partnership-of-necessity as well. She was perhaps aware of the complexity of my motives better than other people. Naomi knows me well. She does know that I am shrewd, practical, and self-serving first, as well as kind and loyal. And what's wrong with that, instead of an idealized portrait of a selfless hanger-on?

Me and Boaz
Do you imagine me as young, or in my thirties, or older? Do you imagine me—authors are perforce omniscient about their characters, but biblical authors habitually withhold the information in my case as well as in others—as good looking or, rather, ordinary or perhaps ugly? To judge by representations of me in Western artwork, book illustrations, and film, most readers imagine me as relatively young, beautiful, and graceful.

And how do you read Boaz? As older than I am, surely, perhaps a really old man, restrained and intelligent, a man who gets me and gets what he wants, all in good time (Ruth 4)—a careful and good man of character? This is his portrait most subscribed to.

I suspect that most readers need to construct both images—Boaz's and mine—as they do in order to construct a romantic love story between us in a way that will be acceptable to stereotypic, Western, gender iconicity: younger woman/older man; she—a good looker, he—the brains; she—passive, he—active. And, according to your individual perceptions, you may also read chapter 3 of "my" scroll (the scene at the threshing floor, at night) as either a sex scene or else as a non-consummation: the story itself is rather vague on what happened between us there and then.

I am not going to tell you what happened: this is a private matter between consenting adults. I would say, however, that you ought to reconsider some of your premises. There is no compelling textual reason to think I was beautiful or sexy; there is no compelling reason to assume Boaz was old or older: if he calls me "daughter" (Ruth 2 and 3), this is an expression of his social superiority over me more than anything else. And as claimed, there's no reason to think me less than intelligent. In chapter 2 I negotiate with Boaz, make him notice me, secure a position with his economic family for the season, secure my livelihood and Naomi's for the duration. And in chapter 3, I go beyond Naomi's instructions: she tells me to lie at Boaz's "feet" and wait to see how he rises to the occasion; I ask him to marry me, directly. Then, later on, I let Boaz do all the work: I know when to speak and when to let others do the work for me. Which leads me to a question: Does the fact that I conduct my business intelligently make me less of a model female character?

Finally, was there love between Boaz and me? Again, at the risk of not satisfying your curiosity, let me adhere to my natural reticence. I'm not the kiss-and-tell type. But please do consider the alternative. If we did not act out of love, if we married and produced a son out of a deeply felt sense of duty—to preserve my dead husband's name, to keep the land in the family, to provide Naomi with stability and continuation—how much more positive shall we both appear then? If I married Boaz for security, in order to solve my survival problems and Naomi's, would you blame me? After all, the god I did eventually come to believe in did not inquire after my motivation for marrying Boaz: he simply "gave [me] a pregnancy," as the good book says (Ruth 4:13).

My Eventual Disappearance

Have you noticed that I am not present in "my" story after I give birth to my son, although Boaz is certainly mentioned later in the genealogy leading up to King David (4:18-22)? In my own story, from that point onward I'm *mentioned* but am no more an *actant*, an active agent. Truly, the local women do tell Naomi that for her I'm more valuable than seven sons, imagine, because I love her (4:15). But who gets to act as the infant's mother? Naomi, not I (v. 16). Who gets to name the infant? This is often a mother's prerogative in the Hebrew bible; for example, my foremothers Rachel and Leah name all their sons and, in the case of Leah, also names Dinah her daughter (Genesis 29–30). But, in my case, the female neighbors do the naming of my son (v. 17). I am excised from the story at this point, until I resurface in the Matthean genealogy of Jesus (as a mother, of course).

Why? Have not the editors called the book after me? They did not call it "Naomi and Ruth," which they could have done: without Naomi, I was nothing; this is one of the reasons why I chose to go with her—remember, necessity motivated me as well as love. The biblical editors named the book after me, "Ruth." And yet, they disappeared me from the proceedings as soon as I fulfilled my maternal duty and bore a son.

Over the centuries, many solutions have been offered to this puzzle: structural, text-historical, text-critical. Recently, some feminist interpreters have understood the ending of "my" story as yet another signifier of the patriarchal framework in which Naomi and I operated. Again, it is not for me to solve this puzzle. I can, though, make a suggestion.

I am of Moabite stock. In the Hebrew bible, quite a few "foreign," ethnically "Other" woman figures are given the task of advancing Israelite/Judahite history, of propagating or aiding it along. Several of those are present here today. Think about Hagar the Egyptian (Genesis 16 and 21), Lot's daughters (Genesis 19), Tamar the Canaanite (Genesis 38), Joseph's wife Asenath (an Egyptian—Genesis 41? or Dinah's daughter?), the midwives for the Israelites in Egypt and Moses' wife Zipporah (Exodus 1–4), Rahab of Jericho (Joshua 2 and 6), David's wife Maacah from Geshur, mother of Absalom (2 Sam.), Solomon's nameless wife identified as daughter of Pharaoh and Solomon's other foreign wives (1 Kings 3–11), Rehoboam's mother Na'amah from Ammon (1 Kings 14:21), Jezebel the Phoenician (1 Kings 16–2 Kings 9), and the foreign women in Ezra and Nehemiah— to mention but several in a long list. We foreign women have had a major national influence: we stood there, in junctions of historic developments, with history written not only in/by our productive bodies but also by our sensibility and sensitivity. And yet, and yet, the ambivalence felt by the stories' writers is such that, in spite of our useful contributions, perhaps because of them, they cannot let us get away with what we did (according to them). They let us play major roles, and then they punish us for it. Hagar is banished from Abraham's homestead. Lot's daughters are implicitly accused of incest and lack of paternal respect. Judah does not marry Tamar, and she remains a single, if honored, mother. Asenath gets an afterlife only much later, in post-biblical literature. Zipporah, well, it seems that Moses may have taken another wife (Numbers 12) but, at the very least and as she herself has told us, he sent her away. David's house is torn asunder because of irregular sexuality. Solomon becomes a religious sinner because of his wives, and the united kingdom splits after his death. Jezebel kills prophets and is killed by the text. Foreign women, Moabites and Ammonites (like me), are seen as a danger to the postexilic community, as in the books of Ezra and Nehemiah. In short, we foreign women exemplify, by our very femaleness and Otherness, a threat to the community's integrity. We are liminal, and thus a temptation. Ironically, we serve as catalysts for creating the society that excludes us. We come from the outside, are assigned non-conformist sexual tasks, and invigorate the local stock, by compliance and obedience (in my case) or by fighting against Israelite/Judahite beliefs. Our role is invaluable but not entirely rewarding. When all is said and done, even in my case, we are not forgiven for fulfilling this necessary function. I, finally, am *absorbed* rather than *integrated*—to the point that I disappear from my own story.

Epilogue
I am Ruth. I have tried to raise some interpretive issues related to reading the book called after me. Much of what I've just told you is, of course, a piece of constructed, subjective, impudent fiction. When all is said and done, you still know very little about my literary, canonized character—about my emotions, motivation, needs, looks, eventual fate. You know even less about my historicity: was I, was I not? Am I, am I not? A fictive or fictitious figment of imagination certainly has a grasp on life that is longer than most. But over and above that? I am quite certain, however, that in interpreting "my" biblical story, many things are generally pre-assumed and prefigured. The interpreters' or readers' times, locations, and interests condition such assumptions and prefigurations. They are also influenced, radically so, by the readers' gender or subscription to conventional gender views. It is perhaps time that we became aware of our responsibilities as gendered [post]modern readers. This is the only point of this retelling of "my" story. Otherwise, obviously, I have no claim on history or on "t/ruth."
     And now it's Orpah's turn.

Orpah: The Exclusion
I'm the one who is supposed to have turned back. Let me state my position, briefly, because I'm still reeling under the impact of

meeting Ruth and Naomi again, after all these years, and am too preoccupied with the impressions of our triple meeting to make a comprehensible presentation. Too much has passed, too much has been attributed to all and each of us, too much "history" has been added to our tales.

I'm Naomi's daughter-in-law and Ruth's blood sister and sister-in-law. Typically, as I've noticed, Ruth didn't tell you that we are paternal sisters, from different mothers but from the same royal father, the then king of Moab. She never refers to that. In truth, my mother's house within my father's house was stronger than Ruth's. This may explain, a little, why Ruth's decision and mine were diametrically opposed to each other: I definitely had a supportive address to return to. At any rate, I turned back and returned to my "mother's house," following Naomi's advice as reported in chapter 1 of the book named after Ruth. I decided to do that instead of proceeding with the two other dear women to Bethlehem, after my husband—Naomi's son—had died. Believe me, it wasn't an easy decision to make. Ruth and I, two half-blood sisters, had been married to two full-blood brothers. When both our husbands died shortly after our father-in-law Elimelech had departed this world, our existence caved in. And I loved Ruth dearly, and I liked Naomi as well. It's simply too painful, after all this time, to even reminisce about the wonderful household our extended family had, with Elimelech as its formal head but with Naomi as its prime mover. I can't do that; it's so depressing to recount how much we've lost with their deaths. (Did I mention that they died because of a mysterious virus, that our house and harvests had to be destroyed because of fear of infection, that even magic didn't help assuage the fears those sudden deaths inspired in the community, that our belongings and assets were fumigated, that we didn't simply *leave* but had to do so, for fear of our lives, because our countrymen began to think that all this bad luck was due to the family's Hebrew origins—a prejudice somehow never exercised during the good years?) Naomi doesn't say so, but *she* had to leave, and we, the dutiful daughters, accompanied her as a matter of course, voluntarily.

So why did I change my mind in mid-course, so that I'd be criticized for going back? . . . got very bad press for that. Second thoughts of a secondary character. Post-biblical Jewish sources derive

my name from the Hebrew word '*oref*, "nape/back of the neck,"
because this is the part of my anatomy Naomi and Ruth saw last,
until this conference (we never met afterwards; we remain close but
life drove us apart). Moreover, it was Naomi's expressed wish that we
turn back. And I took her seriously. Like Ruth, as she so openly
confesses, I needed to do what was right for me at that time of
widowhood, poverty, and rootlessness, with no males left in our
household to protect and feed us. And, unlike Ruth, I made another
decision. I did think that going back to my mother's house would
give me—a childless widow but still capable of conceiving—another
chance in life. You see, I was not as brave as my beloved friend and
sister and sister-in-law Ruth. I was more delicate and, let's face it,
more spoiled than she was. She was much more confident in her
abilities to adjust than I was, or so it seemed. Or perhaps, as she has
said, she was simply more desperate and less certain of her welcome
back home, should she return to her mother's house. Perhaps she felt
that she really had no other viable option but to continue with
Naomi. But I, operating out of fear and anxiety and encouraged by
Naomi to leave, welcomed the chance. I was too scared of the
prejudices against "Others" in Israelite and Judahite societies. I
couldn't face that, and I couldn't face the necessary cultural
adjustments that I'd have to make. For instance, I asked myself,
would I have to worship my ancestral goddess in secret, or worse still,
give her up? And who would marry a widow like me? In my mother's
house, the royal house, although we'd been estranged for years
because of my marriage to a Judahite, I might still be considered the
repentant prodigal daughter; I might still be able to make something
of my life—and certainly, they'd have the means to support me. And I
was so tired of hardship and heartache, so much in need of
consolation and creature comforts!

So I returned and was accepted, as prodigals sometimes are, and
lived in comfort and relative contentment. Happiness, of course, was
too much to hope for: part of me remained with Ruth and Naomi,
although I couldn't find it in me to accompany them on their quest.
And part of me, in spite of everything, always wondered whether I'd
made the right decision. When you come to a fork in the road and
choose the one direction, you never know what you might have
missed!

The African theologian Musa Dube Shomana, from Botswana, has recently established that, for a while, I did try to remain in contact with Ruth. As she recorded, we exchanged letters. Like Ruth, I could read and write, which was far from usual for women in our time. That was a direct outcome of our royal Moabite descent. As daughters of royalty, we were literate. Hence, life circumstances notwithstanding, we could correspond.

Musa Dube managed, through another person, to uncover our correspondence. She did show how we tried to stay in touch, exchange news with, and draw mutual comfort from each other. But this didn't last for long. Xenophobia is not a modern or postmodern invention only. Once we parted at the junction, once I kissed my mother-in-law, Naomi, goodbye, our fates diverged.

I did remarry. Naomi, bless her generous soul, was right in stating this was possible. I did manage to become a mother, fortunately once again. But post-biblical Jewish lore, from the Babylonian talmud to the *Ruth Rabbah* midrash and also elsewhere, has me as the eventual mother of Goliath, defeated by David (1 Samuel 17). Now, look at that. The biblical giant Goliath is defined as a "Philistine," therefore probably of non-Semitic Greek origin. This did not prevent the Jewish sages from making me his mother, making him my son, although I'm a Moabite, hence of Semitic stock. An "Other" is an "Other" is an "Other"; somehow, it seems that no finer distinctions were necessary. Moabite, Philistine, what does it matter? In fact, what is interesting—once again—is not the historical "truth" per se but the Jewish sages' need to posit me firmly as the oppositional matrix to Ruth, my much-loved sister and marriage kin, whom they accepted as one of their own, at least after a fashion if not fully, as she has told you.

I therefore remain an outsider, an enemy. Never mind the fact that, by turning away and returning to my home, I complied with Naomi's wish as explicitly expressed. Never mind the fact that Naomi never ever had anything against me, that I never had anything against her. Never mind that I did love her and Ruth with all my heart. But, when the crunch came, when we faced two possibilities, Ruth was too scared to go back and thought that casting her lot with the unknown (read: Bethlehem) would be better; whereas I was too scared to go forward in the direction of that same unknown. I leave this issue for you to ponder. However, while we're at it, and if your geography isn't too shaky after all this time, let me remind you that Moab affords a wonderful viewpoint for observing the wherewithal of the West Bank from the east. Watching Rahab's story, and furthermore, from the wings—so to speak—gave me much pleasure. And I'm still watching, from the Jordanian kingdom.

To conclude, allow me to add a few words about my mother-in-law, Naomi. Mother-in-law jokes are common and stereotypic and repeated with relish and culturally acceptable, widely so. I'd like to re-emphasize that Naomi, although not a "praying shawl of blue purple," as the Jews playfully say to indicate innocence or purity, was always fair to Ruth and to me. She didn't pull rank unnecessarily, and she didn't put her own interests before ours. This is exemplified by her expressed wish to absolve us from the need to accompany her back to Bethlehem—a wish I honored to the letter, and Ruth disobeyed. Different paths, different destinies . . . I rest my case. Let the floor be Naomi's now.

Naomi: Would You Believe This?

My friend Dave, an art dealer, a man who says his mind loudly and clearly when asked to and even more willingly when he's not asked to, was having a drink with me the other day. In between one dirty joke and another, for this is his way of entertaining his not-so-young female guests (I suppose that you qualify as one of the guys once you're past your prime), he stopped for a breath (I was afraid for a minute he'd choke on his own laughter, in response to his own jokes), and said, "My dear Naomi, it's time you disclosed your part of the story to the world."

I tried to feign innocence. I answered, in studied artlessness, "What do you mean?" Dave didn't even blink while retorting, immediately, "About you and Ruth." So please excuse me, my dear Ruth, whose reserve and discretion are legendary, and all of you, dear ladies. Here's my confession.

Ruth and Orpah were good daughters-in-law. Their mutual bond was strong: Orpah has already told you that they are paternal sisters as well as sisters-in-law. Since their family disowned them when they married my sons, they regarded me as the mother they could share. They were closer to each other than to me, which was understandable, but also made me jealous. In general, though, while I retain my right to complain at all times—which is customary in my source group—there was no real reason to whine. In our family we raise our wine glasses to a habitual toast: "health and love." And this is what we had, all round, in our comfortable exile, on the fleshpots of Moab. Our chief anxiety was linked to the fact that both young couples didn't manage to produce offspring. Ruth and Orpah spent most of their time traveling around consulting medical experts, visiting fertility shrines, conferring with midwives and herbalists, participating in magical sessions. Much money was spent this way, but to no avail. I was beginning to suspect that this was divine retribution for leaving our land, that our god, the god famous for interfering with women's wombs, closing them and opening them at will, was punishing us in the worst possible manner. And I started thinking that we should uproot ourselves again, that we should make *aliyah* as it is now called ("going up," which is our term for immigrating back to our own land), that we should return to Bethlehem if we wanted to break the barren spell that appeared to have settled upon our domestic, otherwise blissful, family existence.

But worse was to come before my thoughts on this matter crystallized. Suddenly everything changed when our husbands, all three of them, died of the plague within the span of one week. We became not only inconsolable but also destitute. We lost our loved ones, we lost our livelihood, we had to sell our properties for a song because we were "infected" and in order to return debts the girls had incurred in their fertility quest. When we stood up from our low mourning couches, after the lamenting women had departed and we were left alone in the silence of what used to be the happy and noisy inner courtyard of our extended family's compound, I knew what I wanted to do. If a new beginning, I said to myself, then in the old country.

I shouldn't have let the girls come with me in the first place. I should have convinced them to stay in Moab, where they really belonged. But I was weak and selfish. After a few days' walk, and with my strength returning slowly, I asked them to go back to their mother's house. I cannot and had never criticized Orpah for abiding by my wish. She did not only what was right for her personally, but also what was right for me. I must confess that, until then, she was my favorite. She was vivacious, outspoken, with a colorful personality, an attractive extrovert. She didn't tell you she was a Hollywood-type, glamorous beauty. She would light up a party by her mere presence. But she was also more than a little spoiled, as great beauties sometimes are. She was built for decoration, not for hard work. Ruth, on the other hand, was plainer and quieter. She never confided in me; there was always some reserve between us. She was quick to take offense and retreat into herself, although she wouldn't complain. An introvert—deep water but no sparkle. Whereas Orpah basically shimmered and glittered, Ruth spent hours brooding, reading, and writing. Girls, don't be insulted by these portrayals; you know that I love you both. And Ruth, especially you, never mind that I once loved Orpah more (all parents have their favorites, only that not all of them admit it to themselves or to others); be patient and listen to the rest of my confession.

Orpah, the one closer to me, understood me perfectly when I asked both my daughters-in-law to leave me and turn back. Orpah, the one I loved most, obeyed. I could count on her selfish inclinations, on her instinct for survival—and I don't mean that in a pejorative sense. And, once she turned to go, I was sure Ruth would follow. To my consternation, my slightly standoffish, quiet, reserved, distant daughter-in-law chose to come with me rather than go with her sister. And she made an oath that bound her to me as a man is bound to a woman, as she told you herself.

To say I was surprised would be an understatement. I didn't understand her motivation at all. Duty and love—yes, these were there, but why carry them so far? Ruth says now that she made a conscious rational choice that was the best for her, that going back would have been worse, that she acted in the interest of her own survival no less than of mine. At the time I was too bewildered to comprehend. Once she had pronounced an oath—and the spoken word as you know has a binding value of its own, it cannot be rescinded—I let her follow me. As we walked and walked, I became aware of the fact that without her I couldn't have made it back to Bethlehem. But now I was mourning Orpah's departure as well as my husband's and sons'; Ruth was a convenience but less meaningful for me. When we came to Bethlehem, when the women welcomed me at

the gate, I didn't even introduce Ruth to them. She was a silent
presence, unacknowledged, by my side (the end of Ruth 1). Ruth,
apologies, I'll always be ashamed of that.

And afterward? Ruth worked for both of us while I moped and
pitied myself. Ruth brought the food; I slid into a depression. Ruth
impressed everyone she met with her dignity and conduct, and I
stayed at the shelter she arranged for us. Ruth made contacts with
my relatives: she went by chance—or was it divine providence?—to
Boaz's field and made his acquaintance, instead of me sending her
there directly with a formal introduction as I should have (chapter 2).
She left every morning and came back every night, never
complaining, gleaning in the fields and going her own way,
respectfully, quietly. I was grateful to her, most certainly. But my
heart, my heart was empty. I didn't feel a thing. I didn't feel love
toward her, or toward anybody else living or present. I was a bereaved
wife and mother and played the part maximally.

Then one day, after several weeks had gone by, everything altered
dramatically. Ruth came home with a piece of information: there was
a plot of land, cultivated by one of our neighbors, that actually
belonged to me as my late husband's surviving heir. I couldn't own it,
because in our culture women don't own land unless the
circumstances are such that no male relative at all exists. Even
Zelophehad's daughters, whose father had no sons, were given the
right to inherit his land portion by Moses (Numbers 27) provided
that they married their cousin (Numbers 36). But I could sell it to
one of our male relatives who could "redeem" it from me (as written
in Leviticus 25) for its value. This discovery, as you may imagine, was
of the utmost importance for me. I'd lost all documents pertaining
to our former glory in Bethlehem long ago and was depressed. And
here, in her intelligence, Ruth not only provided for us on a daily
basis but also found a more permanent solution, at least for a while.

I never was a demonstrative woman. In fact, even when parting
from my beloved Orpah, she kissed me and I didn't kiss her (chapter
1). But this time, I jumped out of bed, where I'd been lying listlessly,
grabbed Ruth, and hugged and kissed her rather emotionally.

And then it happened. All of a sudden, as I was touching Ruth, a
wave of . . . what? came over me. I couldn't understand what was
happening. It was an electric shock, you'd say today, that totally

engulfed me. It was, I said to myself as I was reeling with confusion but in the midst of it the clearest comprehension, *desire* that I felt.

Desire. Not pure, not simple. Me, physically attracted to Ruth? I couldn't have known, I didn't know what came over me, I'd never touched her before, our relationship was almost formal, if full of respect and emotionally sound. This feeling, this sudden desire, this electrifying effect, was devastating.

When I'd collected my wits about me, when my knees stopped buckling under, the question was, What to do? Did Ruth notice, I asked myself? After all, she "clung" to me, like a man to a woman. Did she mean it in that way, I asked myself in bewilderment? If so, she gave no sign, verbal or otherwise. Should I pursue this for a relationship? Please remember, our sages thought nothing of women playing with each other, as they quaintly termed it. All they were concerned about was that this kind of female "foolery" wouldn't intervene with child production with a husband. From this viewpoint, if my desire or sudden illogical passion, born out of a chance physical encounter, were to be consummated, no sin comparable to male homosexuality would have been involved.

I became tense. I pondered this for a week or two, pretending to be almost as depressed as before despite the good news brought by Ruth about my land property and the new lease on emotional life that came my way. Now I suddenly saw Ruth not as a plain introvert but as attractive, sinuous, supple, graceful as she went about her chores. More than once I nearly spoke to her or—better or worse still— grabbed her. In my wild imagination, I saw the two of us establishing a two-woman homestead, perhaps acquiring a child by some means, natural or otherwise or by adoption. In my fond imagination, I saw us establishing a relationship of love. Why did Ruth follow me to a strange land? Why does she feed and comfort me, if not because of love and love alone? She was a generation younger, so what? Men are allowed to have younger lovers; why should women not be allowed that? And nobody should know, nobody would suspect, they'd view us as two bereaved women making the best of difficult circumstances. And all this time I was burning, burning. . . .

After enjoying and suffering from emotional turmoil for some days, I came to my senses. I decided not to ask Ruth for her viewpoint, or emotions. Logic reined me in, although only with great difficulty did I manage to control my desire. We lived then and we live now in a predominantly patriarchal society. Then more than now, a woman needs a man to protect and cherish her. A woman needed and still needs children, at least and preferably a son, to secure her social position and old age requirements. Establishing a two-woman arrangement, be the cover story plausible or not, did not seem viable. I had to concede that to myself. Furthermore, affairs, love affairs, may end. And then what?

I have no idea how Ruth felt about this unrequited love and passion that flooded me all of a sudden. I never discussed it with her: perhaps I should have, maybe then Jewish and Christian history would have been different. My decision, as painful as could be, was to deny myself even the mere chance to realize my passion. My decision was never to mention the revelatory experience I had to Ruth herself. Instead, and partly in self-defense, I pushed her into seducing Boaz at the threshing floor, as reported in chapter 3 of the book named after her. I felt this was a selfless act on my part, excruciating but necessary for all concerned: I didn't trust myself to overcome my desire for much longer if we continued to live together.

The rest is well documented. What happened on the threshing floor notwithstanding (I uphold Ruth's decision to leave that as an oblique and private report), Ruth did marry Boaz and thereafter produced the necessary son. And the field whose ownership Ruth discovered was sold to Boaz as part of the transaction, and I became doubly secure: as an independent widow, and as a foster mother to a male heir.

Ironically, and listen to this, the newborn son is reported as having been born to *me*,

A son is born unto Naomi. (Ruth 4:17)

As Ruth has shown, she disappears from the scene at this point, having given birth to Obed. I am named as the child's practical and practicing mother. The neighboring women, who named the child, said thus to me,

Blessed be Yhwh who has not stopped you from having a redeemer today, and his name shall be established in Israel. And

he shall restore your life, and be the nourisher of your old age,
for your daughter-in-law who loves you, who is better to you
than seven sons, has born him. (Ruth 4:14-15)

Irony indeed. It is I who came to entertain a love and desire for Ruth,
not the other way around. Or is it, did she really love me as I briefly
wanted her to? I've meanwhile recovered from this infatuation by
sheer self-negation and will power; it has passed into the deepest love,
with the erotic potential almost totally gone. Nevertheless, I'd really
like to know. Ruth never said anything. Neither did she refer to this
issue in her presentation to us, as you've undoubtedly observed. I
don't know what to attribute this to. Did she never notice my sudden
obsession with her? Is she too well-mannered and polite to ever refer
to it? Did she decide to keep quiet and pretend indifference on this
point, out of decorum and respect? I'm afraid that her presentation
doesn't supply any answers. Paradoxically, incongruently, I got a little
of what I wanted in those few turbulent days: a son of Ruth, to be
considered my own. The fact that she chose, or agreed, to stay in the
wings after the child's birth, letting me bask in the limelight of
motherhood, may serve as an implicit indication that she knew and
complied, non-verbally, with my passion. Or can it?

    After all is said and done, in my opinion, this is ultimately the key
to my beloved Ruth's character: she was and is motivated by grace
and duty. I've read somewhere I think that the scholar was a Jewish-
American psychologist named Sternberg who was obsessed by
quantifying love scientifically, an interesting theory. According to
Sternberg, love can be typified and figuratively depicted as a triangle.
The triangle's angles are passion, intimacy, and commitment.
Personal temperaments, personal choices, determine the length of
the three triangle sides and the size of the ensuing angles. Ruth's
triangle, I suspect, was very strong on the "commitment" angle. She
spoke little and did much. She presents herself as a self-seeking
intellectual. Her motivation for her deeds and actions, however,
remained secretive for a long while, until today in fact. But was she as
self-seeking as she presents herself? I have my doubts. But if we are to
trust the biblical account, if we read her as consenting to my
monopolization of her own baby, then her social answer to my

irregular and surprising passion is clear. Without any further ado, without verbalization, she gave me the child I craved to raise with her and then disappeared, to come back later in Jesus' lineage, as she's already told us.

To return to my friend Dave, who served as a catalyst for this "confession": so-called lesbian aspirations are common today, while not always acted upon. Many times, as in my case, such aspirations or passions remain dormant, in the realm of phantasy. Sometimes they don't. Many same-sex female lovers have looked to the book of Ruth for a model showing how they could bridge age and culture gaps in a love relationship. As I've tried to explain, the love I felt toward Ruth as the result of a touching accident—a love never consummated, a love never confessed until now, a passion denied, a desire sublimated in the name of the proper social order—remains a private matter. I shall never know whether it was reciprocated at the time, or whether it could have been reciprocated at the time. I too made a choice to deny an inner voice. I don't regret it—what's the use? But contemporary same-sex female lovers might think otherwise, and might imagine that they do have more of a choice at this time.

Dave is ultimately named after King David, like so many other Israelis and non-Israelis in the Western hemisphere nowadays. Dave is a typical macho, vulgar, direct, noisy Israeli living in Europe but more and less than that at the same time. He is totally non-religious. Nevertheless, he has a vested interest, absurd but existentially voyeuristic, in everything pertaining to his biblical namesake King David and his lineage. Like so many males, he enjoys speculating over possibilities of female same-sex love attachments. He'd be even happier if video depictions of his phantasy were available. It's easy to laugh at his preoccupations, especially after all this time. However, his diagnostic powers, his suspicions really, born out of male insecurity in the face of any female alliance, shouldn't be discounted. About Ruth and me, Dave suspected the worst (from his viewpoint). But basically, let's face it, he understands.

SEVEN

∞

I Am the Glow:
Rizpah Daughter of Ayah

*R*izpah (Person). The daughter of Aiah and concubine of Saul ben Kish, first king of Israel. She bore Saul two sons, Armoni and Mephibaal (Mephibosheth). Nothing is known of her life during Saul's reign. During Eshbaal's brief reign, she became the focus of Abner's unsuccessful attempt to depose his inexperienced nephew and rule Israel in his stead (2 Sam. 3:7). By having sexual relations with the former king's concubine, Abner tried to lay claim to the throne by virtue of his possession of the royal harem. During the early years of David's joint reign over Israel and Judah, Rizpah's two sons were ritually executed along with the five sons of Merab, Saul's eldest daughter, in an effort to end a three-year famine that had been plaguing the land (2 Sam. 21:1–14). Rizpah is reported to have kept a vigil over the seven dead bodies, keeping away birds and animals of prey until rain fell and ended the drought—from mid-April until October or November. David then is said to have had the bones of the seven victims gathered up, and to have had them buried along with the exhumed bones of Saul and Jonathan, who had been buried in Jabesh-gilead, in the family ancestral tomb located in Benjamin at Zela. (*Anchor Bible Dictionary* CD-ROM)

This is a scholarly summary, a short encyclopedia entry, of my historical significance, if significant it is. As we shall see, it's more and less than a summary. On the one hand, it leaves out some important details. On the other hand, it prescribes imagined motivations for the male characters' actions, motivations that are not explicitly stated in the biblical text (not to mention other explanations and clarifications by way of gap fillings). Typically, although written by a woman, this scholarly synopsis doesn't refer at all to my imagined motivation but only to the males'. I shall be happy to supplement information on both accounts: that of details and that of my own position.

My name means "glowing coal," much like the "glowing coal" from the sacred altar that a heavenly winged body puts to the mouth of Isaiah in his vision, presumably to expiate his sinning lips and prepare him for his prophetic mission (see Isa. 6:1-7, especially verse 6). What are your associations when a "glowing coal" is mentioned? Mine would be a slow and long burning fire, barely visible perhaps—capable of burning, but after all a remnant, an ember, not a fully developed fire. Hence, by implication, my name refers to a quiet but enduring passion, and also purification by fire, as in the example cited. And these implications of passion, endurance, purification, or expiation suit me well. They sum up my emotions and activities within the framework of my sorry life. Another example of a telling symbolic name; you may nod your heads in recognition after and when listening to the other colleagues who have spoken here as well as to me.

But before continuing, let's give a thought to my pedigree. I'm called "daughter of Ayah," and most commentators insist that Ayah is my *father's* name. They mention that an obviously male person by that name is defined as a Horite (a sort of Canaanite) in lists appearing in Genesis (36:24) and Chronicles (1 Chron. 1:40). Therefore, "Ayah" would logically be my father's name for them. Such a definition would make me a foreign woman by associations, although not too far removed from the Israelites—and note again the preference of biblical scribes to describe female characters not only as Others but also as ethnic foreigners. However, *'ayyâ* is a female form, and as a semantic word (to distinguish from a proper name) means "falcon, kite," something similar to "vulture," at least in poetry. Wisdom, among other things, is so godly that it's not to be found even in

The road not known by a vulture
Nor seen by the eye of the kite (*'ayyâ*). (Job 28:7)

This bird is an unclean bird, forbidden as food in the two great lists of allowed and forbidden foodstuff in the Torah, namely Leviticus 11 (v. 14) and Deuteronomy 14 (v. 13).

You probably guess my contention: Ayah is not my father's name; it's my mother's name. Let me prove this to you by citing some relevant examples. We do know that other women in the bible are given animals' names—Deborah ("bee"), Jael ("mountain goat"), and Huldah (feminine form of the biblical Hebrew word for "mole," as evidenced by post-biblical Hebrew). The same applies for males—Oreb ("raven"), Shaphan ("hyrax"), Achbar or Achbor ("mouse"), Ze'ev ("wolf" or "jackal") are examples that spring immediately to mind. And if you say that some of these names are associated with unclean animals, as they're set forth in the Leviticus and Deuteronomy lists, I'd say this applies to female and male names/animals alike—mole, vulture, hyrax, raven or falcon, and mouse are as forbidden to eat as the *'ayyâ*. Apparently, there's no connection between name giving and food taboos, historical or otherwise: the biblical hyrax person is a scribe, Achbor a royal functionary in Josiah's court, Huldah a prophetess. And if you claim it's more usual to designate a person by paternal lineage, this is of course true; but if Dinah is called "daughter of Leah" (Gen. 34:1, and see her story), and even males can be identified by their mothers, like Joab son of Zeruiah (whose story will come later), there's no reason to assume that this doesn't apply to me too. However, as usual, it's easier for biblical scribes to assume paternal lineage than to admit the less usual maternal lineage in a given case. I proudly correct that: I am Rizpah daughter of my mother, Ayah, daughter of the falcon if you please, which has a bearing on my story as you will hear.

But first, a little personal history, to supplement the "summary" I quote at the beginning of my talk. Indeed, I was a secondary wife to King Saul and had two sons by him. Some authorities insist that I loved Saul very dearly, but let me defer my comments about this for a little while. At any rate, after he had died, his general, Abner, son of Ner, took me as wife, which was seen as his way of challenging Saul's failed successor Eshba'al. Abner was later assassinated by Joab son of Zeruiah, David's general and nephew (2 Samuel 3). What is less known but preserved in a handful of sources if not in the Hebrew bible, is that when David was done grieving for Abner, hypocritically or otherwise—after all, Joab did him a service, one of many, by eliminating Abner—he himself took me for a wife. Be assured that those sources are not interested in my fate: the discussion takes place *a propos* the important question, Was David justified in taking me for a wife, since a father-in-law's wife is prohibited for the son-in-law for reasons of incest? Remember, David was Saul's son-in-law since he had married Michal—whom I knew and liked (and see about this later)—before me. True to form, the sages justify David's action by referring to the custom of kings and aspiring kings to consolidate their political authority by symbolically appropriating their predecessors' women sexually, publicly, as Absalom did to his father (2 Sam. 16:22; see also 12:11-12).

Now, let me fill in the gaps here. Abner ben Ner's name means, "father of the lamp [or candle], son of the lamp [candle]." Biblical storytellers and later interpreters insinuate that Abner's taking me as his wife was done out of political motives, to stress his claim to the throne (remember, he was King Saul's uncle). However, the names provide a subtext: how fitting, how preordained, for a "glowing coal" and a "lamp" to get together! Abner really and truly loved me, as much as Adonijah loved Abishag in a similar situation (1 Kings 2:13-25); even politically minded males act out of emotion sometimes! Nevertheless, in both cases, the biblical scribes and their successors seem to have discarded the personal motives of love and desire under the weight of the political implications: King Solomon, much like Eshba'al before him, preferred to view the desire for a woman (for Abishag, as for me) as threatening political ambition. And both Abner and Adonijah perished, superficially because of their desire for a woman. And yes, Abner's passion for me was indeed reciprocated. Look at our names again: fire and fire came together, a match made in heaven in spite of the circumstances. But *Realpolitik* did intervene; there was no getting away from that.

For there's no doubt that King David's taking me as a wife was politically motivated, as was his appropriation of Abigail after her husband had died (1 Samuel 25) and his reappropriation of his loving wife Michal (2 Sam. 3:14-16), whose love he didn't reciprocate. Inasmuch as David was capable of loving, he loved Bathsheba; other wives, like us, were simply either temporary bedmates or else tokens of his ambitions to merge Israel and Judah into a single, united, functioning monarchy and to regulate his relations with neighboring political entities. Which he succeeded to do, of course, and let me not demonize him on that account.

My life in his harem wasn't too bad. It was routine, with not much contact with the king. The marriage was a matter of formality, basically. And I enjoyed Michal's company, although her relationship with David was much more complex than mine. She longed for him, and he spurned her. Although she's not present here—she died in the biblical text—still, you can find a kaleidoscopic, multi-viewpoint of her life and love in a recent book, *Telling Queen Michal's Story* (edited by David J. A. Clines and Tamara C. Eskenazi). As for me, I mourned my second deceased husband, Abner, for a while. Realistically, though, I said to myself, I did have my two sons, the ones I had with King Saul, and a comfortable life. I survived and they did too, together with their relatives the sons of Merab daughter of Saul, my other stepdaughter. While I had no royal ambitions for myself or for them, I was well aware that they were the only surviving descendants of Saul's house, apart from Jonathan's son Mephibosheth. And I kept my peace.

Until the famine, and the Gibeonites' demand for Saul's sons to be killed as compensation for Saul's disregard for the ancient oath to spare them (given to them on the basis of their lie by Joshua: they claimed they came from far away, hence should and could be spared from the Israelites' holy war and their own extinction) as a remedy for the famine. Now, look how the story is presented in 2 Samuel 21, as if the Gibeonites' demand was a just and moral demand, as if Yhwh's anger was raised by Saul's past action. When? How? Why so long after the events? No answer to that, I'm afraid. A short and fragmented verse (2 Sam. 21:1b) declares divine authority for defining the famine's reason as Saul's bloody extinction of the Gibeonites, but it does *not* condone their demand for revenge. And there's no word as for a possibility that David could sidestep the Gibeonites' demand to kill seven of Saul's sons, none whatever. David was a shrewd and manipulative man: he could have found a less bloody solution if he were so inclined. But he wasn't. He did spare Jonathan's son, this is true, but not mine. And not his sister-in-law Merab's. This option to effect an elimination of Saul's descendants seems to have served him well.

Later generations disliked the story, exceedingly so, if I may pass judgment. There's no trace of it in the Chroniclers' account of David's reign: they pass it over, like they do to other stories that present David in an uncomplimentary light. Josephus Flavius writes—and please note the emphases I introduce to this text's layout in order to point out how Josephus modifies the biblical account in order to exonerate David of any blame in this episode—

HOW THE HEBREWS WERE DELIVERED FROM A FAMINE WHEN THE GIBEONITES HAD CAUSED PUNISHMENT TO BE INFLICTED FOR THOSE OF THEM THAT HAD BEEN SLAIN . . . AFTER this, when the country was greatly afflicted with a famine, David besought God *to have mercy on the people, and to discover to him what was the cause of it, and how a remedy might be found for that distemper. And when the prophets answered, that* God would have the Gibeonites *avenged* whom Saul the king was *so wicked as to betray* to slaughter, *and had not observed the oath which Joshua the general and the senate had sworn to them*: If, therefore, said God, the king would permit such vengeance to be taken for those that were slain as the Gibeonites should desire, he promised that he would be reconciled to them, and free the multitude from their miseries. As soon therefore as* the king *understood that this it was which God sought, he* sent for the Gibeonites, and asked them what it was they should have; and when they desired to have seven sons of Saul delivered to them to be punished, he delivered them up, but spared Mephibosheth the son of Jonathan. So when the Gibeonites had received the men, *they punished them as they pleased*; upon which God began to send rain, and to recover the earth to bring forth its fruits as usual, and to free it from the foregoing drought, so that the country of the Hebrews flourished again.

As you can hear and see, Josephus adds and modifies and deletes specifics and takes away some of the cruelty of the story, not to mention leaving me out of it altogether, so as to lay the responsibility on Yhwh and his prophets, leaving David an orthodox, lily-white agent of god's will and savior "of the multitudes," his people, from hunger and certain death. Nobody asks why and how this suited David, and why he, a man of talent and intellect, saw fit here to surrender to superstition and prejudice.

This whitewashing of David is only partly successful, for later generations were more troubled by David's actions, on various counts. Uncomfortable readers asked embarrassing questions, and they sometimes supplied answers to them. What happened to me, to Rizpah, after Abner's death? (I've already mentioned the traces of information that allowed him to take me as wife, with the possible conflict with incest taboos.) Why did god prefer the welfare of foreigners, the Gibeonites, to that of his own people, the descendants of Saul? Another issue was that of the poor executed men's sin—what was their own sin, even if their grandfather Saul disregarded an ancient oath to the Gibeonites? Other sources deal with the question of letting the sons' bodies hang without burial, which is considered an abomination to god.

Other sources praise me for my actions of religious devotion, as they see it, for according to the biblical text I guarded the hanging bodies for about seven months, preventing the birds of prey and wild animals from picking on them, justifying god's decision on the one hand and never ceasing my maternal vigil on the other hand—so much so, that finally David is put to shame and brings Saul and Jonathan's exhumed remains to burial. While it's not stated that he did bring the sons' bodies to burial, he actually did; and mysteriously, at this point and causally with my persistent action, god finally hears the supplication of the land, no doubt a euphemism for the lifting of the famine (2 Sam. 21:12-15). And many readers rate my actions very highly, claiming that my martyrdom (*sic!*) overrides the abomination, the desecration of god's name by leaving the bodies hanging without burial. As for Christian readers of both genders, amazingly the name Rizpah was a rather popular girl name in the United States in the nineteenth century, in the South but not only there; a survey of Internet pages will show that my name (and story) is borrowed for endowing faith and health communities with dignity and loyalty, once again in the United States.

I am but a glowing coal. My anger, my fire, is subdued, albeit enduring. What I did was in line with a long and time-honored tradition of nonverbal protest. David allowed the execution of men who were not only my own flesh and blood, his wife's (admittedly one of several) sons, his stepchildren, but also his wife Michal's nephews, his dead, loving friend Jonathan's nephews. His sparing of Jonathan's son Mephibosheth the cripple (or should I say, in keeping with current politically correct attitudes, "physically challenged"?) is a fig leaf: David knew full well that Mephibosheth could never be king because of his physical disability (his feet were damaged when he fell, while his nurse tried to save him from the Philistines after his father and grandfather had perished in battle—2 Sam. 4:4). The seven sons given to the Gibeonites for lynching and public humiliation, my sons and Merab's, were able-bodied men. Not only of Saul's family, but David's as well by virtue of marriage. Yet he never hesitated in handing them over and his scribes attributed his action, this removal of potential although paranoiac threat to his reign, to Yhwh's hinted, general, although non-specified approval.

As for me, feminist readers attribute my action in the next summer season, more than half a year, to lofty or deeply inbred maternal emotions. I did stand there, day and night. But let me tell you a secret or two. Perhaps my action was heroic, as pointed out by many: for instance, Jopie Siebert Hommes. But I had additional motives as well, at least two very powerful ones, which I'd like to set forth now, in brief. You may guess that the dry manner I employ for delivering my story hides great emotional intensity, as befits an ember, a trace, a remnant, as befits my name.

My sons were lynched and displayed for all to see, and so were Merab's (strictly speaking, my stepdaughter's sons). I guarded their bodies as well as my sons'. This was my protest action on behalf of my other female colleagues linked with David, his other wives and female relatives by marriage: on behalf of Michal, who was the closest to me, and her sister Merab, and Ahinoam, and Abigail, and the others too. As long as I was there, not speaking, not screaming, not weeping, not asking for anything, David's inequity could not be forgotten. A Gandhi-like operation of passive resistance, you may conclude. And ultimately effective: I couldn't save the boys from their fate, but I could save their memory, especially the memory of my own sons. Why, even their names are recorded, unlike the names of Merab's sons, although not clearly enough. At least my firstborn, Armoni, "my palace," is clearly recorded. Let's drink to his blessed memory.

And let me confess further that, at least during the daytime, my ordeal was made easier by my ability to converse with birds of prey: vultures, falcons, kites, and the like. I am daughter of Ayah. My mother taught me how to converse with birds of prey, her namesakes. I kept telling them, repeatedly and in their own languages, to go away and explained why. They understood: like me, they do care for their offspring under very difficult conditions. And they stayed away. And let me sleep during the day. And then I could go about my guard duty at night. And I persevered, and the lynched boys were finally buried. A fate similar to that of my first husband, King Saul, and my stepson Jonathan: they too were killed, exposed, later buried.

This is a story of royal men, as you may have gathered, more than of women as mothers. I was less interesting for the biblical authors and their successors than Saul and David. Nevertheless, my act of protest captured their imagination. They love selfless drama; this is how they want to image their women, as subscribing to male values to the exclusion of their own well-being or potential wishes. I remain there, glowing quietly, a sore in their—side? Soul? Comprehension? Compassion? Or perhaps as an icon of implied criticism, the woman who knew her practical theology (People should be buried, whatever the cause of their death, divinely ordained or otherwise!) better than the famed King David, let him *not* rest in peace.

In passing, let me refer to a phenomenon mentioned also by several of my colleagues, notably Dinah. Sometimes we so-called tragic Hebrew bible women who never get to utter one single word in our unfortunate biblical story receive a much more empathetic if also no less fanciful treatment not from [male] sages and scholars but from [male] poets and authors. This is especially true, as also in the case of Dinah, when you consider the Hebrew writers of the early and mid-twentieth century, in Israel. I do agree that, as Ofrah Ben Meir, a contemporary theatre scholar from Tel Aviv writes,

> the adoption of the Bible as a cultural starting point was part of an early twentieth-century pan-cultural phenomenon: the national search for roots. Among the characteristics of this phenomenon was the revival of Jewish plastic arts. . . . It is thus hardly surprising that the choice of Biblical iconographic

themes in the Hebrew theatre was not made by chance, but
guided by the national ideology.

Two plays in which I feature come to my mind, and I'd like to
comment on each of them briefly. The first is called "Rizpah
Daughter of Ayah" and was published in Hebrew in 1941. It is
written by a long-forgotten poet/author whose name was Haim
Elchanan, and who wrote under the pseudonym Y. H. Ben David.
This author writes a bad imitation of biblical Hebrew, so pompously
stylized as to make his thoughts unintelligible to any reader; it's
almost impossible for any viewer to relate to the language register of
his play. I have no idea whether this five-act monstrosity, heavily and
internally over-rhymed (remember, biblical poetry seldom rhymes)
even in its stage instructions, was ever performed on an actual stage.
At any rate, it is worth noting that Ben David has Saul as a man who
loves me and has me love Saul passionately, and both of us behave as
true sharing partners. Moreover, in a little twist he introduces—he
has Achish king of Gath, a Philistine, fall for me—he presents me as a
fiery character, as befits my name. Moreover, he has me on good
terms also with Jonathan and other persons linked to Saul, and he
focuses on my relationship with Saul rather than on my later life
history, which is a refreshing approach. If you're interested in reading
this romantic drama, I think that some academic libraries still have
it, and you'll have no trouble in obtaining it: the play as well as its
author isn't much in demand and never was.

Another case altogether is Aharon Ashman's dramatic trilogy
"Michal Daughter of Saul," written in Hebrew and published in Tel
Aviv as well. The first part of the trilogy was actually produced to
great popular acclaim by the *Habimah* theatre in Tel Aviv, in 1941 as
well, and is largely considered the first *original* biblical play to have
been written in Hebrew by a Hebrew author. The performance was
directed by Baruch Chemerinsky. The stage design concept by Genia
Berger transformed the stage into a three-dimensional representation
of King Saul's palace, with all the familiar Orientalist features:
rounded pillars, stairs, and Arab houses. The costumes displayed an
eclectic mixture of Eastern and Greek elements.

Ashman is much better known than Ben David: he's also written
the words for quite a few popular Israeli songs that passed into the

realm of "folk" songs or dances. In addition, if you allow me judgment, he's a better writer than Ben David. He was absolutely besotted with the biblical materials he wanted to make alive again, and knew his Hebrew bible inside out. For instance, in his volume of *Collected Plays,* he has a play on Jerusalem's Wall (in Nehemiah's time) and another one on Alexandra, the last descendant of the Hashmonean (Maccabbean) house. His Michal trilogy constitutes three plays, written between 1938 and 1950, each consisting of three acts. The plays are named "Early Love," "In Palti's House," and "The Rejected," respectively.

Now, Michal is clearly not only the protagonist but also the heroine of Ashman's poetic imagination. He absolutely adores Michal; she is the chief focalizer of his mind's eye. He identifies with her love for David, extols her inner and physical beauty, has hardly any criticism of her. A true romantic he is, tracing her by and large unrequited love for David with sympathy and delicacy. He is biased, then, in her favor, and I'm but a sideline for him. Ashman has me love Saul dearly (like Ben David; I wonder about those men's needs, to present me as such) and act in all my misconceived intrigues with the view to avenge his death and re-institute his dynasty. I must say that, despite his preoccupation with his heroine, he has great understanding and compassion for the likes of me. He presents me as a positively loyal spouse of Saul, a concubine surely but a substitute for Michal's and Merab's and Jonathan's mother, who—in his rendering—falls ill very early on. Indeed, he assigns to me immoral court intrigues, including having sex with biblical and other invented characters, but makes sure his audience knows this is for the purpose of reinstating Saul's house. However, ultimately and in a disgusting moralistic fashion, Ashman has my sons executed by the Gibeonites, and he has me going crazy over this crime as poetic justice for my manipulative transgressions. At any rate, and this must be emphasized (without divulging whether I did love Saul or not), Ashman has such a good grasp of the court situation, fair comprehension of the potential social and emotional context—house of Saul, house of David; all of us were so closely linked by a criss-cross pattern of blood kin and marriage kin relationships; the role of Zeruiah's sons, David's cousins and military henchmen—that his own whimsical presentation of me contains grains of truth if not the

whole truth, in the impossible sense that "truth" can and may be
relativized or invented. Just as an example, not as a substitute for
reading his trilogy (recommended), look at his lines (my own
translation from the Hebrew), as attributed to me and to Michal,
toward the very end of the trilogy (third play, act 3). The place and
time is my guard over the executed sons' bodies, and I'm presented as
a wasted crazy witch. Michal and a trusty old servant are coming to
give me some food to strengthen me in my vigil. I panic, and Michal
entreats me to eat:

> Rizpah (looking commandingly around her): Who's king
> over the beasts of the field? Who controls the winged beasts? I
> am, and no one apart from me! The mountains are for the
> mountain goats! The secret forests for the leopard! For the
> snakes—the clefts of the rocks! The tree tops—for the winged
> fowl! I've installed a boundary, it shall not be transgressed! A-
> yah, A-yah . . .
> Michal: Don't go, mother bird. We're not hunters. We're
> birds as well, storm-escaped birds, wing-broken. Surely you
> recognize us?
> Rizpah: I recognize, I recognize; you're ravens, raven thieves
> . . . you steal, you peck stealthily . . . A-yah, A-yah . . .

I shall refrain from commenting on Ashman's vision of me, and of
Michal and our other family members, at this point. The only issue I
wish to raise is his understanding of my ability to converse with the
human-eating animals by virtue of being my mother's daughter.
Furthermore, Ashman utilizes the onomatopoeic properties of my
mother's name, *a-yah*; do admit, the cry does sound like an anguished
cry, an appropriate refrain for my "madness" at having to guard over
the dead bodies of my and Merab's sons. And this is an implicit
imagining, more creative than that of professional biblical
commentators or early Jewish sages, of my own link with the
animal—specifically winged—worlds, which helped me in my task. In
that, I resemble Zipporah. She flies, I enter into discourse with birds;
we're both bridges between the human and the non-human worlds.
My lips are sealed with regard to a more comprehensive critique of
Ashman's work, although I enjoy his portraiture of me—at least in

part, until he makes me crazy with sorrow. At any rate, I hope that I've established here, if briefly, yet another tenuous link between women and birds. Yes, since I can see Zipporah, Moses' wife, the "bird," the "Bird Woman," if you please, our pilot, among the audience—and I did enjoy her talk about her own experiences, tremendously so. I recall Zipporah's talk as tribute to her own self and the other "bird women," her partners, as well as to my mother, the forgotten *'ayyâ*, the female bird transformed in bible reception and memory into a father bird.

EIGHT

∞

A Double Date:
We Are Tamar and Tamar

*T*amar's story is read but not translated. . . . David and
Amnon's story is neither read nor translated.

(Megillah 4.10)

Love that has an agenda—when the agenda is gone, love fades
away. And [love] that doesn't have an agenda doesn't fade away.
What is love that has an agenda? This is Amnon and Tamar's
love. And that with no agenda? This is David and Jonathan's
love. *(Aboth* 5.16)

I'm Tamar daughter of Hirah (I'll explain later), daughter-in-law to
Judah.

And she's Tamar daughter of David, sister to Absalom and Amnon.

Tamar I and Tamar II if you wish, in biblical chronological order
(Genesis 38 and 2 Samuel 13, respectively). We are both called Tamar,
"date palm," after that stately, tall, fruitful tree that grows in hot
climes and even on the fringe of deserts and in oases, a tree that
requires little water and cultivation to produce its honeyed fruit that
is full of nutrients and energy and can keep well to boot. And there's
one more Tamar in our family, absent today, but we shall talk about
her soon. You may then assume, and rightly, that Tamar is a name
that runs in our family. We have no idea how the tree name was made

into a personal female name—because of its life-sustaining fruit
perhaps? Or because sweetness is attributed to women as a socially
condoned ideal even if it's not in every woman's character (please
remember that Na'amah and Naomi's names may have something to
do with "sweetness," too)? At any rate, we notice that another name
for "palm," similar in sound but probably indicating the male palm,
the word "Tomer" (like the tree under which the prophet Deborah
sat, Judges 4:5), is used as a boy's name in contemporary Israel, while
Tamar continues to be used as a girl's name. Well, as I said, the name
does run in our family. So let's first talk about our individual stories,
then link them to each other and—in particular—to matters of
domestic sexual politics of the less usual kind.

Tamar I

I'm Tamar the Canaanite woman of Genesis 38, who was married to
Er, Judah's first son by the Canaanite daughter of Shua. My marriage
was peaceful, nothing out of the ordinary, and staying with Judah's
extended family in the same household was routine and hard work—
we were agriculturalists and shepherds; women as well as men had to
participate in all work. But we were quite comfortable. Not having
children did mar it somewhat for us, but the doctors said that we
should keep trying some more before getting worried. And as my
husband kept consoling me, their god (my adopted god by virtue of
joining their family) had promised them that if they followed his
commandments, which my husband thought they did, "there would
not be a sterile man or a sterile woman among you, or in your cattle"
(Deut. 7:14). I sometimes thought that, being an outsider and in view
of the piece of scripture just quoted, I was perhaps the sterile one. But
this idle mode of reflection ended abruptly when Er was brought in
one summer morning from the field, dead after suffering a sudden
stroke. He was barely twenty-five, you see; I was devastated with
sorrow, although I was sure that Judah the paterfamilias would take
care of me. Worst was the conventional attitude of people around us,
namely that Er was probably killed by the Hebrew god for being evil.
The Hebrews' tendency to justify their god's behavior even at a cost to
their own self has always been pathological. At any rate, Judah asked
his second son, Onan, my brother-in-law, to perform the task of

levirate marriage with me. You've already heard from Naomi what this means: the sexual union of a sister-in-law and her dead husband's brother (if they share the same space, that is, household; Deuteronomy 25) so as to produce a son that will inherit the late husband's portion of land. An economic-agrarian custom no doubt, but one that was also beneficial for a fresh widow, such as me. And, naturally, I've known Onan for years. But there a funny thing happened. Onan didn't mind being married to me; why should he? After all, he could have other wives as well. He certainly didn't mind having sex; what he did mind, however, was impregnating me. I'm afraid that greed for more land was his undisclosed motivation. Therefore he attempted to avoid having children with me by various means. Some readers vote for *coitus interruptus* as his favored practice, others for masturbation, which came to be called Onanism after him. I can tell you that he used both methods in turn and was quite open about this preference if less so about the actual reason for it, which was never openly discussed. At first he tried to exonerate himself by claiming that I should get over my grief for his brother's sudden death, that I should love him more, that he was concerned for me. Now, all this caused *me* some concern but not too much. I wanted children but was too grief stricken and shocked to give the situation any clear thought. And also, I was sure that if Onan persisted in his refusal to impregnate me, I could possibly steal his seed somehow, when he was less watchful, when he was tired, when he lost control. Who knows? Meanwhile, the sex was good and welcome, a consolation.

When Onan too was brought from the fields in a horizontal position, quite dead from a stroke (surprise), tongues went into overtime, wagging. A dual explanation for this notorious recent double death of two brothers emerged. The household cronies were sure that Onan too was killed by god; they also advanced the notion that, concurrently, I was a Lillith-demon, a husband-killing *vagina dentate*. (Since Lillith is reputed to kill babies in addition to men, this took care of my own childlessness as well.) Imagine my grief.

According to custom, Judah now had to give me to his third and only surviving son, Shelah. Judah procrastinated, imagining that he would thus save Shelah from the she man-eater by the delay. And he sent me back home to my father's house until Shelah grew to be up to the task, as Judah politely explained.

Now, that was bad. My father's house wasn't too happy to receive me, although my father, Hirah, was Judah's friend. First, another mouth to feed, even though there was my capable working body to supplement the mouth. Second, my reputation as husband killer (unearned, let me assure you, as implicitly recognized by the biblical authors who attributed the husbands' death to their god's will or the husbands' own moral wickedness). And third, I'd married into a foreign clan; this in itself branded me as a traitor to my father's house. Do you understand better now why Ruth preferred not to return to "her mother's house," as Naomi wished her to do and as Orpah in fact did? Do you understand how all the difficulties Ruth faced in adjusting to a new place paled into relative insignificance in view of what she faced in returning home? These difficulties I certainly experienced, even though—and symptomatically, the biblical author doesn't mention this at all—my father was Hirah, Judah's best mate and co-adventurer in matey male outings.

So after a while, and after my mother-in-law had died, I took matters into my own hands. I heard my father say (not to me; he ignored me completely while in the household) that he and Judah were going to celebrate the wool shearing of the flock they held in partnership. This, as I knew, would involve eating and drinking, then looking for occasional sexual partners. And I knew what route they'd take, automatically, in order to return from their drinking. So I wrapped myself in a long, long *chador* and seated myself at that certain crossroads, looking as if I minded my own obscure business. Now, even the biblical author knows that I didn't "disguise" myself "as a prostitute," as some biblical commentators are only too hasty to assume. No! Judah *thought* that I was a prostitute (Gen. 38:15) and asked me for the price of my sexual favors: I merely wanted to pretend to be a woman alone, happy to go with any man. So when Judah thought I was a harlot, and started negotiating a price, my response was, Why not? And I entered the spirit of the game; he had no cash or kind on him, as was his habit, so left his identity markers with me as a pawn for later payment. We had sex, I went home, I conceived, I was pregnant, and I held Judah's identity markers. So when he—the brute—sent my father to find me, of course he couldn't, and Judah dropped the search in order not to lose face (please note: "Let us not be scorned," said Judah to my father [v. 23], not suspecting the truth at this stage). Such an ironic comedy of errors,

with me and my father and Judah! But when tongues wagged once
more and Judah discovered my pregnancy, after judging me to death
as an adulteress but getting tangible proof of his own role in it, he
acknowledged that I was more righteous than he in this matter, since
he had withheld Shelah from me (38:26). He never came near me
again, though, for—in truth—I'd made a fool of him. And I was amply
rewarded. Conception, in that ancient world, was a minor miracle.
Bringing a child to full term was another miracle. Having two healthy
twins who survived the birth to become adults was yet another. As I
said, I was amply rewarded for my daring act. The Hebrew god was,
implicitly if not explicitly in words, on my side. I was more righteous.
I had twin sons, Perez and Zerah. Through Perez I became an
ancestress of Boaz, eventually of David (Ruth 4:12, 18-22; 1
Chronicles 2–4), and then of course Jesus (Matt. 1:3). My place in
history is assured for all time. As a consequence of the risk I took,
Ruth could marry Boaz, a descendant of my son Perez. Ruth too took
a grave risk when she went to the threshing floor at night, only to
bear a son later. Indeed, do remember, my name is used as a
blessing—and warning—to her upon her marriage (Ruth 4:12).
Without me, and without Ruth, my namesake Tamar II wouldn't
have been born and wouldn't have come to grief, either.

Tamar II

I'm Tamar, daughter of David. I'm mentioned as David's daughter in
a list, after David's secondary wives and his male children, in 1
Chronicles 3:9, but without maternal lineage. It's as if I have no
mother; the complaint of being, of feeling, like a motherless child has
been aired by several of my august predecessors here as well. At any
rate, at the very beginning of 2 Samuel 13, which is the event I wish
to talk about, this is how I'm introduced:

> David's son Absalom had a beautiful sister whose name was
> Tamar; and David's son Amnon fell in love with her. (NRSV)

Or:

> Now Absalom, David's son, had a beautiful sister, whose name
> was Tamar; and after a time Amnon, David's son, loved her. (RSV)

Or:

> Absalom the son of David had a fair sister, whose name [was]
> Tamar; and Amnon the son of David loved her. (KJV)

So here you have it. I'm the full sister of Absalom, third son of
David, "son of Maacah daughter of Talmai, king of Geshur" (2 Sam.
3:3; 1 Chron. 3:2). So I'm the daughter of a foreign lady, a royal
Aramean, which in my case makes the foreign blood that is endemic
to the Davidic house even greater—although so is the case of my
earlier namesake Tamar, who is altogether an allochtone from the
Hebrew/Judahite viewpoint on her father as well as on her mother's
side!

Now what else do we learn of me, and immediately? Not my age,
not my nature, not anything about my talents or shortcomings, not
anything about my life or inner life. Only what is relevant to the story
to be unfolded—and, to be sure, this is the usual practice for biblical
storytellers. We learn in a hurry that I'm the paternal half-sister of
Amnon, David's eldest son (2 Sam. 3:2, 1 Chron. 3:1) and the
apparent heir to David's throne, the beloved son. And that I'm good
looking. And that my half-brother Amnon "loves" me. And note, in
view of what's to come, how the story in fact begins (and it also ends,
2 Sam. 13:22) with Absalom first, and with me in a secondary place.
Once again, this can give you an insight into the storyteller's
technique. This meticulous ordering of names, of relationships, is in
fact a clue to the storyteller's underlying interests. In other words,
he's not primarily interested in me but, rather, in my brother
Absalom and in his eventually catastrophic relationship with
Amnon, a relationship that has me stuck in the middle.

So let's read the story further (v. 2). Look at these three
translations of the Hebrew text:

> Amnon was so tormented that he made himself ill because of
> his sister Tamar, for she was a virgin and it seemed impossible
> to Amnon to do anything to her. (NRSV)

> And Amnon was so vexed, that he fell sick for his sister Tamar;
> for she [was] a virgin; and Amnon thought it hard for him to
> do any thing to her. (KJV)

> And Amnon was so tormented that he made himself ill because
> of his sister Tamar; for she was a virgin, and it seemed
> impossible to Amnon to do anything to her. (RSV)

All three translations agree that Amnon desired or loved me or both, so much so that he became or made himself ill, but found it "impossible to do anything" to me because I was "a virgin" at the time. So the translators recognize the fact that, in Hebrew, a single verb may ambiguously refer to both love and lust. But they do neglect to recognize that the Hebrew expression rendered "became ill," or "made himself ill," may also indicate, and more precisely, "pretended to be ill"—a possibility I'd like you to consider in view of Amnon's duplicitous behavior toward me later.

At any rate Jonadab, Amnon's companion, cousin, and counselor (and my own cousin then, too) noticed Amnon's strange behavior: Amnon took to his bed and his former personality, of a happy-go-lucky playboy assured that his father would fulfill any of his whims, virtually vanished. He became a brooder or at least looked like one. Everybody at court was alarmed by his behavior and his appearance. And Jonadab, hearing the reason, advised him to request David to send me to his apartments, ostensibly to cook for him in order to make him better. Remember, the women's quarters were separate from the men's quarters within the royal compound, as most of you well know. So this is what Amnon did, and I was ordered by David to go to my brother's apartments. This seemed a little unusual but not really weird, and I was in no position to either refuse or question: for my father, I've always been an afterthought, much like for the writer who recorded my non-maternal existence in the Chronicles lineage. So I obeyed. As I was cooking in Amnon's modern, well-equipped but pristine kitchen (a show kitchen, not used much but befitting for a prince and his parties), listening to the exaggerated groans emanating from his bedroom (and they were too loud for a seriously ill person, much like a dramatically rolling dying hero in a silent movie), for all the world going busily about my task, I was idly wondering about the following intriguing possibilities. Did my father actually believe that I could heal Amnon by my cooking and an accompanying magical ritual, as some modern-day commentators do? Did my father attribute healing skills to me, as is often done to women, and therefore didn't find Amnon's request a strange one? Or was our venerable father simply indulging the spoiled Amnon as usual, not giving as much thought to the motivation behind Amnon's request as to his own fear for Amnon's health? No firm conclusion presented itself. The cooking over, Amnon dismissed all the attendants and servants from his apartment and asked me to come to his sickroom, his bedroom, with the food and to serve it to him personally. Once he got me into his bedroom, he got hold of me and commanded me rudely, directly, to have sexual relations with him (v. 11). I was completely taken aback and refused (vv. 12-13), citing shame and scandal as reasons for my refusal. Also, I said (which came to my mind as secondary tactics; Josephus Flavius, of all people, understood that perfectly!), we could get married; our father King David might allow it. I actually don't know even today whether this might have been possible. In other royal cultures, such as in certain Egyptian dynasties, royal brother-sister incest was practiced to promote power politics and governmental cohesion. But, in ancient Israel and according to biblical laws, incest with both maternal and paternal sisters is generally prohibited (Lev. 18:9; 20:17; Deut. 27:22). Could royal sibling incest and unions be acceptable? This is doubtful, although some authorities may think this might have been allowed for royals. But hark, the men of David's house, as many of us have learned to our cost, often behaved as if they were above the law in their dealings with women—and this includes our venerable father himself. "The deeds of the fathers signal those of the sons"; so it goes in our family.

Amnon wouldn't listen. He overpowered me and he raped me. Let's not dwell on the particulars apart from saying that, thank heaven, it didn't take too long. He was too excited, I suppose, to function properly. Which isn't mentioned in the biblical text, of course, a decorous gap is maintained here, but this may explain to *you* why after the event his "love" immediately turned into "hate." He dismissed me with two words, "get out!" (v. 15). In spite of my protests, this half-brother of mine, the heir to the throne, simply ordered his servant to throw me out. Which was done without further ado.

I found myself in the public arena of the royal compound, feeling confused and exposed. I quickly decided, though bleeding and shaking, that there was an urgent need for me to protect my reputation, now that my virginity was gone. In a flash, I comprehended that publicity of my new state, the loss of my virginity, would be a better response than concealment. I was wearing a "long robe with sleeves" (NRSV) or simply "a long outer garment" (in Hebrew, *ketonet passim,* much like Joseph's unique garment in Genesis 37, and popularly referred to as a "coat of many colors"), which signified visually my royal and virginal state (v. 18) but also made me quite conspicuous. I tore my garment and went into highly visual mourning: I put ashes and my hands on my head and started wailing loudly. And I went on wailing, and screaming and tearing my hair, which was partly a put-on but a great release after all I'd gone through, until I came to my full brother Absalom's house. This was the very last time that my voice was heard.

Absalom immediately understood what happened. He advised me to keep quiet and to forget. He seemed to think that I stood no chance against Amnon, "my brother"—implying that Amnon's status as senior son and heir-apparent to David would make legal redress impossible (v. 20). And therefore I kept quiet, until now actually. No, I kept completely silent, as if I'd been rendered speechless. And I "sat," desolate and mourning—my virginity, my life, the loss of my sense of family and protection—in Absalom's compound.

From this point onward, I virtually disappeared from the biblical story. But this is not the end of the incident. Absalom, who, like me, kept silent for a time, neither forgot nor forgave; and lest you think that I was naïve, although I knew that apart from being angry and hating Amnon on my behalf, "because he had raped his sister Tamar" (v. 22), I also knew that he had always hated Amnon because of the sibling rivalry between them, because of the competition for our father's affection, because of ambitions to succeed to the throne, because Absalom saw himself as a better person than the idle Amnon. And I waited, in confidence, for Absalom's rage to mature, for him to rationalize fully his ambitions while coupling them with the oriental brother's duty to avenge his sister's, thus the family's, honor and drown shame in the transgressor's blood. Virginity could be presented as a precious commodity that ought to be protected, you see, overriding any family feelings. So Absalom didn't take up the matter with Amnon. He didn't take it up with David. For a while. He bided his time. Two years later he murdered Amnon and escaped David's wrath by running away to Geshur, to our maternal royal grandfather (vv. 23-38). Eventually Absalom returned to Jerusalem (2 Samuel 14). However, the chain of events that started with my rape and infamous treatment by Amnon ultimately matured into Absalom's revolt against David and his death, and the elimination of previously born heirs from the inheritance line in favor of our paternal brother Solomon (2 Samuel 15-20; 1 Kings 1-2).

Look again, now, at my portrayal in the bible. I am indirectly (through my actions and, especially, speech) characterized as a strong-minded, shrewd, and sexually moral young woman, although my age isn't specified. I'm presented as intelligent and of considerable rhetorical skills. I'm good looking, an obedient daughter and devoted sister to full and half-brothers alike. But all my virtues do not save me from my fate: to be raped without direct personal redress, to remain with my socially imposed shame without being able to complain until I virtually disappear from the story, and to lose all prospects of marriage and progeny—although it is implied, according to at least one source (2 Sam. 14:27), that my brother Absalom had a daughter and called her Tamar after me. In fact, all the male kin who should have supported me and should have looked after my well-being—my father, David, Amnon, Absalom, Jonadab—betrayed me one way or the other: David by uncritically ordering me to go to Amnon's chambers and by not translating his anger about the rape into action against Amnon (2 Sam 13:21); Amnon by raping then discarding me, both done mercilessly; Absalom by plotting a revenge that would seem conventionally acceptable but, ultimately, would promote his own ambition for the throne without affecting my desolate state. (He could have looked around, discreetly, for a husband to take me off his hands. This is often done, but he didn't, so as to have me remain by his side, a permanent silent reminder of Amnon's transgression.) Jonadab disappointed me by engineering the encounter. No, I was *not* protected by my male kin or by other participating male figures, such as Amnon's attendants. I was and subsequently remained a pawn in the power politics between my brothers, and between them and their king-father. Indeed, indeed, to go back to the story's beginning,

> David's son Absalom had a beautiful sister whose name was Tamar; and David's son Amnon fell in love with her.
> (2 Samuel 13:1 NRSV)

My rape is narrated as a covert, albeit decisive, argument against Amnon's suitability for the throne, an incidental kingpin in the unfolding story of King David's domestic chaos from the incident with the Bathsheba (2 Samuel 11) affair onward and the ensuing political rivalries. My eventual silence and the bible's silence about my ultimate fate, together with the story's extension into both my brothers' doom—Amnon by the hand of Absalom's assassins and Absalom by the hand of Joab—indicate my less than central role in my "own" story, which is, ultimately, more about Amnon and Absalom and their competition vis-à-vis our king-father than about a raped royal daughter. I'm afraid that, from this perspective, my textual fate is no better than Dinah's. But I'll articulate this subject further later on.

Back to Tamar I

All this is well within a framework that attributes motifs of sexual impropriety to David and to his lineage, back and front. This leads us back to the portrayals of our respective fathers and father figures, in and by our stories. Remember, Judah is ancestor to David. What we have to say about our father figures has largely been foretold by the late feminist bible critic Fokkelien van Dijk-Hemmes almost fifteen years ago. She's drawn up an analogy between Judah and David in our stories. She observes that:

- Both lose their two older sons: Judah loses Er and Onan; David loses Amnon and later Absalom.
- The son born of an (originally) illicit relationship makes history: Judah has Perez, of whom David is born; David has Solomon, Bathsheba's son.

- Both David and Judah send their daughter (or daughter-in-law) somewhere on the basis of an incorrect analysis of the situation: Judah in order to protect his son from a potentially fatal sexual contact, or so he seems to think; David in order to satisfy his son's request.
- The way in which they both focalize is distorted. Judah does not seem to know the difference between a prostitute and a sacred woman. David chooses to interpret the "cakes" that Amnon wishes for as "healing food," while remaining uncritical of the wished-for cooking context.
- Both are happy to be sidetracked: Judah with Tamar, and David with Bathsheba. (154)

You have seen that some of Fokkelien's arguments—let her rest in peace, she's been dead for ten years now—are not acceptable to us. For instance I, the Tamar associated with Judah, was *not* a sacred woman (or a prostitute). And so on. But, basically, she has it right. Both our father figures were similar in their sexual attitudes and their attitudes to their daughters (or daughter figures), like other biblical fathers-to-daughters. And while they were supposed to protect us, they didn't. No wonder that our "house," or clan, has foundational stories in which a woman or women—blood daughters such as Lot's daughters (Genesis 25), a daughter-in-law (I, Tamar I), and a daughter figure (Ruth), all of us too foreign—manage to compromise a male—blood father (Lot), father-in-law (Judah), and father figure (Boaz). The male is always and somehow drunk, or seemingly so, taken in by the female[s]. The women are the initiators of this incest or near-incest. But the result, oh the result, is one or two sons to carry on the paternal line down to King David. Is this the divine plan, to carry on our line through dumb, sexually undisciplined fathers and father figures who couple with enterprising kin women unknowingly, unawares, or reluctantly? Shall we listen to Fokkelien van Dijk-Hemmes again, who lampoons Judah thus:

Father goes out on the town
    Splendid idea, that, of Hira's, to have a trip out. I'm not cut out for the grieving widower role, and, well after all, time heals

all wounds as they say. Perhaps the sheep shearing will give me
a chance to chat up some woolly little baa-lamb. I'll have to get
rid of my old pal first, though.

Well isn't that a coincidence! Surely that's Abraham's grave
on the left. What an excellent excuse. And who knows who I
might meet on the way. Great, it worked, Fine, father, off you
trot to your grandfather's grave. I don't know if you'll ever be a
grandfather the way you're going on . . . Now what's that I see?
Something a good upright Israelite should walk straight past.
But who is going to now? And a qedesha like that's just a
common or garden whore anyway. Let's see if it works. Stupid
of me not to have brought anything. Mind you, . . . this kind of
woman will probably do it for free. A religious duty they call it.
Ha, ha, it's all right for these Canaanites, isn't it?

Hm, disappointing. My nice suit doesn't seem to be making
much of an impression. I'll send her something. Hira will
understand, I'm sure. Hmm, kinky, a veil like that. I wonder
what is under it. A nice bit of stuff by the sound of it. She's
asking a lot. Seems like she doesn't trust me. Well, what the
hell, you only live once. Good thing Shelah's safe at home. He
should see this. You look great as a father, caught with your
trousers down. You can forget about the rest of his upbringing.
Just look at David. Dreadful how he fed that lamb to the lion.
Poor old Tamar. No, you'd be better taking the lion in the dark
a few times and . . . Tamar?

Tamar II

Done laughing, ladies? In my story, however, incest is initiated by
the male perpetrator of rape, not by the female (me). Furthermore,
as already mentioned, Judah and David are not the only fathers
who neglect to save their daughters from the machinations of their
own ambitious sons. For in some ways, my story is also reminiscent
of another rape story, that of Dinah and the responses of her
brothers, Jacob's sons, and of Jacob himself (Genesis 34). Do you
remember Dinah's story as she's told it to us? Let me list the
similarities and the differences between the two stories, 2 Samuel
13 and Genesis 34.

1. Dinah is abducted and raped by a male foreigner. I'm compromised by my own family male members (Amnon, Jonadab, and David).
2. "Love" seems to be involved: for my rapist before the event, for Dinah's rapist after the event.
3. Dinah's brothers avenge their sister's rape by killing the rapist and his community. Absalom kills Amnon two years later.
4. Ostensibly the same principle of sister's honor and family honor is at stake. In both cases the revenge advances the brother's or brothers' political, military, and territorial ambitions.
5. In the Genesis story, too, the raped woman is silent—even more so here than in my own case—and her eventual fate is not resolved in the text.
6. Jacob the father knows full well that his sons are responding to more than the family's shame; however, apart from a few futile protestations, he neither rescues Dinah nor comforts her—nor does he stop his sons' murderous ploy against the Shechemites. Neither does David, although he, of all people, could understand what the stakes were.

So here we are, and we—Dinah and Tamar and Tamar—have managed to stay alive, if unwell, in spite of rape and sibling rivalry and paternal weakness, and through scribal neglect, I suppose. No one really cared about us. And as Dinah has already said, that some contemporary critics, females as well as males, maintain that "rape" is a modern invention, not applicable to my or Dinah's or similar cases, really and truly hurts. A reminder: scholarly voices have come forth lately claiming that ancient women were not agents of consent; or that sexuality per se is a post-industrial revolution invention, hence its forceful appropriation is an anachronism; or that the terminology the bible uses is that of physical humiliation in general rather than a specific terminology of sexual assault. Well, what can I say? These denials add insult to injury, literally.

NINE

∞

My Sons, the Generals:
I Am Zeruiah Sister of David

> Peace, the more people participate in it,
> the more space there is for it.
> —*Rivka Guber (1902-1981)*

I am a bereaved mother. Like Rizpah, who has already told us her story. And like her, I belong to a royal family—the same and another family. And unlike her, nobody remembers me much.

I am Zeruiah (pronounced *tseruyah*). I'm known as sister of David more than daughter of Jesse, my father. No wonder: first because David, bless him, turned out to be such a prominent figure in his own time and even more so later. Who would have guessed, when we grew up on the outskirts of Bethlehem? And, as you may know, there was some confusion about our paternity. My sister Abigail, naturally a sister to David too, is called "daughter of Nahash" and not "daughter of Jesse" (2 Sam. 17:25; 1 Chron. 2:16). Later generations had great worries about that paternity problem, and some sages managed to save Jesse's honor by identifying him with Nahash with the aid of a nice *pilpul* (in Hebrew: a sharp, acrobatic, "peppery" turnabout of logic). The truth of the matter is that in our family sexual mores were a little lax— David wasn't alone in that!—and sexual scandals tended to be swept under the metaphorical rug. Some attribute this tendency to our heritage; we do derive from our ancestress Ruth the Moabite. Please excuse me, Ruth, for bringing this up. You do know that my opinion of

147

you is quite different, and there's no such edge to it. You all may, then, consider that my being named as David's sister might have had other reasons than the wish to glorify my own ancestry: at the beginning as well as at the end of the day, the biblical text has no interest in me per se.

So why bother to hide the suspicion about my paternal ancestry? Not only because of David's honor, certainly not because of mine. The main reason is that my three sons—Joab, Abishai, and Asah'el—were professional soldiers in David's employ. And they are named after me, "sons of Zeruiah," and not after my late and unlamented husband.

Our first kings were extremely tribal in their choice of officials and military companions. Much like other totalitarian rulers of the time and even today, nepotism was at least partly motivated by the notion—at times mistaken—that blood ties facilitate trust and loyalty. In our case this kind of loyalty wasn't practiced by all or else was carried to extremes by our male relatives, as we shall remind ourselves shortly. Be that as it may, Saul appointed his uncle Abner as his chief of stuff (1 Sam. 14:50)—the same Abner who later took our friend Rizpah, secondary wife to Saul, to be his wife (2 Sam. 3:7), and David chose my three sons as his most trusted soldiers (2 Sam. 2:18), although, true to his political and suspicious nature (some call him cautious and savvy rather than suspicious), he also instituted a parallel organization of mercenaries and foreign professional soldiers under Benaiah as soon as he could do so.

My sons' loyalty to David surpassed servility to the extent of self-eradication. Joab, my eldest, killed both Abner—some say he did that with Abishai's help (2 Sam. 3:27-30; 1 Kings 2:32)—and Amasa (2 Sam. 20:10), his cousin, my sister Abigail's son, my nephew and David's. He caused Uriah, David's loyal soldier and Bathsheba's husband, to die so that David's face in this affair could be saved (2 Samuel 11). He also killed Absalom son of David, his favorite nephew, because Absalom had rebelled against his aging father and nearly succeeded in securing the kingship prematurely for himself (2 Samuel 18). David, whose dark doppelgänger Joab became already in his early twenties, resented him for killing Absalom against his wishes (although, like engineering Uriah's death, that served David well) and also seemed, publicly at least, to resent him for Abner's death (ditto, for an imminent threat of the Saulide house was thus removed). My nephew Solomon, upon coming to the throne, claimed that David commanded him to kill his father's cousin Joab as revenge for his blood guilt acquired by killing those enemies or inconveniences to David. Perhaps it would be a wise political move of cleansing his own name and the new regime, based on the new powers rather than the old tribal connections. Perhaps Solomon resented Joab's affiliation with and support of his half-brother Adonijah, whom he later killed as well. And thus my son Joab, having served David and his house with such selfless devotion, was taken from his refuge by the altar and summarily executed (1 Kings 2).

My son Asah'el, the youngest, was killed by Abner in a personal battle at the beginning of David's reign. In truth, Abner did try to dissuade Asah'el from the duel, but my youngest was always impetuous, confident in his agility (he was a celebrated short- and long-distance runner, like "one of the gazelles in the field," 2 Sam. 2:18). Asah'el wanted Abner's blood; Abner knew he himself was older but more experienced. Asah'el left Abner no choice, he made it a matter of survival for the older man, whereas for him it was a matter of jest and honor. Asah'el died (2 Sam. 2:27-30), which made it possible for Joab to murder Abner later under the unsaid pretext of avenging Asah'el's blood.

Who is left? Yes, my middle son Abishai. He too was fiercely faithful to David and close to Joab, although always secondary to him in hierarchy and significance. A real muscleman, without Joab's brains or Asah'el's charm, but a military hero of renown. He saved David's life by jumping into the military fray for him (2 Sam. 21:17; 23:18). He was weapon happy, quick to anger and to kill: in the old days, when they were still fugitives, he would have killed King Saul when the opportunity arose had David not talked him out of it (1 Sam. 26:7-9); and later, during Absalom's revolt, he would have loved to kill Shim'i for the grave sin of cursing David (2 Sam. 19:22). Abishai's escapades earned him a legendary reputation for martial prowess. For instance, he is reputed to have led a campaign against Edom that resulted in eighteen thousand Edomite casualties (1 Chron. 18:12). Like Joab, Abishai miraculously survived all the battles and wars he undertook on David's behalf, undoubtedly in spite of his mindless physical courage. (Joab, it seems to me, escaped because of his intelligence and trickery, although he didn't lack physical and spiritual courage either; his brother, and excuse this mother's realism, escaped by luck, as well as stupidity.) However, somehow, Abishai managed to retain the good will of all who knew him. In spite of his close association with Joab, in spite of his participation in many of Joab's exploits and shady plans, the resentment David felt against him was contained. Unlike his two brothers, Abishai died normally, naturally, an unreflective old man pleased with himself and with his life's exploits.

Some biblical scholars claim that, as the king's sister, I must have enjoyed certain privileges and honors had I lived at court instead of remaining in Bethlehem. Let me emphasize this wasn't so. In ancient Israel, unlike in ancient Egypt for instance, the king's sister had no official status. Furthermore, David and I were never close. He was the youngest of my seven brothers (1 Samuel 16; 1 Chron. 2:13-15); he was always in the field or shepherding flocks; he was a dreamer, the butt of family jokes. As I've said, who would have guessed he'd turn out to be so exceptional? So there was no emotional bond between us. Later, after making Jerusalem his capital, David changed and became even more remote. And his philandering never endeared him to me, too much like our mother and a reminder of our family's uncertainty about my and Abigail's parenthood. So he did look after me financially, I must acknowledge that, and we did see each other on rare family occasions and religious festivities. But that was all.

You may rightly ask whether I have any special privileges, or status, because all my sons were royal officials and close to the king. To begin with, certainly, I was glorified for having produced such heroic sons, and I did enjoy the attention. But I noticed, as time went by, how the respect shown to me became more and more forced—how the more my sons' reputation for fierceness and cruelty spread, the more the fear people felt about them was extended to me. The sons had a network of information services, spies if you will, that helped them safeguard David's kingship. (My brother David was by no means as popular in his lifetime as the biblical stories suggest. He inspired ferocious love in some, and an equal measure of furious loathing in others. You couldn't remain indifferent to him, that's true. There are enough subtexts in the bible to corroborate this understatement.) Thus, as knowledge of my son's information set-up spread, I became more and more isolated, even from my neighbors and female cronies. And they, my sons, seldom had time to visit their mother; they were too busy worshipping David to have families of their own and to give me grandchildren. David was their life.

Worse than all for me was charting their personal progress along the trajectory of so-called justified violence, justified *jihad* (Arabic: "holy war") or *Ḥerem* (Hebrew: "dedication") or what will you. And here I underwent a laborious trajectory of my own. To begin with, during the bad times of tribal then national danger from many external but neighboring enemies—Philistines, Edomites, Amonites, Canaanites, to name but a few—one had no choice but to be patriotic. We imagined that no peaceful solution was viable, that the land was too small, that we'd be thrown into the sea if we didn't manage to limit our enemies' aspiration by chasing them from our land deep across boundaries and frontiers into their own territory. War was heady then, a powerful tool for national unity in spite of the hardships and the real danger. I was so proud of my sons' contribution! I was the mother of heroes! But then, as more peaceful times came but the military ethos hardly changed, and defense turned into expansionism, when survival metamorphosed into ambition, lack into greed, loyalty into *dibbuk* ("obsession"), my views gradually changed. The men of my family never had enough, were never satiated. From killing on behalf of their own sons, cousins, nephews, uncles, and friends, or respected colleagues, they progressed into killing those same persons if they seemed to thwart their plans (remember Uriah, Bathsheba's first husband?). Violence in the house of David bloomed forth; my sons contributed to it considerably by not only heeding their master's voice, but also divining his unspoken wishes before he even had time to formulate them in his head. There's true devotion for you, and no mistake!

Violence breeds violence. This is certainly a cliché that's worth repeating; I feel nauseated because it happens again and again. I lived to lose two sons to the violence they encouraged by not considering peace as an alternative to a previous way of life. I was and am highly critical of my brother David and all three of my sons the generals— like many Jewish mothers, I wish they were medical doctors instead! Nevertheless, I did and do love them, still. And I mourn their way of life and the untimely and ungainly passing away of Joab and Asah'el every day of my long, long life.

So what do you do when this is what you are, an unsung bereaved mother—unlike Rizpah, not even the subject of plays or further stories—a genetrix of such aggression and brutality enacted by her sons? First you reflect, with sadness. You ask yourself questions. Did later generations forgive me for bringing such violent sons into this world? Perhaps not, but I don't figure in the popular imagination in spite of my family connections. Perhaps yes, since my name recurs in the names of certain Jewish sages—R. Berechiah son of Zeruiah, R. Yitzhak son of Zeruiah, R. Shmuel son of Zeruiah. And a certain rabbi, much later after the Middle Ages, writes about his (granddaughter) Zeruiah. Now, when a singular name such as mine is re-used for little girls, and sages become known by their maternal lineage thus, it may mean that I'm at least partly forgiven. Which reminds me: some scholars insist that my name is derived from a Hebrew verb that means to "flow, bleed," plus the shortened form *yâh* (for Yhwh, our god's most holy name), that is, "Yhwh caused [blood] to flow." This derivation seems to me a direct if perhaps unconscious reference (it is uttered under the umbrella of scholarly investigation) to my maternal position of matrix to three blood-shedding sons. So the problem for me was, how to atone for my sons' sins? In other words, how to transform myself from "god caused to flow" to another possible name derivation, that is, "*yâh* caused to heal" (from the Hebrew צרי (*tsori*) ("medicine" or "healing agent"). So I looked for a way.

And this surely came. Many centuries of mourning and reflections later I happened to hear the story of a woman called Rivka (Rebekah) Guber.

This is the woman I chose, and here's a short biography adapted from the Israel Postal Authority description and originally written by Yigal Almagor (Ruimy) of Di Zahav, a settlement in the south of Israel. For, as you know, prominent persons are now eternalized by having their portrait on a stamp (and let's not dwell on the manner of eternalization this affords).

Rivka Guber was born in 1902 to a family of Jewish farmers who for generations had lived in the village of Vilaszashatanovo Witbesc in the Ukraine's Charuson County. She worked in the fields and with domestic animals from an early age. She completed elementary school in her village and went on to finish high school and two years of university education in the county's central district of Watrinoslav. During the Bolshevik revolution her father, along with all the adults of the village, was recruited into the war, and the village itself changed hands from one to the other combating forces. In 1921 she married Mordechai Guber, a yeshiva graduate and a Hebrew teacher. They immigrated to the then British-ruled Palestina/Eretz Israel and in 1925 settled in the southern town of Rehovot. Rivka worked as a teacher while her husband became an agricultural instructor. Later they left Rehovot in order to help establish a *moshav* (cooperative settlement more flexible than a *kibbutz*), and in 1939 they were among the founders of another *moshav* in the south.

During World War II Rivka left her husband and her small children to volunteer in the British Army. Let me add in passing that women as well as men did that, joining the Jewish Brigade as well as other units of the British army. Unlike some of them, Rivka returned safely. But in Israel's war of independence (1948–49) she lost her two sons, Ephraim and Zvi. A *moshav* was named in the brothers' memory, *Kfar Ahim* ("village of the brothers"). During those years, Rivka served as an educator and principal at the *Ahim* ("brothers") School in Kiryat Malachi, in the same area. She devoted herself, together with her husband, to the integration of immigrants, mainly in the Lachish area.

In 1956 the Guber family donated their house and flourishing farm to the *Magen* ("shield") Fund and moved with their daughter, Chaya, to a remote area of the Lachish region where they helped establish a string of *moshavim* and the city of Qiryat Gat. After retiring they finally moved to a senior home in Tel Aviv. But even then, Rivka continued traveling and helping. She wrote many books in Hebrew. One of them, the story of the moshav named after her dead sons, was translated into English.

In 1976 Guber became an Israel Prize winner for her vast contribution to the integration of new immigrants, especially from Muslim countries and in Israel's south. In recognition of her labors, in 1979 she participated in the official Israeli entourage accompanying the then-Prime Minister Menachem Begin to the United States to sign the Camp David peace treaty with Egypt. She died in 1981. In Israel she was and is still lovingly known as "The Mother of Sons," a title bestowed upon her by David Ben Gurion, Israel's first prime minister.

Rivka Guber, as you can see, resembles me in some ways although the differences are great. Or shall I say, I resemble her, since of the two of us she's the more formidable? Look here. Rivka and I come from agricultural stock. We were both "mothers of sons" who died in Israel's wars of independence. I remained almost cloistered in my village at the south of Israel, not far from where she was. She turned her grief into energy and into helping others. Her circumstances were undoubtedly more conducive to such transformation of emotion into action: she lived in another time. But, as well, her character was so much stronger than my own brooding character.

I'm not ashamed to say that I became her anonymous shadow, her groupie. Wherever she went to help, there was I. Volunteering, taking care of babies instead of taking care of the grandchildren my sons the generals never gave me, always glad of doing the most menial tasks, always keeping my anonymity, never even trying to have a conversation with the great woman.

This was and is my salvation. Rivka is my model, as I've said. After she died, I continued her work with the new waves of immigrants to Israel, Russians and others from the former Eastern Bloc and Ethiopians. But I don't go to console bereaved families of Israeli soldiers who continue to "fall" (this is the Hebrew euphemism) in the wars of contemporary Israel. I couldn't do that without divulging my own opinions about wars in general. Instead, I'm a permanent fixture at the "women-in-black" demonstrations. Those women have been assembling, since the early 1990s, almost every Friday afternoon at busy Israeli city junctions, silently protesting against the cyclic violence between Palestinians and Israelis. We're sometimes mishandled, spat upon, verbally abused. But no matter: the mothers will prevail. We want our sons to forgo war ideologies. We want our sons to live long and to die of natural causes.

This is how I atone for the blood guilt of my military sons, and my royal brother, and other male members of our family. A blood guilt that is still enacted anew every day, and rotting our earth, and devouring our sons.

TEN

∞

I Am the Rat:
Huldah the Prophet

*T*his is the story in which I participate, as briefly given in the
book of Kings and more or less copied in the book of Chronicles
(2 Kings 22:14-20 = 2 Chron. 34:22-28)

Round about 625 BCE King Josiah of Judah was busy renovating
the Jerusalem temple. By that time the northern kingdom of Israel,
our sister state, had been out of business for about a hundred years.
We used to look down our noses at what we'd call the riffraff that
inhabited that land, around Samaria and Beth El, which we claimed
as our own. In fact, our snobbish attitude was exaggerated. It was a
well-known secret in Jerusalem—for us, the navel of the world—that
we shared a common religio-cultural heritage with that "riffraff," and
that much innovative literature, prophetic and legal, has come down
to us from there and appropriated as original to them by the high
and mighty Jerusalem scribes and Torah teachers.

It is in the nature of such renovation projects that even the
farthest corners of a building get attention, and even the temple's
inner sanctum, the holy of holies usually accessible to certain priests
only, has to be gingerly entered by builders and their overseers. So
even the lazy and fat priests—with their job guaranteed by heredity,
and with their shares of meat and flour assured as long as there
continued to be human misery and ensuing ritual, that is, sacrifice—
were galvanized into a spring cleaning of their own. Or so the story
goes. And a "book" was found in the temple, a scroll, really. Gossip

had it that the "book" was either newly manufactured—perhaps by some dissenting Jerusalem priests, or by provincial priests—or else it was smuggled out of the outskirts of Samaria just a little while before. At any rate, this "book" in the temple was written in an autobiographical mode, ostensibly by our revered leader Moses—yes, Zipporah, by your husband. In passing, it must be noted that Moses has always been more popular in the north than in Jerusalem; for our priests, Moses' brother Aaron was the more important brother. At any rate, the "book" more or less contained the nucleus of the book of Deuteronomy, as we know it today from the biblical canon.

King Josiah was extremely shocked when the "book" was read to him (like so many of his class, he was a capable man but illiterate). Indeed, the passages that threatened such frightening curses for those who didn't follow Yhwh's ways (now to be found in chapter 28 of Deuteronomy) were too frightening to even contemplate, and Josiah knew full well—as did Jeremiah (note his description in Jeremiah 7 and 44, for instance), as did other prophets—that Yhwh was a revered divinity in our beloved city but not exclusively so. Worship of the Queen of Heaven continued undisturbed in the temple, side by side with Yhwh's worship. That dual worship (if you're asking me, of course it made sense to worship a male and female divinity concurrently; I myself served and loved the Asherah cult because it was so peaceful and family-oriented, as Jeremiah witnesses against himself!) was precisely what the Deuteronomic authors viewed as a deadly sin. So Josiah was frightened. The situation, he feared, was hopeless. His pious (or would you say, responsible and realistic as a leader?) attitude was: if the "book" were right, and the people had never behaved in accordance with the divine word, divine retribution would now surely and inevitably befall them and him. Therefore, he sent emissaries to seek God's guidance. The officials were dispatched to me, to a woman prophet, to Huldah.

Most biblical commentators have found that choosing me as a prophet, to be asked for Yhwh's advice, was odd. The grounds? First and foremost, because I'm a woman. And second, because I'm not otherwise known as a prophet. Therefore, from ancient times onward, commentators have been pondering this question, notwithstanding the fact that female prophets are known in the bible as well as in other writings of the ancient Near East. The Jewish sages wrinkled their noses with distaste, virtually and perhaps also in reality. Why not seek God's counsel from Jeremiah or Zephaniah, both prophetically active at the time, rather than an otherwise unknown woman?

Let me classify the reasons given, keeping my tongue firmly in my cheek for the duration.

1. For this emergency, a male prophet wasn't immediately available. Jeremiah was out of town. He'd gone to visit, perhaps to lead back to the land of Israel, the ten tribes lost when Samaria fell to the Assyrians, about a hundred years before our time. Note the connection made, in a roundabout way, between the "book" found in the temple and Jeremiah's presumed journey. Surely Rashi, a medieval Jewish commentator, does *not* believe that the "book" found is [part of] Deuteronomy; surely such a commentator would attribute Deuteronomy squarely to Moses, as an orthodox Jew should, without questioning. And yet.... Another commentator is perhaps a little more careful when he surmises that at the time Jeremiah was perhaps in Anatoth, his own village, or happened to go to an unspecified location on a professional mission, whereas I lived in Jerusalem itself and could be consulted without delay. This latter commentator (Radak) goes even further by referring to the matter once more, hence lending it emphasis: there happened to be no [male] prophets in Jerusalem at the time. Period.

2. Perhaps the officials, or the king himself, expected that an interview with me would be less cruel than with either of my canonical counterparts. Look at Rashi again: "Our sages said, for the woman is more pitying than the man; that's why he [Josiah] didn't send for the Prophet Jeremiah."

3. Or else, horror of horrors, although no written teachings of mine have been preserved, I was a respected prophet nevertheless. (We have to remind ourselves that judgments upon personalities and their place in history vary between contemporaries and future generations). So the rabbis say:

Three prophets were prophesying in Jerusalem in the days of Josiah. They are: Jeremiah, and Zephaniah, and Huldah.

Jeremiah was prophesying in the public places; Zephaniah—
in the synagogues; and Huldah—to the women.

Interesting, isn't it? Anything, but anything to make me less
important than my male brethren-in-trade!
      The tendency to belittle my stature is apparent in the actual
biblical story as well as beyond it. In the biblical story, this is how I'm
defined:

So the priest Hilkiah, and Ahikam, Achbor, Shaphan, and
Asaiah went to the prophetess Huldah—the wife of Shallum
son of Tikvah son of Harhas, the keeper of the wardrobe— who
was living in Jerusalem in the Mishneh, and they spoke to her.
(2 Kings 22:14)

Hilkiah and those whom the king had ordered went to the
prophetess Huldah, wife of Shallum son of Tokhath son of
Hasrah, keeper of the wardrobe, who was living in Jerusalem in
the Mishneh, and spoke to her accordingly. (2 Chron. 34:22 NJPS)

Now look here. Nobody has ever heard of my husband, right? Not an
insignificant public servant, the keeper of the wardrobe (of the priests,
in the temple). But what has he got to do with the prophecy? I'm not
provided with a lineage; he is, although Chronicles bungled the names
somewhat. Anything, anything to displace some attention to him. One
rabbi, though, actually refers to my genealogy from Joshua and Rahab.
Rahab, you venerated foremother, you've already told us how often
you're mentioned as foremother of prophets, including me. But this
honor of providing me with a lineage other than by proxy (through my
husband) comes after the bible. Truly, are the biblical priests covertly
pretending that they heard about me through my association with my
husband, whom they met daily? Should we take seriously the implied
contention that I was unimportant? I have evidence that subverts the
ludicrous attempts at devaluing me. My evidence is of several kinds:
spiritual, literary, and geographical.
      To begin with, there's no denying that the bible actually calls me
"[female] prophet" and that Yhwh speaks through me and I deliver an
oracle to the priests, and to Josiah. Later generations acknowledged

seven biblical female prophets—Sarah, Miriam, Deborah, Hannah, Abigail, Huldah, and Esther—although only three of us are actually termed "prophets" by the biblical text (Miriam and Deborah, apart from me). Or there's another list of nine female prophets: Sarah, Rebekah, Rachel, Leah, Miriam, Deborah, Hannah, Abigail, and yours truly.

Further, there's the little problem of the word "Mishneh," which is used in the bible to designate my dwelling in Jerusalem. Rashi links it to the temple itself: according to the Mishnah the two southern gates to the Temple Mount were called the "Huldah Gates." If this tradition be sound, then it lends more credibility to my stature not only during my lifetime, but also in succeeding generations down to the second temple era. Wouldn't you agree? But Rashi also offers another solution for the Hebrew word "Mishneh": outside the gates, or "between the two walls [of the city]" (for 2 Chron. 34:22). Note, gentle ladies, that Rashi relies here on a Hebrew root that may mean "two" or "second," which seems to be part of the word "Mishneh." But he has a further problem: that root, or a homonym thereof, may also mean "to study," as in the word "Mishnah." Indeed, the Aramaic Targum translates here: "and she [I!] was sitting in the house of study." So Rashi goes into a song and dance, explaining—following the Mishnah just mentioned—that I did have an office in the temple but, for reasons of modesty, it was blocked in the direction of the Sanhedrin's (religious council's) office.

So, from here to there, on the one hand I'm undervalued or devalued. On the other hand, I get an office in that male bastion, the temple of Yhwh in Jerusalem, my own office not far from the holy of holies. I, a mere woman, get closer to the essence and center of our religion than my husband, who's decorated with an unstable genealogy (note the different names in the parallel Chronicles account) and is a glorified dresser to the priests. There are minor differences between the Kings and the Chronicles accounts on this point, but they are immaterial; and the pedigree remarks themselves have no significance beyond the realm of easy identification for the priests', or biblical authors', gratification. The sages and commentators deconstruct their own efforts of minimizing my role. And with time it is I who gets all this and two, not one, two gates in the Temple Mount named after me.

Ultimately, my authority rested with the contents of my divinely inspired message. Ultimately, its impact is related neither to my husband's position nor to my gender. May I also remind you that my association with the temple, through my marriage in the biblical text and in my own right beyond it, is far from unique for a Jerusalem prophet, which is immediately apparent by analogy to several other great prophets. Think about Isaiah, Jeremiah, and Ezekiel. I'm in good company here, although nobody would supply *me* with a priestly lineage. But it matters not; to be a descendant of Rahab is preferable.

In the best tradition of Isaiah, Jeremiah, Amos, and Hosea, I was fully committed to my unpopular role. You realize that by being approached I was made involved in matters of state. I delivered an oracle to the king's emissaries, and I did that fearlessly and directly. My words foresaw the destruction of Jerusalem, although—since I admired and adored Josiah, whom I met regularly for chess games and philosophical discussions—I was able to declare that the king himself would die in peace (2 Kings 22:20; 2 Chron. 34:28). As you well know, this last prophetic detail did not come to pass: Josiah died fighting an Egyptian king at the Battle of Megiddo (2 Kings 23:29-30; 2 Chron. 35:20-24) in 609 BCE. This was the beginning of Judah's fall; less than three decades later the Babylonians conquered our beloved city and demolished the temple. The destruction was horrendous. Exile followed.

Many biblical commentators say that the non-fulfillment of my prophecy concerning the king's fate marks it as a genuine political prediction delivered prior to the events rather than in hindsight, as is so often the case with the political "prophecies" of my male colleagues, always keen to blame their human flock rather than their divine shepherd. Do you think that there must have been a mistake in my delivery? Let me pretend that there was. Let me announce that unlike you, esteemed convener, in your similar situation with King Saul, I took another kind of initiative here. You may claim that you didn't hear the actual message Samuel delivered to Saul, that you could only guess by Saul's reaction, that the only way you could console Saul somewhat was by offering creature comforts, acting like a regular Jewish mama: Eat, my child, eat! But we'll soon hear your version of the story. I couldn't do that. I knew the truth about

Josiah's untimely death, and I knew that nobody else would, unless I
made it public. And I knew that Josiah's spirit and planned political
and religious reform, not to mention public morale, would fail if he
and his advisers and the priests and the people heard the divine
truth. So I shouldered the guilt. I lied. And I suffered, since I knew
that the divine will won't change, that retribution would come. Like
Abraham, I did try to argue with Yhwh, to negotiate, but to no avail.
My reward, short-lived as it was, consisted of the little good I could
do in face of the unchangeable and indomitable. I was successful,
even though the truth proved to be a heavy burden, for the king, for
his part, accepted the oracle of his trusted friend as an authoritative
message. Thus I went on to play quite an important role in the
institution of Josiah's reform; and whereas, like all women, I was
excluded from officiating in the cult itself, as the king's special
adviser I got to have my office at the temple. And a reputation for
generations to come. Which was small consolation and no more.
Moreover, with Josiah's death the possibility for including women
among the temple personnel died as well. It took centuries and the
destruction of the second Jerusalem temple until women were
included again in the services and cultic personnel of the synagogue.
And that tradition died once more with the advent of the orthodox
rabbinic system, at least officially and until recent times, when
women began to officiate as rabbis and singers in progressive Jewish
communities of the West. I see myself as a forerunner of this trend—
not because I was a prophet, but because I had an office in the
temple. And therefore, you can guess what my occupation is at this
time, although I've changed the unsavory name that scriptures gave
to me. I was a rat—see my behavior about the divine oracle—but am a
rat no more.

One of my subtexts for making my story public knowledge,
including the heretofore concealed part, was to illustrate to you how
at times exegetes and commentators attempt to minimize female
roles in history but, even as they're busy so doing, they actually
sabotage their own efforts. In my case, my post-biblical stature grew
beyond recognition. So much so that a grave was invented for me, in
the Jerusalem hills, not far from the graves of the Davidic kings. The
grave is mentioned mainly in early rabbinic sources from Eretz Israel,
in various places in the Tosephta and in the Mishnah. This is such a

great honor—the ultimate crowning glory, you may chuckle. But let me protest. You see me in front of you, alive. There's nothing in the bible about my death, or burying place. We managed to run away as the temple was being destroyed. We left with Jeremiah and the others going to Egypt. We continued to wander from there. However, I do understand why a grave was invented for me. There are so many graves in Jerusalem, some attributed to specific [usually male] royals or prophets: Absalom's grave, Uzziah's grave, Ezekiel's grave, and many more. There's consent among scholars that such graves—and the patriachal/matriarchal graves around Shechem, Elijah's grave on the Carmel (remember he went riding up to Heaven?), and many graves of rabbis in the Galilee, to mention but a few—are imaginary in as much as archaeological and inscriptional evidence is not available. Folk traditions identify burial places so that they can serve as focal points for prayer and healing. The persons ostensibly buried in such places become "saints" in popular belief, although both sainthood and grave-worship are foreign to our religion. (Isn't this why nobody knows where Moses is buried apart from Yhwh himself, in order to abort the possibility of grave-worship or sainthood, particularly viable in his case?) This practice of naming graves reflects a genuine need, sometimes commercial interests (have you ever been to a festival on a saint's day, let's say to the R. Shimeon son of Yohai in Mt. Meron, near Zephat/Safed? So many beggars, such commercialism!). I hate that, and I can only guess that somebody, somewhere, perhaps a woman or women, saw a grave and found it useful to name it after me—not your typical female model, not a model for motherhood, not a liminal woman, not a sinner, but nevertheless a model and an exceptional one: a temple official and a prophet. So be it then. A need will be filled. And while the women come to my false grave for advice and oracle and solace, dressed in modest clothes and wearing headscarves and sunglasses, and they lie down on it and beat their breasts in supplication and pray and give alms to the beggars, I'll continue to gaze at this idolatrous phenomenon with amazement, for a while. And I'll say to myself, I can't foresee when this idolatry will end. And I'll nod my head sadly, then drive down to have a good gossipy session with my foremother and near-neighbor, Rahab of Jericho.

ELEVEN

∞

Love Me Tender, Love Me True . . . :
I Am an Anonymous Woman
from the Song of Songs

Who can live without love?
—*Rhetorically, from an exasperated woman friend,*
after quite a few vodkas

Everybody needs a little help sometimes
—*Charlie Brown, "Peanuts"*

Preamble

Let's say, for the sake of my presentation, that the biblical book
variously known as the "Song of Songs," or "Song of Solomon," or
the "Most Sublime Song," is a collection of heterosexual love lyrics
(although, as you may imagine, it can be adopted or colonized for
homosexual love as well). Let's say that it harks from various eras,
locations, settings. Let's assume that "love" includes spiritual,
emotional, erotic, and sexual baggage. Let's discard, for now, the
widespread but erroneous notion that the SoS (yes, I do prefer to
abbreviate it thus—Help!) is one unified love story between, say, King
Solomon and a provincial damsel; or perhaps it is the tale of a
romantic triangle: Solomon, a young provincial woman, and a
provincial shepherd—when either the one male figure or the other
finally "wins" the woman. Let's assume, for now, that no wedding is
involved, no societal stamp of approval (and the ensuing mandatory
babies; no "Be fruitful and multiply" here!) is bestowed upon the

lovers. Let's forget that for generations upon generations in Judeo-Christian cultures the SoS signified some kind of a love story between the human and the divine. Let's suspend disbeliefs that originate in many generations' wisdom and folly and start afresh. Let's agree, for the duration, that what you see is what you get—and this can be, it really is, as good as it gets.

What I mean, and believe me I should know, is not only that love in the SoS is a many-splendored thing but also that the splendid poetry refers to more than one couple, more than one relationship: which is the nature of a *collection*. And the wonderful, exceptional unifying element of this collection is the apparent notion that female lovers are more outgoing, braver, more direct, and more risk-taking than their male counterparts. Furthermore, they are more articulate as poets, but on the poetic capabilities of women you've already heard from Adah, Zillah, and Zipporah. And this state of affairs runs counter to the whole bible, where male literary ability far outshines that of females, although female literariness is at places stated, as in the case of a Miriam or a Deborah—albeit grudgingly; see Exodus 15 and Judges 5, where, in both texts, the male figures of Moses and Barak respectively are added as the songs' poets and performers. As for performing song and dance, there's recognition of such female skills and their place in culture throughout the Hebrew bible; this I must admit.

Why am I telling you all this? Simply as a preamble for presenting my own story, which is recorded after a fashion at the beginning of chapter 7 of the SoS. There I appear, out of nowhere, as an addressee of a request, of a command:

Come back, come back, the Shulammite, come back so that we can view you! (SoS 7:1; Eng. 6:13)

This is how I'm addressed in this song, not as Shulammit, a personal name to so many girls born in Israel of the mid-twentieth century. No, I'm called "*the* Shulammite," which could mean, in Hebrew, a woman from a place or group called "Shulem" or "Shulam" or the like. Is this a ploy, once again to render a woman effectively nameless? My predecessors have already waxed eloquent over this Hebrew bible praxis, or ploy. Be that as it may, let me assure you

Shulammit is the name I've used to refer to myself, all these centuries from a long time ago. But in the poem I answer coyly, not asserting my true name but going along with turning my name into a tag:

What shall you view in the Shulammite?

Whereby my interlocutors answer,

The dance of the two camps. (7:1)

Note that, so far, neither the biblical text nor I have told you whom the request comes from: this will come later in my story. At any rate, silently and obediently, I begin to dance. Or so it seems, since the poem goes on to describe me as dancing, with the description moving from my toes upwards. And before I go into analyzing this description of my own body, of my own self, let me make a little detour, much as my colleagues have done, so that my own reflections on this matter are made more comprehensible.

Do See Me in Context, Please

An enthusiastic description of the physical attributes of a loved person seems to be part and parcel of love poetry. For the sake of convenience I shall adopt the Arabic term *wasf*, which designates a descriptive love poem, as is often done by bible interpreters. Listen to this example, conveniently taken from the tale in the *Thousand and One Nights* that our friend Zipporah has utilized for her own story. Here comes the description of naked Bird Woman, as first seen without her wings (feathered dress) by Hassan of Basrah:

The . . . damsel . . . was the loveliest creature Allah had made in her day, and indeed she outdid in beauty all human beings. She had a mouth magical as Solomon's seal and hair blacker than the night of estrangement . . . her brow was bright as the crescent moon . . . her eyes were like eyes wherein gazelles scan, she had a polished nose straight as a cane and cheeks like blood-red anemones . . . lips like coralline and teeth like strung pearls . . . and a neck like an ingot of silver, above a shape like a

wand . . . her middle was full of folds, a dimpled plain . . . and
her navel an ounce of musk, sweetest of savour could contain.
She had thighs great and plump, like marble columns twain or
bolsters stuffed with down . . . and between them a somewhat,
as it were a hummock great of span or a hare with ears back
lain while terrace roof and pilasters completed the plan; and
indeed she surpassed . . . with her beauty and symmetry.

I shall come back to this description later on, since I must
compare it to my own in the SoS. But let me continue with my
methodological reflections for the time being. In poetry extolling
spiritual love, the convention of describing a lover's body parts is often
retained as well, although there the convention functions as an
allegorical base for covert allusions, as so many times in both Jewish
and Christian exegeses; but those need not occupy us here. It is
customary to extol and glorify those physical attributes that make
the loved one—usually the female—desirable for the [male] lover.
Frequently extravagant comparisons, metaphors, and hyperboles
form the description's core.

If we look closely enough at such "descriptions," though,
something strange will emerge. No realistic picture is actually
obtained through the description: by the poem's end we still have no
idea what the loved person looks like, in the sense that no *coherent* or,
if you wish, photographic visual image is communicated. It seems
that the details given are primarily designed not to supply a
snapshot, so to speak, but to involve the listener or reader's senses
and emotions, inasmuch as those details presumably reflect the
heightened emotional state of the assumed speaker. The actual so-
called description may be well ordered, traveling with a manageable
road map over the physicalities referred to, thus conforming to a
transparent descriptive model. Conversely, it may be excitedly
haphazard, thus supplying an additional (structural) proof of the
irate mood of the speaking lover. The tone, however, is almost always
serious, celebratory, idealizing—as befits a lethal (subject) matter like
love.

"Almost always" allows for exceptions or, rather, a counter-genre
that rises out of the mainstream and deconstructs it. In order to be
effective, such a subversive counter-description would use the chief

literary conventions of the parent genre so that the former is
recognized as a legitimate offshoot of the latter. And yet, the counter-
description would introduce a certain shift by departing from one or
more of those same conventions. Thus, by bringing in a seemingly
minor change (or minor changes), the whole "snapshot"—rather than
some of its components—can be transformed into something else.
Indeed, it is possible to radically alter the basic meaning (on the
poet's side) and response (on the reader's side) of a *wasf,* or any other
poetic work, through relatively minimal transmutations. The change
might indicate, simply, a transition in mood, an additional angle,
rather than a radical alteration of viewpoint; on the other hand, it
might signify criticism of a literary or social convention—or both.
Adherence to a recognizable literary convention, together with
recognizable departures from it, may result in a *parody* of that same
convention or genre—if and when (a) it can be established that a
writer is deliberately parodying, that is, imitating a style; and
especially (b) if the reader discovers the "imitation" to be an amusing
or humorous comment on the values of the original literary form.

There are three *wasf*-type poems in the SoS—in 4:1-5 (with a part
parallel in 6:4-7), in 5:10-16, and in the last passage, "my" passage,
7:1-7. The first one deals with a female lover's figure, as does the
poem about me. The middle one deals with a male lover's figure.·
This two-to-one ratio can hardly be accidental, despite our
expectation that more male descriptions will be forthcoming, since
the chief voices in the SoS are female voices. Traditionally, *wasf*
poems deal with female beauty rather than with its male counterpart.
Neither does the placing of the *wasf*s within the SoS seem unplanned:
they function as kingpins for the concentric, chiastic structural core
of the whole work. Chapters 4 to 7:1-7 are the SoS central section
that begins and ends with female-figure *wasf*s, while a male-figure
wasf stands at the center (5:10-16) of this central section. The
arrangement seems justified in view of the prominence of the female
figure and voice throughout the SoS. Highly fitting, wouldn't you
say? On second thought, however, the question arises: why is another
extensive female-describing *wasf*—the one describing me in chapter
7—necessary in addition to the first one (in chapter 4)? One plausible
answer is that the second rounds off the structure of the whole poem
(the SoS in its entirety), for it places a female *wasf* in two symmetrical

positions within the text. Yet, this does not exclude another possibility that I'd like to explore: although "my" poem deals with the same subject matter (a female lover's desirable physical charms and their impact), it also adds fresh insights to the previous catalog. It would be my task in the following remarks to demonstrate that the fresh material introduced by "my" *wasf* in chapter 7 is motivated by insights into the comic elements of my dancing figure. I would claim that "my" poem's tone is ribald and the humor sexual, although not to the point of actual obscenity. (That some contemporary commentators, mostly males, but not only, *do* see it and other parts of the SoS as pornographic will have to be taken into account nevertheless; later, though, if you don't mind). As far as I'm concerned, when I look at the mirror, this poem sets up to me and of me, and I see myself as a hilarious parody, so much different from the other and previous two *wasf*s (which, as I shall readily show, are closer to one another than to "me," their humorous counterpart).

On Sexual Humor

Sexual humor may be blatant, scurrilous, coarse, lecherous, outspoken, irreverent, exuberant, vicious. Therefore, defining it as a guideline for understanding "my" poem, or any other biblical passage, might arouse emotional and, consequently, also academic resistance in you, my honorable listeners. Can love be funny? Should it be; should we laugh at it? Are we justified in ascribing jocular tendencies to biblical literature, well known for its lofty, didactic nature? Should the scriptures laugh at love in such a manner? And what about the sanctity of the biblical text and the allegorical interpretations attributed to the SoS, including our passage, since early antiquity? Furthermore, and from another angle altogether: if we assume a "lowly" humorous intent on the assumed author(s)'s part, do we not enter the most dangerous ground of authorial intent, which is to be trodden at one's peril only, preferably not at all? Even when we limit ourselves to dealing with the readerly response rather than the "author's intent," the attribution of sexual humor to "my" passage remains problematic. For it can, and should, be argued that a joke is effective and, indeed, recognizable as such only when it is funny. We hardly need Freud's authority to know that when a joke or comical remark requires extensive explanations, it does not work. Therefore, if my *wasf* of SoS 7:1-7 has not been recognized as a humorous piece or a parody of its original genre until now, does not that mean that it simply is not funny? Last but not least, since I'm alive and well and speaking in front of you, and prepared—nay, anxious—to concede the possibility of a humorous approach of sorts, should we not dwell a little bit on what such an application of sexual humor to my erstwhile dancing figure does to my own emotions— depending, of course, on the sort of humor I can detect?

Now, a word of warning if you don't mind. Excessive reverence toward ideologies and their supportive texts excludes the recognition of humor. For, whereas ideology is a rationalized (if not always rational) response, humor functions as a subversive agent of the conscious (so, quite reasonably, following Freud). Humor may attack and even cancel out conscious ideological stands. It follows that in order to see the humor of "my" *wasf*, be it to my or your or our personal taste or otherwise, we must suspend our respect for the scriptures and their universally assumed didactic intent at least for a short duration. Only for a while, though. Love, we must remember, is predominantly a serious, even sacred matter, and its complexity admits suffering and tragedy as readily as fun and comedy. It is perhaps worth noting in passing that, in keeping with this train of popular thought, we tend to be profoundly moved by love tragedies, even though love comedies may give us more pleasure (of another kind altogether). Needless to say, in the SoS, love and its physical manifestations are treated most seriously, barring our instance and perhaps a couple of others. Just my luck, and I mean it!

The Other Wasfs as Keys to Understanding My Own

"My" poem is thus a parodic, self-deconstructing piece: it is constructed as a double entendre: its form and imagery are those of a descriptive adoration poem, whereas its purpose is different from the latter's. In Freud's terms, we are here dealing with a juxtaposition of technique versus purpose. Understanding the tongue-in-cheek execution (yes!) of the *wasf* genre lies in comparing it to the other two occurrences of the same genre in the SoS, 4:1-7 and 5:10-16. Superficially, all three share the same motivation and basic technique. When we look at the details, however, we find that the differences between the three poems are considerable, especially in the case of "my" poem (7:1-7) vis-à-vis the other two.

I shall here reproduce the text of the three *wasf*s, for your own convenience, side by side, and then proceed to make comments on them. While I do that, you can refer to the written texts to follow my analysis.

SoS 4:1-7 (on a female)	SoS 5:10-16 (on a male)	SoS 7:1-7 (on a female)
1. Ah, you are fair, my darling, Ah, you are fair.	10. My beloved is clear-skinned and ruddy,	1. Turn back, turn back, O maid of Shulem!
Your eyes are like doves Behind your veil.	Preeminent among ten thousand.	Turn back, turn back, That we may gaze upon you.
Your hair is like a flock of goats Streaming down Mount Gilead.	11. His head is finest gold, His locks are curled And black as a raven.	"Why will you gaze at the Shulammite?"
2. Your teeth are like a flock of ewes Climbing up from the washing pool;	12. His eyes are like doves by watercourses, Bathed in milk,	"In the Mahanaim dance." 2. How lovely are your feet in sandals,
All of them bear twins, And not one loses her young.	Set by a brimming pool.	O daughter of nobles!
3. Your lips are like a crimson thread,	13. His cheeks are like beds of spices,	Your rounded thighs are like jewels, The work of a master's hand.
Your mouth is lovely.	Banks of perfume	3. Your navel is like a round goblet
Your brow behind your veil	His lips are like lilies;	Let mixed wine not be lacking!—
Gleams like a pomegranate split open.	They drip flowing myrrh.	Your belly like a heap of wheat Hedged about with lilies.
4. Your neck is like the Tower of David,	14. His hands are rods of gold, Studded with beryl;	4. Your breasts are like two fawns, Twins of a gazelle.
Built to hold weapons,	His belly a tablet of ivory, Adorned with sapphires.	5. Your neck is like a tower of ivory,
Hung with a thousand shields —All the quivers of warriors.	15. His legs are like marble pillars Set in sockets of fine gold.	Your eyes like pools in Heshbon By the gate of Bath-rabbim,
5. Your breasts are like two fawns,	He is majestic as Lebanon,	Your nose like the Lebanon tower
Twins of a gazelle, Browsing among the lilies.	Stately as the cedars.	That faces toward Damascus.
6. When the day blows gently And the shadows flee,	16. His mouth is delicious And all of him is delightful.	6. The head upon you is like crimson wool,
I will betake me to the mount of myrrh,	Such is my beloved, Such is my darling,	The locks of your head are like purple
To the hill of frankincense.	O maidens of Jerusalem!	—A king is held captive in the tresses.
7. Every part of you is fair, my darling,		7. How fair you are, how beautiful! O Love, with all its rapture!
There is no blemish in you!		
(Some lines are repeated in 6:4-7)		

[translation: NJPS]

Look at the three poems, the two "female" ones flanking the
"male" poem. Each one is comprised of seven (!) verses. Now, I do
know that the division of the biblical text into verses is much later
than any imagined time of composition; but still, since the number
seven carries such weight of magic and perfection, I'd like to think
this span of the *wasf*-type love poem is not accidental. However, let us
continue. All three poems begin by stating that the female lover and
male lover are visually, aesthetically, beautiful. This is explicitly so in
4:1a (twice) and 5:10b. In 7.1b the statement is featured but is
limited, since here the notion of beauty is focused on my feet and/or,
by metonymy, footwork (meaning dance steps). All three end, again,
on a similar general note. The female lover's aesthetics are reiterated
in 4:7, after the overall picture's seductive and sensual value is set
forth (4:6). The male lover of 5:15a-16 is monumentally handsome,
all sweetness and light. However, in my own case, where the
description of my dancing figure ends, a comment is added. The
comment (in 7:8) is analogous to the proper ending of the other two
poems: aesthetic pleasure is viewed as the forerunner to sensuous and
sexual pleasure. You can see that the comment, although properly
speaking outside the poem's boundary, is articulated more explicitly
and daringly (7:8-10a) than in the other two passages. The ending is a
genuine expression of desire, probably uttered by a male voice to
begin with (vv. 8-10a):

> Your stately form is like the palm,
> Your breasts are like clusters.
> I say: Let me climb the palm,
> Let me take hold of its branches;
> Let your breasts be like clusters of grapes,
> Your breath like the fragrance of apples,
> And your mouth like choicest wine. (NJPS)

And then I'm reported as answering, saucily,

> Let it flow to my beloved as new wine gliding over the lips of
> sleepers. (v. 10b)

A rather obvious reference to love consummation through
"climbing," tasting, drinking, smelling—wouldn't you agree? No

wonder the passage is considered by some commentators as corrupt beyond understanding; the sexual innuendos are too outspoken. All in all, "my" poem's forwardness is achieved by a combination of tone and imagery that departs radically from those that conclude the other two *wasfs*—as we shall see in a little while.

In chapter 4 the physical "description" starts with the head and proceeds downward, more or less in an orderly north-to-south fashion. The bodily inventory ends with an allusion to the female lover's breasts (4:5) but does not proceed to her body's nether regions. Can this be the result of accident? Should we assume that for some obscure reason only part of this specific poem came down to us? The existence of the circular ending (4:6-7), which, strictly speaking, lies outside the *wasf* proper—it starts and ends with the general notion of the lover's "love-liness"—makes such an evaluation a remote prospect. The poem seems to be a complete one, even though this isn't true for the female lover's body. What, then, can be the reason for the incompleteness of the lover's "photograph"? Clearly, the body parts described are those unclothed, visible—or, in the breasts' case, partly so—to the eyes of the beholder. This seems like a public concession to modesty, although metaphorically veiled allusions to the consummation of the speaker's passion are, of course, contained in 4:6: what do we imagine the *mountain* of myrrh and *hill* of frankincense to be, in such a context? And may I remind you of what caught Hassan's sight so poignantly in naked Bird Woman: "and between them [her thighs] a somewhat, as it were a hummock great of span or a hare with ears back lain while terrace roof and pilasters completed the plan"? Oh well, referring/not referring directly to a locus of female physical delights, an apparent concession to politesse, one may speculate, is probably motivated by reverence or, at least, a put-on, socially conventional attitude. At any rate, the loved one is perceived by the poem's listener or reader as a sculpture, a bust—not a complete person, hardly a body to be made love to, an inventory of body parts that don't make up a whole. Since the love object lacks some vital parts (even if they are referred to obliquely), the declared passion of the assumed speaker becomes hardly credible: the constraints of chastity serve as a deconstructive (in the literal sense) and conventional (in the social-sociological sense) agent.

A similar attitude guides the male lover's physical portrayal in 5:10-16. Like the previous (female) one, this *wasf* commences from the head downward. Unlike the former, it supplies a head-to-toe rundown. Yet, there is a vast difference between the terms used for depicting the male lover's head and those referring to the rest of his figure. The first section (vv. 11-13) has the same kind of sensual imagery already encountered in chapter 4. Several repeated metaphors seem to belong to a set stock. Their distribution within a specific poem, though, exhibits some variation in application. Thus the comparison of eyes to doves recurs twice (4:1; 5:12). Running water may feature in a metaphor depicting eyes, as does' milk (5:12). Elsewhere, the milk is involved in the depiction of teeth (4:2). Aromatics (4:6; 5:13), fortifications (4:4; 5:13c), and mountains (Gilead, 4:1; Lebanon, 5:15) are recurrent features as well. The imagery roundly appeals to the senses: visual (color), tactile, olfactory, auditory, and, perhaps, also gustatory. It seems that the description is aimed at promoting touch, notably of the hair tresses. In contradistinction, the second section (vv. 14-15a) represents the lover's torso and legs as a monumental sculpture made of precious building materials, metals, and gems. This has the effect of involving two senses only, the visual and tactile, thus impoverishing the picture and divesting it of more comprehensive sensual impact. The overall impression one is left with is that of the cold beauty and maddening unavailability of a statue, rather than with the live warmth of a human being. Instead of celebrating desire, the literary convention of the statue promotes a distancing of the love object; instead of describing the physique of the love object to a sensual/sexual end, the poem brings about a dislocation of emotion from the sensuous to the purely aesthetic. In other words, no "real" picture emerges, no "real" lover is portrayed, no point of reference outside language/literary idiom is presented to the reader to hold on to. It is indeed possible to fantasize about making love to a statue, as has been done within the realm of literature and outside it. Nevertheless, most people would sooner prefer an actual flesh-and-blood model, even if somewhat blemished. Thus modesty is retained and desire contained, at least as far as social convention and public appearance are concerned. The price for such containment is a certain lack of descriptive specificity, which may result in the reader's, or listener's, diminished sensual involvement.

"My" poem, the poem of Shulammit without "the," in chapter 7, is altogether different. Like the male *wasf* of chapter 5, it alludes to the whole body. Yet, unlike the other two *wasf*s, it starts with the feet (7:2) and proceeds upward, to the head and hair (7:5b-6). Could it be argued that, since I am presented as a dancer, this is the "natural" course the description should follow? Perhaps. Still, the departure from the *wasf* procedure better attested in the SoS (from the head downward) seems to imply more than an innocent break induced by the difference in situational context. Since the reader is now spared no physical detail—including an explicit reference to my navel (or, according to other commentators my vulva; v. 3a)—it seems that here modesty is forsaken in favor of the involvement of the senses, the sexual motivation (of the speakers), and the expected response in kind (by listeners and readers).

Modesty and sexual decorum imply at least professed reverence toward the object of desire. Once this conventional reverence is discarded, a lighter mood may set in. Reverence does not necessarily exclude joy. It more often than not, however, does exclude humor. Neither does joy always imply humor, although it might. Let's not be simplistic: humor isn't about light-hearted jokes only. So if you're as satisfied as I am at this point that the mood of "my" poem is much lighter and more irreverent than that of its counterparts, the road is open to showing that it is not only that, but humorous as well. This, together with an affirmation that the type of humor involved is anchored in jocular/sexual—rather than visual/aesthetic—allusions, requires taking a closer look at the details of the visual descriptive procedure that caresses my body from toe to hair.

I, Shulammit, the Dancer

Let me remind you that "my" poem begins with an invitation to me to perform once more "the dance of the two camps," and my own verbal response—a question for a question—to that inviting challenge (both parts of the dialogue are in verse 1). It is far from clear who and of which gender the speakers challenging me are, although, as it transpires, I comply with the invitation and begin dancing. Let me recreate the situation for you, then. I'm called upon to perform a solo dance in between two "camps," that is, two rows of spectators. The audience is active and noisy, slightly drunk. An extensive running commentary accompanies my dance, a commentary that becomes more and more daring as my dance becomes faster, the atmosphere warms up, and the drink flows. This "commentary" is far from solemn, as befits such an occasion of dance and drink. Imagine not one voice, but a multiplicity of dialoguing voices here, with each voice encouraged to be flippant by other, presumably also male, spectators. The mood is wild and the situation nearly gets out of hand. This poem is neither a wooing procedure (chapter 4) nor a longing evocation of an absent and sought-for male lover (chapter 5), but a close scrutiny of a present, live woman in public performance. Me.

The poem begins, conventionally enough, with descriptive and metaphorical materials that feature in the other *wasf*s. It commences (like 4:1) from the notion of my aesthetic beauty, this time dealing first with the feet (7:2a). The next item, my thighs, is again depicted in terms similar to those we have already encountered: they are compared to exquisite jewels. Similarly, we remember, the male lover's torso and limbs were covered rather than revealed by presenting him as a statue made of gems and precious metals (5:14-15a). And here, at this point exactly, the masking of the love object's body by items of clothing or comparison to artifacts ends, for the dancer's navel or vulva—mind you, my very own—is boldly introduced (7:3a). It is conceivable this boldness is inspired by the scanty dress sported or not sported by me at the time: I concede that it was a little on the flimsy side but would absolutely reject as beneath contempt allegations of my dancing naked, or stripping as I went along. Furthermore, even nakedness or near-nakedness does not wholly justify a description of what cannot be seen, inasmuch as clothing does not necessarily restrict the imagination. You'll probably agree with me that the verification of this point is less important than diagnosing the description's audacious tone. Moreover, and listen to this, some modern commentators understand the next line, "let drink not be lacking" or some such (3b), as an allusion to my womb's juices, symbolized by (mingled) wine. I would like to suggest that, while I was dancing and listening to the "encouragement," the actual expression hit me as well as a double entendre. Wine was indeed called for to be served to the speaker(s) and spectators by way of

self-encouragement, and, at the same time, this is a sly reference to my
sexuality, enhanced by my dance and the resulting flying garments.
When you dance as I used to, with love, with abandon, like King David
in front of the divine ark (2 Samuel 6), with dedication, the last thing
on your mind is physical modesty. You dance, you worship. You may
expose parts of your anatomy by mistake. Or they may move
suggestively, which for the spectators may amount almost to the same
thing, perhaps the better for being imagined further. Anyway, such a
double sense, as Freud points out, is characteristic of a certain type of
joke, whose enjoyment is almost exclusive to those present but often
proves elusive for those absent from the original scene.

Next in the descriptive line is my dancing belly, likened to a
mound of wheat bordered by lilies (3c-d). Again, the description is
forward and quite transparent: behold my stomach and my pubic
hair. It appears that I'm described as far from slim. Learned lines
have been written about my Rubens- or Botticelli-style "statuesque"
figure, and the changing tastes and fashions in female beauty over
the ages. For all we know, the ancients (and especially the Arabs;
look again at Bird Woman's description) might have indeed
preferred fat and healthy-looking to skinny women. But, who
knows, perhaps they did not. As you can still see, I am and always
was a lady of obvious corpulence, but to interpret the reference to
this as an adoring remark seems even to me to be conditioned by the
wish to view the running, football-style commentary on my dancing
as straightforward praise, much like the other *wasf*s. However, if
you're willing to consider "my" poem as a humorous offshoot of the
wasf convention, much like some of Shakespeare's sonnets—a parody
that uses conventional materials and form while, simultaneously,
departing from the parent norm—another picture emerges. Look,
for instance, at Shakespeare's Sonnet 130, in modern spelling for
your convenience:

My mistress' eyes are nothing like the sun;
Coral is far more red, than her lips red:
If snow be white, why then her breasts are dun;
If hairs be wires, black wires grow on her head.
I have seen roses damasked, red and white,
But no such roses see I in her cheeks;

And in some perfumes is there more delight
Than in the breath that from my mistress reeks.
I love to hear her speak, yet well I know
That music hath a far more pleasing sound:
I grant I never saw a goddess go,
My mistress, when she walks, treads on the ground:
And yet by heaven, I think my love as rare,
As any she belied with false compare.

Well, isn't this an attack on popular Elizabethan beauty ideals, carried out through the formal medium of a love sonnet (and this even before entering the fray of questioning the eternal bard's pretense of heterosexuality as decoy for homosexuality; or reading this poem as masked praise for a man!)? I presume you're all computer literate so you can follow up this poem, for a commentary and further elucidation, on the Internet. Shakespeare's sonnet operates as a gentle reprimand to older and contemporaneous conventions of love description, as does "my" SoS poem. I, the dancing woman, Shulammit, am frankly fat; my belly in dance motion as seen or imagined is big and quivering, recalling an unstable and untidy mound of wheat gathered on the ground. I daresay that I must have looked comical! The only things about me that are depicted as truly beautiful are my feet and artistic-looking thighs. Still, at one and the same time, I'm viewed as energetic, scantily dressed or not at all, and—most important and much like Shakespeare's anonymous mistress—immensely desirable. Otherwise, why bother with a blow-by-blow account of my dance?

Next come my breasts, "the twin fawns of a gazelle" (v. 4). On the face of it, this is the exact parallel of 4:5, as well as a foil for the corresponding image of the male lover as a fawn (2:9, 17; 8:14). So much has been written on the specific meaning of this image, with no consensus reached. What may the images of "young twin gazelles" evoke in your imagination? Symmetry? Color? (Slightly darker than the ideal of Shakespeare's time, white breasts, if not his own ideal?) Smallness? Beauty and grace? Jumping movement? If one takes the situational context into account and gives up the notion of producing an identical sense for both occurrences (7:4 and 4:5) of the comparison—a fresh and humorous, slightly comical possibility

emerges. I'm dancing, like a dervish; I'm in constant motion.
Together with the rest of my body, my breasts move fast, much like
frolicking fawns. This seems to be titillating for my audience, but
might look ludicrous as well. At any rate, it is as good a pretext as any
for them to laugh, aloud if through a seemingly respectable
metaphor, at my charms. The laughter, let us remember, does not
cancel out the effectiveness of those same charms. If anything, it
might indicate a modicum of excited embarrassment on the part of
the speaker(s) and audience.

Humor may indeed function as, and be motivated by, an
unconscious mask or mask for the unconscious. This is especially
valid for contexts high in sexual tension and fraught with the anxiety
of exposing one's feelings prematurely. As Freud has observed, the
comic in sexuality and obscenity should be considered for its
functioning as release of strong desires. So my neck is next likened to
an ivory tower (v. 5a), a variant of "the tower of David" in 4:4 and
Bird Woman's neck. Now, although this "tower" imagery occurs in
both *wasf*s, mine and in chapter 4, one is not absolved of finding its
poetic function within each, without presupposing that both
functions are identical. How does likening a woman's neck to a tower
constitute a term of praise? My neck is certainly exaggerated, it is
tower-like, whereas the image in 4:4 is complete. There the female
lover's bejeweled neck is like a tower adorned with warriors' shields,
and therefore a comprehensible female power image; my own neck is
unadorned, opaque. Not to beat around the bush, it is simply
disproportionately long—and I accept this criticism. My neck is too
long for the rest of my body. I've always regretted this fact.

What about my eyes and nose (the rest of v. 5)? The pools of
Heshbon—a town in Transjordan—don't feature elsewhere in the
bible as an epitome of famous beauty. Hence, this item is even more
obscure than the (admittedly difficult) conventional comparisons of
the female or male loved person's eyes to doves (4:1; 5:12), or doves
washing in water and milk (5:12). Are the points of reference the size
or limpidity of the pools, to which my eyes might be compared to
advantage? Not so, truly—such an interpretation seems to be drawn
from the need to constitute that as a term of praise. In fact, public
water places outside the gate of Heshbon, like those outside the gates
of other cities, were used for drinking, watering of animals, washing

bodies and clothes, and clearing debris. The waters were probably
turbid rather than serenely limpid. And why Heshbon? It is a foreign
town, and the foreigners' water is by definition much dirtier than
ours, to be sure! And so were my eyes, much more turbid than the
spectators'/readers', a natural result of my strenuous exertions. By
now I am perspiring freely, my figure is far from the dignified female
or male love objects enjoying a lofty statuesque repose (in chapters 4
and 5). Forsooth, while I'm dancing with all my might, and my head
is already spinning with the excitement and circular movement of
this spin, the thought fleets through my mind that I'm probably
looking ludicrous—that by now my appearance perhaps deserves or
may provoke the derisive comments. But this is a fleeting cognitive
moment only; I swiftly return to executing dance arabesques.

Next is my mountainous nose. Now, that the ancients did not
admire enormous noses any more than we do nowadays sounds
reasonable. Whether it is so or not, any attempt to explain away the
"Lebanese" mountainous dimensions of my nose remains
unconvincing. The fact is that I'm in good company with some other
desired ladies, when I admit that, like them, some of my physical
features are far from conventionally handsome. Think again about
Shakespeare's "Dark Lady" that I've already quoted for you; or
another woman from the SoS, the dark girl from chapter 1 who says
about herself—

> I am dark, but comely, O daughters of Jerusalem
> Like the tents of Kedar,
> Like the marquees of Solomon.
> Don't stare at me because I am darkish,
> Because the sun has gazed upon me. (v. 1:5-6a)

True, I do dance well and suggestively (v. 2a) even today, after all those
millennia. True, my thighs used to be like artistic jewels (v. 2b). My
navel and/or vulva are guessed to be generous (v. 3a-b)—so far on the
credit side. On the other hand, my belly is fat and jumpy like my
breasts (vv. 3c, 4), my neck is (disproportionately?) long, my eyes by
now turbid, my nose is outsize (v. 5). In terms of slang, I was and still
am "a mixed bag," and it is allowed, within the particular life-situation
of public dancing, to poke fun at the dancing me, the object of

personal and communal voyeurism and barely disguised desire. The license for jocularity and laughter is and was indeed derived from the situation, inasmuch as it is related to the distortion or caricature of previous, conventionally used metaphors (Lebanon, tower, fawns).

Verse 6 ostensibly deals with my head, then proceeds to my hair. I think, however, that the Hebrew *karmel*, "Mount Carmel," which presumably refers to my whole head, does not make sense as such unless somebody is poking fun at me yet again—an exaggerated head seems to go together with an exaggerated nose. And yet, if you read here a minimal correction of the Hebrew *karmel* to *karmil*, which is the biblical alternative to and later equivalent of *shani*, "crimson" (in Hebrew), another picture of me emerges according to most translations:

> Your head is like crimson (or purple),
> Your hair like royal purple soaked in the troughs.

In this reading, both parts of the verse refer to my hair (as they should, but let me explain, perhaps in a different manner). At this point most commentators talk about the reddish henna (red dye) properties of my glinting hair; you know that henna has been used throughout the Middle East and beyond for hair-dyeing for millennia. There's a reddish variety that is the primary and also a blackish variety; brides would have their palms dyed with henna prior to their wedding, in the so-called female henna ceremony, signifying their transition from an attached to a betrothed female. Let me tell you, however, that the color reference in this instance is mistaken. Many Oriental women of my acquaintance have and still do dye their hair with henna—for health, for luck, for hiding gray hairs. However, this was not the case here. I never did dye my hair to a reddish color because I liked its dark hue too much. So no color reference was intended here—it couldn't have been. And the translations are definitely wrong. Rather, the poem's reference is probably to threads or woven cloth, soaked in troughs (see also Gen. 30:38, 41, and Exod. 2:16) during the dyeing process. Let me restore the correct meaning—as I see it—to this verse, while correcting the punctuation of the Hebrew text ever so slightly.

Your head is like the Carmel mountain
And your hair like royal purple,
Held in the [soaking] troughs.

Purple and—to a lesser extent—crimson were worn exclusively by
royalty and nobles; who else could afford those luxuries? This
explains the expression "royal purple." After restoring the text and
imagery at this point, and in keeping with the tone and mood of
previous metaphors, things become clearer. I've been dancing for a
while now. My tresses, to begin with perhaps well-groomed and set,
are now wet with perspiration, much like packs of thread soaked in
the dyeing vessels. Beautiful? Even I wonder. Attractive? Well, that is
in the eye[s] of the beholder[s].

Indeed, indeed. There is no reason to assume that the picture I
present by now is aesthetically captivating. Rather than a recognition
of pure aesthetics, other responses might be evoked within the
spectators' psyche by the dance: laughter of an uncertain source;
desire; embarrassment caused by that same desire for a dancer who is
provocative and appetizing, yet far from conventionally good
looking. At least, this is implied by the non-conventional "praise."

Thus we get to the finale of "my" *wasf* or, we should now say, the
parody proper. Verse 7 sums the picture up: I, Shulammit, am
considered fair and sweet (note the visual and taste properties)
inasmuch as sexual pleasure is concerned, which really is the point of
the whole poem. And lest we err, the appendix to the description
states the speaker or speakers' intention even more explicitly.
He(?)(They?) has/have laughed at my dancing without undue
reverence seemingly not because of disrespect. The laughter seems to
spring from the incongruity of my appearing comical—even
ridiculous—as well as sexy. Ultimately, it is the sexy-sensual feature
that prevails. The pastoral comparisons and metaphors of verses 8-
10—the palm, the vine, the vine clusters, the wine together with the
focus on my breasts—all point to sexual intoxication and make it
clear that the speaker or speakers' intention and, perhaps my own,
Shulammit's, too, is to bring passion to its consummation. The aim
of "my" poem, then, is serious. Yet the means is jocular and
completely devoid of the idolization and reverence typical of, for

instance, 4:1-7 (where the sexual goal is overtly identical) and 5:10-16 (where it is not stated overtly as such). Serenity, it transpires, befits the artistic evocation of artworks (which is certainly the statues of chapters 4 and 5); humor is eminently more suitable for dealing with a flesh-and-blood object of desire.

So Where Does All This Lead Us?

"My" poem of 7:1-7, together with its appendix in verses 8-10, is a parody of the serious *wasf* genre. I find it possible to define it so not as a result of speculations in regard to its author's intent but, rather, through a light-hearted analysis of how the imagery functions within the given literary and real-life context. To draw a loose analogy, the poem relates to its counterparts in chapters 4 and 5 much as the humorous Shakespearean love sonnet that I've quoted relates to its serious equivalents within the repertoire of the same poet. Once again, please look. Shakespeare can be quite conventional in pining, or opining, about his lover's eyes—

> Thine eyes I love, and they, as pitying me,
> Knowing thy heart torments me with disdain. (Sonnet 132)

But is as capable of loving with a twist:

> Shall I compare thee to a summer's day?
> Thou art more lovely and more temperate:
> Rough winds do shake the darling buds of May,
> And summer's lease hath all too short a date:
> Sometime too hot the eye of heaven shines,
> And often is his gold complexion dimmed,
> And every fair from fair sometime declines,
> By chance, or nature's changing course untrimmed:
> But thy eternal summer shall not fade,
> Nor lose possession of that fair thou ow'st,
> Nor shall death brag thou wander'st in his shade,
> When in eternal lines to time thou grow'st,
> So long as men can breathe, or eyes can see,
> So long lives this, and this gives life to thee. (Sonnet 18)

Other poets may use the same lyrical conventions, tongue-in-cheek or not. Now, if we do not hesitate to retain the title "love sonnet" for some of Shakespeare's light-hearted lines, we should not refrain from accepting "my" poem for what it is either: SoS 7:1-7, and what seems like a commentary on it or its conclusion in verses 8-10, is a jocular/comical treatment of the theme of love, through form and imagery similar to other treatments, but in a different mood. Is the change brought about by authorial design, and what can the possible motivation for such an admittedly deviant presentation be? I shall deal with these questions shortly. Meanwhile, let it be stressed that the deviations of "my" poem from the norms inherent in and displayed by its counterparts, if and when those are recognized as deviations by the listener and/or reader, are proof enough that low comedy is at play here. However, in order to recognize the humor of "my" piece, one has to forgo two separate sets of prejudices. First, that no passage in scriptures can or should treat love and sex jokingly and with good cheer, especially a passage from an opus that has received such extensive allegorical treatment as the SoS. And second, that love and desire themselves should be treated with respect in any type of literature, if they aren't to be demoted from eroticism to pornography. I believe that these two kinds of objection have hindered many readers from admitting the true nature of "my" passage, and from laughing openly together with the voice of the assumed speaker(s).

I would like to conclude this part of the argument by drawing your attention once more to the two non-biblical authorities on love and sexuality already mentioned, Shakespeare and Freud. Shakespeare pokes fun at his love object in Sonnet 130 in no uncertain terms. Yet, in the concluding couplet he celebrates the fact that all her physical faults, funny and maddening as they are, do not have any bearing on his love for her. Here's the concluding couplet once again:

And yet, by heaven, I think my love as rare
As any she belied with false compare.

The implied protest against conventional, idolized, idealized images of love and of the love object, similar to those expressed in love poetry of the *wasf* type and intentionality, speaks for itself. Nevertheless, the humorous attack on social and literary convention retains the traditional formal guise of a sonnet, and, through an explicit twisting of stock metaphors, a reversal of meaning is achieved. The criticism is leveled through humor, but its serious message is unmistakable. I suggest that "my" *wasf* operates in a similar manner. And then, let's look again at how Freud sums up the question of "sexual" humor, the existence of which in "my" passage I have tried to demonstrate. Verbal sexualization and obscenity offer the amplest occasions for obtaining comic pleasure alongside pleasurable sexual excitement: they can show human beings in their dependence on bodily needs (degradation) or reveal the physical demands lying behind the claim of mental love (unmasking). In my opinion, these two quotations sum up the case for a comic/humorous tone of my *wasf* admirably. And this is not without analogy in, say, other corpora of Judeo-Christian love poetry. Consider, in addition to Shakespeare, the metaphysical poet Andrew Marvell's (1621–1678) poem "To His Coy Mistress":

> Had we but world enough, and time,
> This coyness, Lady, were no crime.
> We would sit down and think which way
> To walk and pass our long love's day.
> Thou by the Indian Ganges' side
> Shouldst rubies find; I by the tide
> Of Humber would complain. I would
> Love you ten years before the Flood,
> And you should, if you please, refuse
> Till the conversion of the Jews.
> My vegetable love should grow
> Vaster than empires, and more slow;
> An hundred years should go to praise
> Thine eyes and on thy forehead gaze;
> Two hundred to adore each breast,
> But thirty thousand to the rest;
> An age at least to every part,
> And the last age should show your heart.
> For, Lady, you deserve this state,

Nor would I love at lower rate.
But at my back I always hear,
Time's winged chariot hurrying near;
And yonder all before us lie
Deserts of vast eternity.
Thy beauty shall no more be found,
Nor, in thy marble vault, shall sound
My echoing song; then worms shall try
That long preserved virginity
And your quaint honour turn to dust,
And into ashes all my lust:
The grave's a fine and private place
But none, I think, do there embrace.
Now therefore, while the youthful hue,
Sits on thy skin like morning dew
And while thy willing soul transpires
At every pore with instant fires,
Now let us sport us while we may,
And now, like amorous birds of prey,
Rather at once our time devour
Than languish in this slow-chapt power.
Let us roll all our strength and all
Our sweetness up into one ball,
And tear our pleasures with rough strife
Through the iron gates of life:
Thus, though we cannot make our sun
Stand still, yet we will make him run.

Wouldn't you agree that desire and many faces of humor, from satire to parody to ironic self-awareness and more, intermingle here to cancel out visions of aesthetic beauty, especially since the concern for lost time is so foregrounded?

Reintroducing Gender

Dear Ladies. So far, and without saying so directly, my reading of all three SoS *wasfs*, and especially "mine," 7:1-7, has not been scholarly and highly serious and far from gender-free. It was in fact a male reading. I've assumed the artificial guise of a male reader, since the voice articulating the parody seems to be a male voice commenting on a female figure; most of the commentators explaining the passage have been males; the pertinent literary analogues from Western literature were composed by males (Shakespeare, Marvell); and I used Freud as chief authority for psychological interpretation.

However, a male reading is, naturally, not the only option. I will therefore briefly transform myself now into a female reader and, from this perspective, entertain the notion of viewing the SoS and "my" own poem as a piece of female composition. Such a transformation makes not only good sense for me but is actually called for by the text as well. Amazingly for the widely agreed upon patriarchal background of the Hebrew bible, the female figure(s) in the SoS is (are) much more dominant than the male (males). As biblical scholar Francis Landy says in his book on the SoS, *Paradoxes of Paradise*:

> The woman is the more interesting because she is the more active partner, nagging [*sic!*], restless, decisive. The man on the other hand is predominantly passive and complacent . . . his most memorable cry is the fourfold repetition of . . . "Return" in 7:1. . . . Even when he is stirred into ineffective wooing, we hear it only through her mouth (2:10-13; 5:2); her voice thus mingles with his, and we cannot tell whether it may not be her wish-fulfillment.

Thus it seems that the predominance of the female(s) in the SoS, as against the lesser role(s) assigned to the male(s) in it, can hardly be ignored even by those who do not espouse feminist causes. Because of this predominance, and some additional factors that I won't go into, it is now commonly argued that female authorship—perhaps enveloped by male editorship, like the rest of the Hebrew canon—should be considered for the SoS or most of it. It is conceivable that the SoS was dramatized and sung to a bride inside her mother's compound just before she was led to her groom—although, as I've stated, the SoS seems to be a celebration of free love, *not* necessarily leading to a wedding—when women played the roles of all parties mentioned, including the male roles. Such a hypothesis would satisfactorily explain quite a few aspects of the SoS: the female voices' boldness, the frequent mentioning of the mother's home but no mention of a father's home, the female predominance, the freedom of speech implausible in mixed company. It would also explain the daring sexual humor attributed to a male voice through the knowing filter of a woman's perception and dramatization, like a play within a play, a parody within a parody. The message would be clear. Females are not ignorant of the problematics of male sexuality. They realize that males may resort to an idealization of their love objects or, conversely or even at the same time, attempt to devalue them. Alternatively, females may poke fun at those same male love objects publicly in order to unmask the male desire and accompanying embarrassment. Women may object to both male manners of coping out of the desire situation. The female voice(s) behind the literary male voice(s) of the SoS in general, and implicit in "my" *wasf* in particular, seem(s) to be advocating a firm view. It is possible to be an attractive female without becoming or pretending to become an idol or a statue; it should be possible for males to desire without either putting their women on pedestals (thus conforming to convention; whose?) or denigrating their appearance (by resorting to sexual humor). A woman (or women) putting such a message across through a male voice—and such a reading makes sense for a female reader—will make her message much more poignant than if it were delivered directly and explicitly and didactically by a female speaker. After all, when all is said and read and performed, "biblical women" such as I still remain within the boundaries of patriarchy and its confines. And so, for that matter, aren't we all, readers of both genders? We all know about stereotypic patterns of sexually motivated, public male behavior. A female reader could satisfactorily sum the case up thus: sexual humor of the ribald male variety exposes desire instead of masking it. A parody on a *wasf* type male-voiced poem, done female style, doubles the fun and the exposure of literary convention and its underlying social conventions. Would you, my dear colleagues, be prepared to entertain the notion that the original audience of my recorded dance were women, that the dance was performed in the harem-like women's quarters, that the female spectators pretended to emulate what they perceived (for better or for worse) to be stereotypic male behavior, and that the joke is in fact richer that it seems at first and second and third glance?

Finally: Pornography?

When does love, desire, mutate into pornography? That is not so easy to determine. It's a matter of taste, of time and place, of personal or collective sensibilities and norms. Pornography is exposure—of bodies, of emotions, of sexual behavior—often designed to stimulate sexual desire in others. For some, it's also the explicitness and the *amount* of exposed flesh and the mode of such anatomical exposure. Whether the exposure is done by verbal or visual means, both modes invite a gaze. And perhaps the nature of the gendered viewer, the nature of the gendered gaze in male-male, female-female, female-male, and male-female pairs of gazer and gazed-at also contributes to the unease one may feel at being gazed at.

"My" poem, as you've seen, exposes me and may even be undressing me and makes me—the subject of a dance sequence—into the object of a gaze. Whose gaze? I've given you at least two options. Why? As release for pent-up desire, a cover-up for genuine or imitated sexual tension. So the question begs itself: is this presentation of me, a presentation that shows so much, pornographic?

For me, the exposure of desire is no big deal; had I not wished to be physically exposed I wouldn't have become a dancer (and please, reducing or elevating me to a belly dancer is beyond the point). I'm no Barbie or skinny model, as you can see and as you've heard. I'm an all-adult woman and lots of woman at that. And I take pride at being desired potentially or actually. So being seen, taking a risk at the gazers' responses, is part of the game. I don't feel "pornographied" by that, not even insulted by the ribald humor, especially since I know its origins. What makes this bearable for me is the knowledge that no violence is implied by the description of my dance: there's no threat to my existence, no veiled proposals of using power to extinguish the force of my dancing being, just a rather implicit sexual proposal at the end. And pornography, especially hard pornography, is more about control and violence and subduing the sexual "partner" than about sexuality and desire. So, certainly, I don't feel "pornographied" by the poem's gaze, be it gendered as it may.

On the other hand, there's still something I wish to add on this topic by way of my presentation's closure while going back to its beginning. For a couple of decades now feminists have rejoiced in the SoS, making it their own. They enjoyed the centrality of female figures in it and all that this implies, so unusual for the Hebrew bible at large. But recently, once again, some readers have challenged this view, claiming the usual biblical male authorship and perspective for the SoS collection as a whole, including "my" poem, and they've been reading it as soft or hard pornography, as dictated by personal temperament. I invite you, my patient listeners, to read the collection once again. You will, most certainly, find some passages that will strike you as cruel to their female heroine—as, for instance, when a woman seeking her lover is beaten up and partially exposed by the city's guards (chapter 5), or as "brothers" attempt to control their nubile sister's virgin sexuality (chapters 1 and 8). And love, it must be said, even in the SoS, doesn't lack a dark side. However, read it as I have, again and again—and having performed that public dance while listening to the comments, let me assure you, no violence passes *between lovers* here. And unless you're upset or titillated by exposed flesh—especially female flesh—beyond a proverbial naked ankle, unless you consider any talk of love and sex as somehow an invitation to go further into the available dark corners of your own mind with it, may I invite you to enjoy the SoS with me, knowing full well that human complexities ensure that love and sex remain paradoxical and ambiguous, a pleasure and a pain?

Back to Me

I'm a dancer. And although timeless, I had to retire after a long and illustrious solo career. So I did. I opened a dancing school for professionals and amateurs. We teach belly dancing, of course; this is an increasingly popular dance mode not only with Eastern but also with Western young women. It doesn't require a sylph-like figure and is a confidence-builder for its practitioners; lots of craft and physical, sensuous fun here, not to mention the custom of Arab men of putting money into the dancing woman's costume, or cleavage, or whatever, during performances. Some women come to practice their bodies for their stripping performances in various joints, an exhibition of a different sexuality altogether. Next come the classical dancers, a more dedicated group whose members put so much into their art, sometimes beginning while still young children. Here aesthetics overrides sexuality almost completely, although sensuality certainly remains present. And I have a small class for paraplegics, and yes, dancing with a wheelchair can and should be fun. These are the afternoon classes, mostly for women and in groups, but at times I still work individually with a promising student or two. In the evening, though, the whole school changes. Mixed-gender, mixed-age groups come in for a different type of dance on different days. It may be ballroom dancing on the one night, with mostly seniors, some coming in couples, some singly. Oh, the number of couplings made here! Or it may be a Latin night, with younger people and a different style of dancing: more energetic, less polite. Or a Spanish night, when the gazing at performers far outstrips the actual dancing by the crowd. Or a night of Israeli folk dances, some to the words of the SoS itself, some invoking my own name. I walk around, fanning myself with that delicate Spanish fan I've adopted years ago, encouraging people to move, checking that they're having a good time, listening discreetly to some comments made by the ones sitting down on the ones dancing, smiling to myself. And listening to the music, which I've collected over time in my many dance tours all over the world. And my feet, my feet, they keep the rhythm, they still seem to want to dance of their own accord. And as the evening wears on and deep into the night, and the air heats up, and the atmosphere becomes fragrant and loaded, and couplings are made for a while or for longer, and sensuality becomes sexuality, I feel good. I'm still Shulammit, the dancer. This is my world.

TWELVE

I Am the Convener

Preamble

My good ladies. It's my turn to speak up, having remained in the wings all this time. This has been a non-hierarchical occasion, as befits even a historically proto-feminist gathering, which, as I see it, is what we've been having. We've conducted ourselves over the last few days as equals, without paying much attention to any type of seniority—of age, or social status, or marital status, or economic status, or whatever, then or now. Which is as it should be. Each one of us has told her own story, undoubtedly written and rewritten in her mind and in other people's minds many times over time, with memory being created and recreated as a matter of upgraded routine. However, as the initiator of this august and exceptional gathering, please let me have the privilege of summing up our proceedings. My "speech," then, will contain two parts: in the first, I shall tell my own story, as you have done concerning yours, in my case operating from two parallel texts. And in the second, I shall recount how I came to entertain the notion of this gathering, and what—as I hope—we've achieved during our meeting, apart from having fun! In so doing, I consider myself—I can assure you of it—only as a first among equals; and I do hope that you air your own feelings in our final, farewell "round-table" session.

Witching It, in the Bible and in Josephus Flavius: The Stories

This is the first story in which I feature, as translated into English. Here it is, a copy for each one of you. Let me read it to you without comment, while you follow it from the printed handouts. The handouts, as you can see, have the Hebrew and the English versions side by side (Hebrew, of course, is less of a problem for you than for some of the later bible commentators; you can follow, you don't need me to read it aloud). I'll read the English text. This has been our language in this gathering because it has become the *lingua franca* of the West, where we all live nowadays. I've rearranged the text visually to foreground some literary matters, such as the direct speech passages allowed by the author to the literary actors. So here we go.

Now Samuel had died, and all Israel had mourned for him and buried him in Ramah, his own city. Saul had expelled the mediums and the wizards from the land. The Philistines assembled, and came and encamped at Shunem. Saul gathered all Israel, and they encamped at Gilboa. When Saul saw the army of the Philistines, he was afraid, and his heart trembled greatly. When Saul inquired of the LORD, the LORD did not answer him, not by dreams, or by Urim, or by prophets.

Then Saul said to his servants,

"Seek out for me a woman who is a medium, so that I may go to her and inquire of her."

His servants said to him,

"There is a medium at Endor."

So Saul disguised himself and put on other clothes and went there, he and two men with him. They came to the woman by night. And he said,

"Consult a spirit for me, and bring up for me the one whom I name to you."

The woman said to him,

"Surely you know what Saul has done, how he has cut off the mediums and the wizards from the land. Why then are you laying a snare for my life to bring about my death?"

But Saul swore to her by the LORD,

"As the LORD lives, no punishment shall come upon you for this thing."

Then the woman said,

"Whom shall I bring up for you?"

He answered,

"Bring up Samuel for me."

When the woman saw Samuel, she cried out with a loud voice; and the woman said to Saul,

"Why have you deceived me? You are Saul!"

The king said to her,

"Have no fear; what do you see?"

The woman said to Saul,

"I see a divine being coming up out of the ground."

He said to her, "What is his appearance?"

She said,

"An old man is coming up; he is wrapped in a robe."

So Saul knew that it was Samuel, and he bowed with his face to the ground, and did obeisance.

Then Samuel said to Saul,

"Why have you disturbed me by bringing me up?"

Saul answered,

"I am in great distress, for the Philistines are warring against me, and God has turned away from me and answers me no more, either by prophets or by dreams; so I have summoned you to tell me what I should do."

Samuel said,

"Why then do you ask me, since the LORD has turned from you and become your enemy? The LORD has done to you just as he spoke by me; for the LORD has torn the kingdom out of your hand, and given it to your neighbor, David. Because you did not obey the voice of the LORD, and did not carry out his fierce wrath against Amalek, therefore the LORD has done this thing to you today. Moreover the LORD will give Israel along with you into the hands of the Philistines; and tomorrow you and your sons shall be with me; the LORD will also give the army of Israel into the hands of the Philistines."

Immediately Saul fell full length on the ground, filled with fear because of the words of Samuel; and there was no strength in him, for he had eaten nothing all day and all night.

The woman came to Saul, and when she saw that he was terrified, she said to him,

"Your servant has listened to you; I have taken my life in my hand, and have listened to what you have said to me. Now therefore, you also listen to your servant; let me set a morsel of bread before you. Eat, that you may have strength when you go on your way."

He refused, and said,

"I will not eat."

But his servants, together with the woman, urged him; and he listened to their words. So he got up from the ground and sat on the bed.

Now the woman had a fatted calf in the house. She quickly slaughtered it, and she took flour, kneaded it, and baked unleavened cakes. She put them before Saul and his servants, and they ate.

Then they rose and went away that night.

(1 Samuel 28:3-25 NRSV)

I am that woman, of course. And now, still without comment, let me read to you Josephus Flavius's rewrite of the same story. Here's a handout again, this time in Greek—Josephus's language—and in English. Once again, I'll read the English text to you; and I've modified the text somewhat while working with the sources as taken off the Web. Some phrases and passages are italicized, so as to draw your attention to matters that, having finished the reading, we shall discuss as examples of obvious differences between the two stories about the same event and the same actors.

Now Saul, the king of the Hebrews, had cast out of the country the fortune-tellers, and the necromancers, and all such as exercised the like arts, *excepting the prophets*. But when he heard that the Philistines were already come, and had pitched their camp near the city Shunem, situated in the plain, he *made haste* to oppose them with his forces; and when he was come to a certain mountain called Gilboa, he pitched his camp over-against the enemy; but when he saw the enemy's army he was greatly troubled, *because it appeared to him to be numerous, and superior to his own*; and he inquired of God by the *prophets* concerning the battle, that he might know beforehand what would be the event of it. And when God did not answer him, Saul was under a still greater dread, and his courage fell, *foreseeing, as was but reasonable to suppose, that mischief would befall him, now that God was not there to assist him*; yet did he bid his servants to inquire out for him some woman that was a *necromancer* and called up the souls of the dead. So that he might know whether his affairs would succeed to his mind; *for this sort of necromantic women that bring up the souls of the dead, do by them foretell future events to such as desire them.* And one of his servants told him that there was such a woman in the city Endor, *but was known to nobody in the camp*; hereupon Saul put off his royal apparel, and took two of those servants with him, *whom he knew to be most faithful to him,* and came to Endor to the woman, and entreated her to act the part of a fortune-teller, and to bring up such a soul to him as he should name to her. But when the woman opposed his motion, and said *she did not despise the king,* who had banished this sort of fortune-tellers, and that he did not do well himself, when she had done him no harm, to endeavor to lay a snare for her, and to discover that she exercised a forbidden art, in order to procure her to be punished, he *swore that nobody should know what she did; and that he would not tell any one else what she foretold, but that she should incur no danger.* As soon as he had induced her by this oath to fear no harm, he bid her bring up to him the soul of Samuel. She, *not knowing who Samuel was,* called him out of *Hades.* When he [Saul] appeared, and the woman saw one that was *venerable, and of a divine form, she was in disorder;* and being astonished at the sight, she said, "Art not thou king Saul?" *for Samuel had informed her who he was.* When he had owned that to be true, and had asked her whence her disorder arose, she said that she saw a certain person ascend, who in his form was like to a god. And when he bid her tell him what he resembled, in what habit he appeared, and of what age he was, she told him he [Samuel] was an old man already, *and of a glorious personage,* and had on a *sacerdotal* mantle. So the king discovered by these signs that he was Samuel; and he fell down upon the ground, and saluted and worshipped him. And when *the soul of Samuel* asked him why he had disturbed him, and caused him to be brought up, he lamented the necessity he was under; for he said, that his enemies pressed heavily upon him; that he was in distress what to do in his present circumstances; that he was forsaken of God, and could obtain no prediction of what was coming, neither by prophets nor by dreams; and that "these were the reasons why I have recourse to time, who always took great care of me."

But Samuel, seeing that the end of Saul's life was come, said,

"It is in vain for thee to desire to learn of me any thing future, when God hath forsaken thee: however, hear what I say, that David is to be king, *and to finish this war with good success*; and thou art to lose thy dominion and thy life, because thou didst not obey God in the war with the Amalekites, and hast not kept his commandments, as I foretold thee while I was alive. Know, therefore, that the people shall be made subject to their enemies, and that thou, with thy sons, shall fall in the battle tomorrow, and thou shalt then be with me [in Hades]."

When Saul heard this, he could not speak for grief, and fell down on the floor, *whether it were* from the sorrow that arose upon what Samuel had said, or from his emptiness, for he had taken no food the foregoing day nor night, he easily fell quite down: *and when with difficulty he had recovered himself,* the woman would *force* him to eat, begging this of him as a favor on account of her concern in that dangerous instance of fortune-telling, which it was not lawful for her to have done, because of the fear she was under of the king, while she knew not who he was, yet did she undertake it, and go through with it; on which account she entreated him to admit that a table and food might be set before him, that he might recover his strength, and so get safe to his own camp. And when he opposed her motion, and entirely rejected it, *by reason of his anxiety, she forced him,* and at last persuaded him to it. *Now she had one calf that she was very fond of, and one that she took a great deal of care of, and fed it herself; for she was a woman that got her living by the labor of her own hands, and had no other possession but that one calf; this she killed, and made ready its flesh,* and set it before *his servants and himself.* So Saul came to the camp while it was yet night. (italics added)

Now, my friends, differences and inconsistencies aside (we shall go into that in a minute), you'd think that here Josephus would end his treatment of my story. After all, he's not known as a great appreciator of female nature. And yet, he goes on to recommend me—I shall read the relevant passage to you later—and then proceeds to wax lyrical about the doomed King Saul's courage, which is much more his style. But let's leave him here and continue to look at the two synoptic stories I've just presented to you—the biblical story first.

The Biblical Story
The original story is worth noting for its problems. The setting is clear. We're some time at the beginning of the tenth century BCE. Having forbidden on pain of death magic of any kind, King Saul finds nevertheless that he needs an answer to his question, What is going to happen in the battle with the Philistines? He has tried asking Yhwh, by technical (dreams and priestly lots; that is, magical practices incorporated by the cult and thus legitimized) as well as prophetic means, to no avail. That his servants know of me, of my proficiency in my chosen vocation and the validity of my results, as well as my reputation for discretion, is clear. So he disguises himself and comes over to my place. Here I, and my sisters in trade, score immediately: it would seem that magic isn't forbidden because it's ineffective but, on the contrary, because it's a heretical but successful competition for institutional (that is, priestly) Yahwistic magic. And yes, without going into the question of attitudes to magic in the Hebrew bible at this point, suffice be it to touch on several issues briefly. One, as is so well-known, non-native Israelite magic is so vehemently forbidden time and time again, with great detail (Leviticus 20; Deut. 18:9-14), that the proscription itself is great testimony for magic's continued existence in the substrata of Israelite cultures. Two, magic is associated with males as well, but especially with females. Three, so many commentators and translators enjoyed calling me a "witch," a pejorative term that, in view of Christianity's

persecution of "witches" in the old as well as the "new" Western worlds in premodern times, covers every female non-conventional behavior—from knowledge about herbal medicine to loose social mores to female wisdom in general. And finally, my own specialty, as can be gleaned from the Hebrew text, was the raising of spirits in order to foretell the future—a practice imitated even today in so-called spiritual séances all over the world, with more often lesser than greater success but allowing for fraudulent and profitable enterprises. What we, I and my sisters in trade who are legitimate practitioners (to distinguish from deceitful claimants), do is acquire knowledge; in that sense, we do influence fates. Knowledge may help, or it may not; knowledge doesn't automatically endow the knower with control, as is clear from Saul's story. At any rate, this is far removed from the claim Ezekiel makes, namely that we can change destinies (Ezekiel 13). We simply don't have this kind of power; we're merely vehicles for transmission of meta-natural information. This is to some degree talent and to a certain extent a matter of technique, which I shall not divulge here. Professional secrecy, you understand. And as is well-known from cases of genuine (to distinguish from false) psychics, we're not always successful when acting on behalf of our anxious clients. While success is rightly considered a measure of reliability, meta-natural worlds aren't easily controlled.

So back we go to Saul and his request. At first I refuse. I don't recognize him—and am scared, since while I do practice my trade regularly and for a living, I tend to be careful. Who knows what the king's spies are up to? (A little paranoia never hurts.) But Saul insists and swears by Yhwh (acceptable to me; I'm not a pagan, merely not a member of the priestly male class), and I comply. Note how, throughout the story, the biblical author allows me a voice, that is, direct speech, whenever my response is called for, which is similar or even equal to the legroom given to the other main [male] figures: Saul and Samuel and Saul's servants. I'm therefore moved to summon the required spirit.

Here the story falters, and in a big way. How is it clear to me as soon as I successfully summon the spirit that the inquiring client is King Saul? How can I *see* a spirit, by definition a body-less apparition? Furthermore, a *divine* spirit should be doubly disembodied! How can the apparition be so physical? How can it be perceived precisely as an

old man dressed in a coat? How can *I* see him, whereas Saul
apparently doesn't? And how can Saul converse with and hear him,
whereas I—who sees—don't hear his speech? And what are the
implications of this complex situation for death and afterlife
theologies in the bible?

The rabbis and medieval Jewish commentators, bless them, drew
firm if not altogether substantiated conclusions. As Rashi succinctly
writes, following earlier versions:

> Three things were said about the *ôb* (Hebrew "spirit"): whoever
> brings it up sees but doesn't hear its voice; the one asking for it
> hears it but doesn't see it; therefore he [Saul] asked what he
> [Samuel's apparition] looked like. And any other doesn't see
> and doesn't hear. (Rashi for 1 Sam. 28:14)

Other sources, from the Mishnah to the Midrash, in addition to
Rashi, concur and also have other solutions. For instance:

> How did she [I] know [that she conjured Samuel up, and that the
> inquirer was Saul]? Our rabbis said, what happens to a king
> doesn't happen to a commoner. To the king—his face is upwards
> and his feet downwards, as usual; but to the commoner—his feet
> come up and his face down. (*Tanḥuma Buber Emor*, 4)

At any rate, as you can see, this is the extent of my service: I make
contact between the two men, the dead and the soon-to-be dead. In
that sense, I don't claim to be a "medium" as contemporary mediums
claim, when they act like ventriloquists and maintain that a dead
person's spirit talks through them, having lodged itself in them for
the duration. No: you may say that I'm just a communication expert
connecting two spheres of contiguous realities, the normal and the
meta- or paranormal. And also, remember, Saul used to be an ecstatic
and on occasion hung out with prophets' bands—even the bible
doesn't hide this detail of his early monarchic period (1 Sam. 10:11,
19:24)—so, presumably, he's able to handle the situation.

Complicated, isn't it? At any rate, Samuel has his depressing say.
Saul believes him and is greatly disheartened, so much so that he falls
on the ground, dejectedly. Although I don't know what exactly

transpires, it's true that I don't hear what Samuel says (exactly as the rabbis maintain); I hear what Saul's question is. And I guess at the answer by his grief-stricken reaction. He seems heartbroken, wretched, miserable. So I blackmail him into eating, the maternal soul that I am. I offer him meat, a fatted calf, and freshly baked crackers. Since I know the political and military situation—the Philistines are camped nearby—I say to myself, I'm probably administering a last supper rite to the condemned man; this makes my cooking-and-serving activities even more poignant for me. Saul and his servants eat, and they depart the same night. Soon Saul and his sons die in battle, on the Gilboa, just as Samuel has foreseen and foretold. The actual fortune-teller then, the real medium, is Samuel's apparition. In this story, magic has been almost totally appropriated by the Yahwistic narrator in favor of the Yahwistic prophet/seer. I don't mind really, since—*pace* so many readers—I was and still am a Yhwh believer myself.

So let's sum up this story. I don't have a name in it, that's true. Like so many of us, and this has been said here again and again, I remain nameless. The rabbis called me Zaphaniah, "god hides," perhaps in unconscious recognition of my religious subscription to Yahwism, or else, simply describing their own theological reflections on and emotional response to the proceedings. Incidentally, the rabbis transform me into a mother to Abner. Now I wonder, is this in recognition of my maternal behavior as well as constituting promotion from anonymity to membership in Saul's family? Remember, Abner son of Ner is identified as Saul's uncle or cousin (1 Sam. 14:50-51). The repressed has the uncanny ability to resurface. Indeed, this is how Saul's servant knew about me and about my occupation: I'm a member of Saul's clan and, therefore, escaped somehow the general ban and death sentence for witchcraft. It is encouraging to notice that, although my family ties are repressed in the biblical story, the storyteller—unlike later generations—is respectful toward me and toward my trade. I'm not presented as a "witch." This, for instance, is the definition given to the short entry on me in the scholarly, respectable *Encyclopedia Judaica,* and you can also consult Pseudo-Philo, who, to his heart's content, names me "Sedecla" and claims I deceived Israel with my sorcery for the stereotypic forty years! No—in the bible I'm presented as effective and kind. I'm allowed participation in dialogues. You don't get many details about me—age, appearance, circumstances—but that is usual. Saul and Samuel are the story's focus; I'm just a vehicle. And many details remain murky, and the theological implications for life/death ideologies remain quite puzzling and certainly unresolved.

Josephus's Retelling

Now, let's move on to Josephus's retelling; please refer to the handout you have and especially to the emphasized passages and phrases. Josephus seems to have been motivated by greater and also lesser issues: some theological, others ideological, yet others emanating from the reasonable wish to make the story more accessible as well as inoffensive to his contemporaries, Jews and non-Jews alike. When I read his recount, the first structural feature that strikes me is Josephus's amplification of it. His story is so much longer than its biblical counterpart and fills in gaps by way of psychologizing the main characters' (including my own) literary behavior. The second feature worth noting in Josephus's recounting is as follows: all my direct speech acts are transformed into indirect, reported speech acts—apart from once and briefly when I ask, shocked, "Are you not King Saul?" Dialogues and direct speech acts are allowed, in this recount, only to Saul and to Samuel. Which re-places me, if you wish, on the margins of the narratological scheme. This simple literary device demotes me to secondary place, Josephus's charitable opinion of my conduct notwithstanding.

Moving to matters of contents and ideas, Josephus's compassionate empathy for Saul's plight is conspicuous. This empathy is greater than the biblical storyteller's and blossoms, at the end (which I've not reproduced for you), into a veritable paean for Saul's courage and manly virtues. Josephus's sympathy, unmistakably and apart from any partisan views he may have held with regard to King David and his dynasty, is on Saul's side. Thus he explains Saul's mind-set at length and minimizes his transgression of appealing to a "necromancer," as he calls me, as much as possible. Further, Josephus attempts to explain problematic issues in the biblical text that troubled the rabbis as well—such as explaining clearly (and against the biblical text itself) that only the *soul* of Samuel is conjured and speaks,

thus creating a problem for the visual element; substituting the
Greco-Roman "Hades" (underworld) for the Hebrew *Sheol*, of which it
is not clear whether it refers to "grave," "pit," "underworld," or
whatever; gratuitously offering that the apparition told me who he
was, thus I could also conjecture who Saul was; that Samuel was
wearing a "ritual" mantle, thus referring to his appearance while alive;
and so on. So, while Josephus keeps to the main story line, he adds
and modifies, thus appeasing his assumed readers while creating new
comprehension problems in relation to the biblical text.

Let's see what actually happens to me in his retelling. Josephus
retains my anonymity. He denies me direct speech, as noted. I become
"disordered," hysterical, upon seeing Samuel's "soul" (and logic be
hanged). But Josephus allows me reported dialogue with Samuel's
"soul," which is what the bible as well as the rabbis deny: in his
version, I see Samuel, recognize his glory (although, initially, his
name doesn't ring a bell with me!), and hear his voice before he and
Saul resume their audience. After the audience is over, I "force" Saul
to eat and manage to convince him to do so single-handedly,
although in the biblical story both I and his servants nag and then
convince him to do so. This admits my power, don't you think?

Thereafter, a funny thing happens to Josephus. In the biblical
story, I give Saul a fatted calf I had at home and some crackers. Let
me repeat what Josephus writes at this point:

> Now she had one calf that she was very fond of, and one that
> she took a great deal of care of, and fed it herself; for she was a
> woman that got her living by the labor of her own hands, and
> had no other possession but that one calf; this she killed, and
> made ready its flesh, and set it before his servants and himself.

Well, if so far he has diminished my figure in the story while
amplifying it almost against his convictions (remember, he lets me
speak with Samuel), all of a sudden the tide turns. I'm a working
woman; I give Saul my last possession, such is my generosity. In fact, I
enact, or pre-enact, the proverbial admonition of Nathan, the
prophet to King David, when he accuses David of overbearingly
taking possession of Bathsheba, Uriah's one and only wife (as far as
we know):

And the LORD sent Nathan unto David. And he came unto
him, and said unto him, There were two men in one city; the
one rich, and the other poor. The rich man had exceeding many
flocks and herds: But the poor man had nothing, save one little
ewe lamb, which he had bought and nourished up: and it grew
up together with him, and with his children; it did eat of his
own meat, and drank of his own cup, and lay in his bosom, and
was unto him as a daughter.

And there came a traveller unto the rich man, and he spared
to take of his own flock and of his own herd, to dress for the
wayfaring man that was come unto him; but took the poor
man's lamb, and dressed it for the man that was come to him.
And David's anger was greatly kindled against the man; and he
said to Nathan, As the LORD liveth, the man that hath done
this thing shall surely die: And he shall restore the lamb
fourfold, because he did this thing, and because he had no pity.
And Nathan said to David, Thou art the man.
(2 Samuel 12:1-7a KJV)

With one movement of the writing quill I'm promoted to extreme
generosity while also being demoted to working-class existence. And
the promotional trend continues. Listen to how Josephus
pontificates, by way of a conclusion and just before he comes back to
praising King Saul's behavior:

Now it is but just to recommend the generosity of this woman,
because when the king had forbidden her to use that art
whence her circumstances were bettered and improved, and
when she had never seen the king before, she still did not
remember to his disadvantage that he had condemned her sort
of learning, and did not refuse him as a stranger, and one that
she had had no acquaintance with; but she had compassion
upon him, and comforted him, and exhorted him to do what
he was greatly averse to, and offered him the only creature she
had, as a poor woman, and that earnestly, and with great
humanity, while she had no requital made her for her kindness,
nor hunted after any future favor from him, for she knew he
was to die; whereas men are naturally either ambitious to please

those that bestow benefits upon them, or are very ready to serve
those from whom they may receive some advantage. It would
be well therefore to imitate the example and to do kindnesses
to all such as are in want and to think that nothing is better,
nor more becoming mankind, than such a general beneficence,
nor what will sooner render God favorable, and ready to bestow
good things upon us. And so far may it suffice to have spoken
concerning this woman.

Josephus attributes to me unlimited hospitality and generosity.
Already the biblical story has me behave much like Abraham, a
legendary host who offers divine messengers, and perhaps Yhwh
himself, a comparable meal of meat and flour crackers (Genesis 18,
also echoed in Josephus). But, as we have seen, Josephus takes the
matter further. He makes me poor, so as to emphasize my generosity,
compassion, and concern as a result of—get this!—deeply rooted fear
of god. This converts me from a lowly practitioner of an illicit
vocation into a shining example for all to emulate! Josephus calls my
trade "art," that is, there's a hint that at least it's a legitimate pursuit
(in the spirit of his time and place?). *Pace* the rabbis, he's concluded
that I could hear Samuel's words, thus knew of Saul's predicted fate.
This enables Josephus to moralize and stress that my behavior, as
generous as it is, could not have been motivated by greed or hoped-
for reward or any other selfish intent: in his version I know Saul is to
die shortly, hence can't hope for personal benefits.

It's always gratifying to receive a compliment, especially from
unexpected quarters. Nevertheless, being a far from naïve person, I
can't help but ponder Josephus's motives for praising me so highly.
This praise doesn't help him in further glorifying Saul's character,
which he does anyhow. That he fairly legitimizes my "art" and draws
it into the circle of less-shady, certainly Yahwistic practice, still
doesn't explain his making me into a god-fearing, maternal
saint. Furthermore, I doubt whether his implied audience, his
contemporaries, probably elite males, would have been overjoyed at
being lectured to heed the example of a poor, marginal, working-
class, anonymous female "necromancer." Consequently, I can do no
more than guess at or speculate about Josephus's motives for

foregrounding my figure in such a fashion. Perhaps he can do so because I insist on *feeding* Saul, which renders me sexless (if not genderless), as presumably nurturing mothers are. Perhaps he's being moody and atypical and follows Qoheleth in thinking something like "poverty and goodness are better than wealth and non-understanding" ("Better is a poor and clever child than an old and foolish king, who cannot be careful any longer"—Qoheleth. 4:13, my translation). Perhaps making a [sexless, faceless, ageless] female practitioner of magic into a shining moral example suits Josephus's didactic purpose, for a moment. Let's leave the matter at that. His output, although I find it inexplicable, is beneficial for my insecure reputation. But is it true?

My Own Version, in Brief

For myself, let me insist that the romantic fable Josephus concocts is way out. Let me set the record straight. The biblical story is more on the mark. I was a well-known, "wise" woman whose talent it was to establish communication between the here and the beyond. As such, I was of service to Saul and Samuel who, because of their mutual enmity and the life/death boundaries that separated them from each other, required my mediating services. I saw but didn't hear (and didn't tell). I was kind to Saul, but who wouldn't be kind to such a tragic, obviously disturbed royal man? As for the text's preservation of my anonymity, for once that proved useful. Against the current and future ban on female "sorcery," I could keep my identity undisclosed. Thus I escaped the fate of many an alleged Western "witch" in the days, and years, and generations to come.

Confidentiality has always been and still is invaluable to me. So let me leave out desirable data, such as my real name, marital status, past and current places of residence, and so on. Let me just divulge that I am a communication expert, working in that field all this time, with a difference: my communication skills transcend into a fourth and fifth dimension, if you wish. And while secrecy hardly becomes a communication industry employee—publicity is more in that line!—it does enable me to respect other persons' privacy. On the other hand and paradoxically, and here I deconstruct myself, I'm so curious about other people—this comes with the trade as well—that I've

convinced you, dear ladies, to come and tell your own stories here.
And this falls under the "truth in advertising" rubric, among other
things. Hear hear, I'm beginning to ruminate. Let me stop that.
Anyway, how I got the idea and motivation for the present gathering
is another story altogether.

The Impetus

My inspiration for arranging this gathering came from two sources:
an artwork and a book, both created by women and about women.

I love art, especially art by women. Far be it from me to enter the
scholarly fray of questioning what "female art" is (or, for that matter,
what "female literature" is). In Judy Chicago's case, there can be no
mistake. Here's a passage out of her official biography, as published
on her official Web site:

> Judy Chicago is an artist, author, feminist, educator, and
> intellectual whose career now spans four decades. Her influence
> both within and beyond the art community is attested to by
> hundreds of publications throughout the world. Her art has
> been frequently exhibited in the United States as well as in
> Canada, Europe, Asia, Australia, and New Zealand. In addition,
> a number of the books she has authored have been published
> in foreign editions, bringing her art and philosophy to
> thousands of readers worldwide.

Chicago, a Jewish American, interests me especially because of her
"Dinner Party" project. Let's read on:

> In 1974, Chicago turned her attention to the subject of
> women's history to create her most well-known work, *The
> Dinner Party*, which was executed between 1974 and 1979 with
> the participation of hundreds of volunteers. This monumental
> multimedia project, a symbolic history of women in Western
> civilization, has been seen by more than one million viewers
> during its sixteen exhibitions held at venues spanning six
> countries. . . . The importance of *The Dinner Party*, along with
> Chicago's role as the founder of the Feminist Art movement,

was examined in the 1996 exhibition, *Sexual Politics: Judy Chicago's* Dinner Party *in Feminist Art History*. Curated by Dr. Amelia Jones at the UCLA Armand Hammer Museum, this show was accompanied by an extensive catalog published by the University of California Press. In 2004, *The Dinner Party* will be permanently housed at the Brooklyn Museum as the centerpiece of the Elizabeth A. Sackler Center for Feminist Art, thereby achieving Chicago's long-held goal of helping to counter the erasure of women's achievements.

In this work,

> The goal of *The Dinner Party,* which is a symbolic history of women in Western civilization, was and is twofold: to teach women's history through a work of art that can convey the long struggle for freedom and justice that women have waged since the advent of male-dominated societies, and to break the cycle of history that *The Dinner Party* describes. *The Dinner Party* is a work of art, triangular in configuration, 48 feet on each side, that employs numerous media, including ceramics, china-painting, and needlework, to honor women's achievements. An immense open table covered with fine white cloths is set with 39 place settings, thirteen on a side, each commemorating a goddess, historic personage, or important woman. Though most are largely unknown, their names should, in my estimation, be [as] familiar to us as the male heroes whose exploits we absorb from childhood through art, myth, literature, history, and popular entertainment. *The Dinner Party* suggests that these female heroes are equally worthy of commemoration, as are those hundreds of others (999) whose names are inscribed upon the Heritage Floor. This lustred porcelain surface serves as the foundation for *The Dinner Party* table and the many important human accomplishments it symbolizes.

I'm greatly interested in history: this is directly related to my profession, for whoever is interested in the future must learn about the past. I was overjoyed to hear that Judy Chicago brought together history and females in art, although I've never seen the work itself outside a book. (Has any one of you seen it? I do hope to visit it now that it has acquired the permanent home it deserves). Moreover, I said to myself, by sitting women at the same table, by spacing additional women's *names* elsewhere and all over in the installation, Chicago managed to effect a virtual gathering of female heroes from across times and spaces.

Then one day I was reading a book by Natalie Zemon Davis, the university professor who wrote the celebrated *Return of Martin Guerre*. This academic book is based on historical data, an event that occurred in the sixteenth century. The narrative, set in medieval France during the Hundred Years' War, records (while utilizing verified historical sources) the alleged homecoming of a French peasant turned soldier after many years of absence. After his return his wife finds him an improvement, in bed and in all other respects, from the husband who has left for the front. She resolutely ignores the villagers' suspicions that he is an impostor. The end, of course, isn't a happy one, in keeping with the historical facts and the inevitable consequences of imbalanced quest for identity. The book reads like a novel and, for me, raises issues about war and religious violence in general—understandable since I was involved in the Saul/Samuel affair—and about gender relations and in particular about women and men at war, and truth and falsity, and matters of identity, given or assumed. In 1983 the book was made into a French film, directed by Daniel Vigne, and with Gérard Depardieu and Nathalie Baye in the main roles. Have you seen it? I enjoyed it tremendously, perhaps because I'd seen the film before I read the book. In 1993 it was remade in English by Jon Amiel, set in nineteenth-century post-Civil War Tennessee, thus updated to the American Reconstruction as *Sommersby*, starring Richard Gere and Jodie Foster. Both films are available as VCR and DVD versions. Don't rush to see the latter, if you're interested in my advice!

I hereby declare myself a groupie of Zemon Davis. Her next book I found even more to my taste. That book is called *Women on the Margins: Three Seventeenth-Century Lives*. It recounts the biographies of three women: the [German] Jewish Glikl bas Judah Leib, widely known as Glückel from Hameln; the [French] Catholic Marie de l'Incarnation; and the [Dutch] Protestant Maria Sybilla Merian. The three women wrote diaries, autobiographies, or other extended documents about their unique quests and ways of life. All three women—each in her own way—were adventurous, resourceful, and successful in what they set out or happened to do. And all three, once again each in her own way, were intensely religious or at least deeply rooted in their own particular religious tradition.

Zemon Davis convenes the three women together, after a fashion. She begins the short prologue (four pages) to her book thus:

> *Place*: Thoughtland
> *Time*: October 1994, Heshvan 5755
> *Persons*: Four women past sixty. Three of them stand near a well-thumbed manuscript, sometimes addressing each other, sometimes musing to themselves. The fourth listens for a time from the shadows.

Zemon Davis has the women argue back and forth, critically, about how they are represented in her book while she, "the fourth" who's "in the shadows," is silent but listening all the while. They complain; they have reservations about their own descriptions, about the company they have to keep in the book. Finally she, the author, intervenes in their conversation to apologetically ask them to suspend their suspicions concerning her project about them:

> It was an adventure following you three to so many different climes. . . . At least you all admit that you loved to describe your world. Glikl and Marie, how you loved to write! And Maria Sibylla, how you loved to look and paint! . . . Give me another chance. Read it again.

Reading this prologue was too much. Connecting Zemon Davis and Chicago, I thought to myself: Natalie Zemon Davis gave new literary voice and life to her historical women of letters, since they are long dead and buried and this can only be done through their literary legacy. She could convene her three subjects together, synchronically, only in her imaginary and virtual "thoughtland." Judy Chicago could do it in a mixed media artistic installation for the world to see and be amazed and reminded of women's history through the lenses of a woman artist. But we, in a way, we could do better! We, woman figures of the Hebrew bible who were never killed by the text and are therefore still alive, we who were never or only seldom have been given our voice in the canonical texts, we who've suffered either neglect or else inappropriate attention during centuries of biblical reception, we can do it differently. We can meet in person and exchange our views concerning our own careers in person. We've all read the literatures about us in a variety of religious traditions produced over time in the Western world. We've often been critical about how we were [man]handled in and by the original texts as well as by their interpretations. We can provide our personal antidotes to the stories about us, in the interest of historical veracity (whatever that may mean) as well as contemporary readers. And our own sense of justice, and curiosity, of course. If identity and memory are matters of construction and reconstruction, we're entitled to our personal views as well, and we're entitled to a hearing, even if of a limited scope. This can be therapeutic, I reflected. And the more I contemplated the idea, the more savory it became. How I wished for at least some of us to meet and exchange views and stories!

I know full well that the continued existence of all of us here is meta-real, caused by the biblical authors' neglect to kill us off. In our cases, the death of the authors didn't imply the death of the author's subjects; on the contrary, such neglect transported us from textual objects into supra-natural subjects. As integrated as we may seem to be in the modern and postmodern age, we are aliens from the past and from the future. Our clandestine existence had and has to be protected. So I went to work in the footsteps of Chicago and Zemon Davis, using my unique skills and contacts and, certainly, the Internet. And I found some of you, and cajoled and persisted. And I found this remote place, and the funding, and organized it all. And thank you for coming and for sharing your stories with all of us. Love and shalom to all of you, be blessed. The rest is meta-history or midrash or both, whatever you prefer. Less colorful than *The Dinner Party*, less varied than *Women on the Margins*, but our very own.

THIRTEEN

❧

Goodbye

Convener's note: I'm trying to summarize here our last session, as I have it
from the transcription of the audiotapes we recorded during the conference.
In most instances participants' actual contributions to this final discussion
were shortened. Our main topic of conversation was how we could cluster
ourselves into categories that would make sense and cohere our views of
ourselves, and of others like us.

Naomi

So here we are. Let's regroup, according to our personal history, in
order to heighten the links that tie us together.

A large group of us belongs directly to the kinship system and
lineage of King David: Tamar daughter-in-law of Judah; Ruth and I
through her; Orpah as maternally associated with Goliath, who was
killed by David; Zeruiah sister of David; and Tamar daughter of
David. Rizpah may belong to us too, since the story about her is
David's doing and, according to her, she was a wife of his. Shall we
call ourselves the David-related females?

Rizpah

But perhaps I do belong, more appropriately, to another group. Both
our esteemed convener and I belong to Saul's history: I was his
secondary wife before becoming Abner's then David's wife; the
esteemed medium encountered Saul on the eve of his decisive battle
and death. We are Saul-related females.

Or then again, perhaps we should break through the biblical
barrier of depicting us as male-relational and opt for subject
categories instead? This would put me in a specific class with

Zeruiah. We would form a bereaved mothers category. And you,
Naomi, would partially belong with us as well—you lost two sons in
quick succession, although the son Ruth bore would redeem you out
of our class. Oh well, there's no escaping from it: this is once again a
male-related category. We're the bereaved mothers of sons. And by
the same indexical token of loss, and once again not escaping the
male-related category, you and I, Naomi, are obviously to be classified
as widows too.

Rahab

Indeed, there seems to be hardly any escape from this male-relational
mould into which the bible fits us. Let's say that I wish to be grouped
together with Huldah, to bask in her prophetic glory. Remember, I'm
named as foremother of no less than eight priests/prophets. And,
after all, Huldah too is considered a descendant of mine in post-
biblical literature, as I recounted and as acknowledged by her. So I
have a right, and in that case, we have a rare phenomenon: a
celebrated and public-life-oriented female genealogy starting with me
and going down hundreds of years later all the way to Huldah. But
on the other hand, I can be grouped with Zipporah and Ruth, for
together with the two of you and five others—Asenath wife of Joseph;
Shiphrah and Pu'ah, the midwives who saved Hebrew babies from
Pharaoh (Exodus 1); Pharaoh's daughter, who saved Moses (Exodus
2); and Jael, who killed Sisera (Judges 4–5)—I'm mentioned as a
righteous convert to Judaism. This tagging as female converts will
undoubtedly satisfy sanctimonious tendencies of Jewish and
Christian orthodoxy alike and will completely override my whoring
past, relegating it into insignificance. Dwelling for a moment—by
your leave—on the whoredom subject, I can be categorized as a
sexually liberated woman, together with Madam Potiphar, and, if you
wish to do so without stigmatizing and shaming, also together with
Ruth (remember her activity on the threshing floor?), Tamar
(considered by Judah a whore or sacred prostitute and certainly an
out-of-wedlock mother), and Shulammit of the SoS. But then again,
Tamar daughter-in-law to Judah and Ruth and I belong to Matthew's
genealogy of Jesus, which is another male-relational grouping.

Tamar Daughter of David

We speak quite a lot about bereavement, sorrow, loss, suffering. Properly speaking, my dears, I must admit that the best (actually worst, but let it be) place for me is to remain within the hateful category of victims of sexual violence, together with Dinah. Not a good place, to be sure, although I keep good company even while in that group.

Dinah

Tamar, how can I console you? A hateful position indeed. How I understand you, having had to cope with violent brothers and an ineffectual father myself as well? Will it help if you remind yourself that you belong to the house of David? Possibly not, considering the violent nature of that royal house. Will it help to remember, at least, that the violence perpetrated by the males of the Davidic lineage was directed at their own gender too and not only at ours? Will it help if I asked you to join me in the rape crisis center, so that we can help others overcome what we had to undergo? We do belong together, you and I, and even in that sorry categorization, we can still be of some use.

On the other hand, I must admit that my eventual fate is a little better than that of yours, Tamar daughter of David. According to later, post-biblical traditions I belong to the foremothers of significant people; even a mother of a tribe am I. So on that count, I belong with Tamar daughter-in-law to Judah, Rahab, and Ruth. Perhaps also with Adah and Zillah, mothers of such talented offspring who, in the bible, invented various aspects of human culture.

Adah

Hey, hey—didn't we say that we were in point of fact the creators of culture, rather than mothers of male culture creators? Let me register a rebellious sentiment here. In the sense of our music/dance achievements, we belong with female prophets such as Miriam and Deborah, we truly do! And, needless to say, with the world-famous dancer Shulammit.

Zillah

Adah, I second your motion. And in the sense of practicing birth control, surely, we belong together with Rahab—she must have practiced the art in her profession—and with our lady of love from the SoS, and perhaps also with Madam Potiphar. And what about our esteemed convener: doesn't she know anything about herbalology and sex, in her capacity as a sort of wise woman?

The Convener

Indeed I do, as a byline. How do I wish to be categorized? As a professional woman perhaps. And then I'd be flanked by Rahab, obviously, but also by Adah and Zillah. And Zipporah, who from Bird Woman turned into a pilot-cum-businesswoman. And Huldah the prophet, a prophet and temple administrator and teacher rather than a professional "wife," identified by her relation to her husband as the biblical text does. And Shulammit, the dancer.

A professional status entails issues not only of female poverty or wealth, not only of a liminal status in a male-governed and marriage-and-children-oriented society, but also of class and other points of social mores. In a society where maternity was deemed the major female role, although women were certainly required to help with the family's productivity as well, and where maternity was presided over by anxious paternity claims, how did women fare when their profession rather than children formed the core of their inner world? What does it mean, being a professional female whose male connections pale by analogy to their vocation? A problem, this, more then but also in the now and, I daresay, in the foreseeable future.

Orpah

And what about supposed ethnicity? Piety aside, what about a category of foreign women, that is, non-indigenous women of geographically neighboring areas who joined the Judahites or the Israelites, usually by marriage but at times by deed (as did Rahab initially), thus playing a role in the chosen people's history? Admittedly, my own role as such a foreign woman is small. However, let's see who's with me here: Ruth, and Tamar daughter-in-law to Judah, and Madam Potiphar, and Zipporah—and Rahab. A goodly crowd, wouldn't you say?

Shulammit

My dears, have you considered two other parameters—one concerning love, the other age? I'm proud to group myself with Ruth, who loved Naomi—and perhaps with Naomi who, at least in the story she told us if not in the biblical text, loved Ruth. And I'm proud to be associated with Madam Potiphar, who loved Joseph so well that she risked all for her passion. As we all know, not many biblical women are acknowledged as having a capacity to love so well (or so badly); if they do love so well, like Michal daughter of Saul who loved David unwisely but passionately, their fate is a personal tragedy.

And age. In readerly imagination I'm forever fixated as a young lover: in my teens, like the celebrated Juliet, or in my early twenties. How old were you, my loves, when your biblical stories were recorded? Who knows? Not much is indicated in this regard. Dinah and Tamar daughter of David, to follow conventional wisdom, were attractive and unmarried, under their father's roof and jurisdiction, hence young. But how young? And Ruth, having been married for several years, couldn't have been very ancient, given the young marriageable age of those times. Zipporah must have been a youngster when she met Moses. Neither could Orpah, or the first Tamar, or Madam Potiphar be out of their twenties, at the very most. Naomi, Adah and Zillah, Rizpah, and Zipporah at the end of her career, and certainly Zeruiah, having raised children to maturity and in some cases having survived their deaths, must have been older— but then again, how old? As to our respected convener and Rahab and Huldah, I have no idea whatsoever about their age. Let me not fall into the male trap that equates female wisdom with post-sexual old or older age.

Huldah

And please excuse me for not being as serious as my profession would call for. Would it surprise you if I complained about the biblical vagueness concerning physical beauty or its lack, as far as most of us are concerned? It was later sources only that imagined Ruth as beautiful, as she has told us. Shulammit, our Lady Love, is extolled as beautiful—or at the very least desirable. But even Madam Potiphar, the arch-temptress, isn't beautiful in the bible itself. Not to mention Tamar, and Tamar, and Dinah . . . or Zipporah? or Rizpah? This is my complaint. While beauty is evaluated as a source of attraction, so few biblical females are described as beautiful. And those who are—such as Rachel, Abigail, Bathsheba—aren't with us today. Has it occurred to you that I was a knockout in my time, or shall we too subscribe to the male view of dichotomized brains and beauty in females? And Rahab, well, even the rabbis thought her sexual attractiveness had been legendary—before she converted, of course. Otherwise, the world being what it is, could she have established her own particular trade with business acumen but without beauty? Perish the thought; endow her with good looks, so that conventional wisdom would survive. Please excuse me, Rahab: surely you understand that you're not the butt of my irony.

Ruth

Mind you, Huldah, once again, that the need of the Jewish sages to make me good-looking equals the need of many other readers to establish a true romance between Boaz and me. Vanity aside, I never was good looking. "Interesting" (in the American sense) is more like it. So let's be careful about this topic. On the other hand Orpah was a real dish, but, certainly, they couldn't afford to recognize it.

Zillah

How about sisterhood as a classificatory measure? The sisterhood of sharing one household, perhaps the same husband, or first-level kin ties? You've heard what Adah and I had to divulge about our family origins. In some post-biblical sources Ruth and Orpah are made into blood sisters as well, in addition to being sisters-in-law; they admit here to being half-sisters. So there's another cross-reference, another category if you will: a horizontal sisterhood, a real one, in addition to the vertical, or looser, genealogical kinship that Naomi, for instance, spoke about. Not links through the males in our lives, not a "sisterhood" in the sentimental sense adopted by early feminists of the twentieth century, but blood and survival ties are what bind many of us together.

The Convener

Have we become feminists, then? Maybe it's time for us to stop, before we get embroiled in that question. We've managed to evade the *F* word almost completely, using it once only in the expression "proto-feminist." Let us break up now; let us leave this issue to our eventual readers, if it does matter. Besides, Zipporah is waiting, and we have to vacate the premises and return to our individual mysterious lives, wherever we've chosen to dwell.

This is endgame. Let's not become over-emotional or soppy. Let's not gush, or slosh, or shed tears. We shall meet again, in the year 2525 perhaps. What is another half a millennium or so for our ilk, paradoxically made immortal by lack of inscribing? We'll have more to tell then. Those of you who wish to remain in touch will exchange addresses, e-mails, and means of contact. The others won't. And this is as it should be.

Back to the mainland, then.

Zipporah

I'm ready. But before we board, before I fly you over, let me quote a few lines from an Israeli song to you, by way of personal leave-taking. Not great poetry, you'll surely agree, but topical.

> We have two ways of playing.
> One, with pre-written notes.
> And sometimes there are no notes
> No notes, and you have to play without notes.
> This is what we did this time.
> And although strings popped,
> The melody was good
> And it is well heard, all over,
> And we shall continue to play it.
> For this tune, it can't be stopped.
> This tune, it can't be stopped.
> Must continue playing, must continue playing,
> Because this tune, it can't be stopped.

The Convener

Let me add a poetic line too, by association. In the late Hebrew poet, Nathan Alterman's, words:

> The song isn't over, it's just beginning!

Let's go!

Selected Sources

Note: All sources appear in the order of relevant subject matter for each chapter. Web site links worked as of September 2004.

Abbreviations in Sources

b.	Babylonian Talmud (*Bavli*)
m.	*Mishnah*
t.	*Tosefta*
y.	Jerusalem Talmud (*Yerushalmi*)

Preface

Some Web pages for religious art:
http://www.zeitun-eg.org (for Gustave Doré's Bible illustrations in vizbible.zip)
http://www.smc.qld.edu.au/relart.htm
http://religion-cults.com/art.htm
http://www.textweek.com
http://www.aphids.com/susan/relimage
http://www.monsmart.com/gallerysos.html (for the Song of Songs)
http://www.religiousmall.com
http://www.etown.edu/vl/worldrel.html
http://religion.rutgers.edu/vri/arch_art.html
http://www.louvre.fr
http://www.christusrex.org/www2/art/index.html
http://www.religiousresources.org/index.php
http://www.ac-nice.fr/chagall/histabr.htm
http://perso.wanadoo.fr/maurice.lamouroux/files/ill_e%20AT.htm

Kugel, James L. *The Bible As It Was*. Cambridge: Harvard Univ. Press, 1997.

On narratology:
Bal, Mieke. *Narratology: Introduction to the Theory of Narrative*. 2nd ed. Translated by Christine van Boheemen. Toronto: Univ. of Toronto Press, 1997.

On reading gaps:
Sternberg, Meir. *The Poetics of Biblical Narrative: Ideological Literature and the Drama of Reading*. Indiana Studies in Biblical Literature. Bloomington: Indiana Univ. Press, 1987, chapter 6, 186–229.

On violence and war:
Camp, Claudia, and Carole R. Fontaine, eds. *Women, War, and Metaphor.* Semeia
Studies 61. Atlanta: Scholars, 1993.

On autobiographical criticism:
Kitzberger, Ingrid Rosa, ed. *Autobiographical Biblical Criticism: Between Text and Self.*
Leiden: Deo, 2002.
Anderson, Janice Capel, ed. *Taking It Personally: Autobiographical Biblical Criticism.*
Semeia Studies 72. Atlanta: Scholars, 1995.

Rashomon:
Rashomon is a 1950 Japanese film directed by Akira Kurosawa, considered more than a
classic. In essence, the facts surrounding a rape and murder are told from four
different and contradictory points of view, as well as a chilling scene in which a dead
witness tells his story. In the end there is no one to trust; it all depends on whom you
believe. It is suggested, then, that the nature of truth is something less than absolute.
Pay attention to how the characters flash back to their story (http://www.foreignfilms
.com /films/1735.asp and many other sites).

Contemporary feminist-Jewish midrash—some examples:
Angel, Leonard. *The Book of Miriam.* Buffalo, N.Y.: Mosaic, 1997.
Baskin, Judith. *Midrashic Women: Formations of the Feminine in Rabbinic Literature.*
Brandeis Series on Jewish Women. Hanover, N.H.: Brandeis Univ. Press, 2002.
Callaway, Mary. *Sing, O Barren One: A Study in Comparative Midrash.* SBL (Society of
Biblical Literature) Dissertation Series 91. Atlanta: Scholars Press, 1986.
Frankel, Ellen. *The Five Books of Miriam: A Woman's Commentary on the Torah.* New York:
Putnam, 1996.
Hyman, Naomi M., ed. *Biblical Women in the Midrash: A Sourcebook.* Northvale, N.J.:
Jason Aronson, 1997.
Ronson, Barbara Thaw. *The Women of the Torah: Commentaries from the Talmud, Midrash,
and Kabbalah.* Northvale, N.J.: Jason Aronson, 1999.
Rosen, Norma. *Biblical Women Unbound: Counter-Tales.* Philadelphia: Jewish Publication
Society, 1996.
Wenkart, Henny, ed. *Sarah's Daughters Sing: A Sampler of Poems by Jewish Women.*
Hoboken, N.J.: Ktav, 1990.
Wiskind-Elper, Ora, and Susan Handelman, eds. *Torah of the Mothers: Contemporary
Jewish Women Read Classical Jewish Texts.* New York: Urim, 2000.
Wolkstein, Diane. *Esther's Story.* New York: Morrow Junior, 1996.
———. "Queen Esther." In *A Feminist Companion to Esther, Judith and Susanna.* Edited by
Athalya Brenner. Feminist Companion to the Bible 1/7. Sheffield, UK: Sheffield
Academic, 1994.

Women in Judaism:
Naomi Graetz. See http://www.bgu.ac.il/~graetz/

Author's original publications, extensively revised for this volume:
Brenner, Athalya, and J. W. van Henten, "Madame Potiphar through a Culture Trip,
or, Which Side Are You On?" In *Biblical Studies/Cultural Studies: The Third Sheffield*

Colloquium, edited by J. Cheryl Exum and Stephen D. Moore, 203–19. JSOT
Supplement Series 266. Sheffield, UK: Sheffield Academic Press, 1998.

————. "Wide Gaps, Narrow Escapes: I Am Known as Rahab, the Broad." In *First
Person: Essays in Biblical Autobiography,* edited by Philip R. Davies, 47–58. Sheffield,
UK: Sheffield Academic Press, 2002.

————. "Tamar." In *Women in Scripture,* edited by Carol Meyers, 161–62. Boston:
Houghton Mifflin, 2000.

————. *The Israelite Woman: Social Role and Literary Type in Biblical Narrative.* Sheffield,
UK: JSOT Press, 1985, 59–60, 72–74 (on Huldah and The Convener).

————. "'Come Back, Come Back the Shulammite' (Song of Songs 7.1-10)." In *On
Humour and the Comic in the Hebrew Bible,* edited by Yehudah T. Radday and Athalya
Brenner, 251–75. JSOT Supplement Series 92. Sheffield, UK: Almond, 1990 (on
the anonymous woman in the SoS).

Introduction

Fragmented women:

Exum, J. Cheryl. *Fragmented Women: Feminist (Sub)versions of Biblical Narratives.* Valley
Forge, Pa.: Trinity Press International, 1993.

Nameless women:

Meyers, Carol, ed. *Women in Scripture.* Boston: Houghton Mifflin, 2000.

Reinhartz, Adele. *Why Ask My Name? Anonymity and Identity in Biblical Narrative.*
Oxford: Oxford Univ. Press, 1998.

On Jephthah's daughter:

Exum, J. Cheryl. *Fragmented Women: Feminist (Sub)versions of Biblical Narratives.* Valley
Forge, Pa.: Trinity Press International, 1993, 16–41.

Chapter 1/Adah and Zillah

For the names Adah and Zilla:

Cassuto, Umberto. *From Adam to Noah: A Commentary on the First Chapters of Genesis.*
Jerusalem: Magness, 1944.

For women singers and Na'amah:

Meyers, Carol. "Na'amah 1." In *Women in Scripture,* edited by Carol Meyers, 129.
Boston: Houghton Mifflin, 2000.

Midrash on Adah and Zillah as Lamech's co-wives:

Genesis Rabbah 23.2, *Yalkut Shimeoni* for Job, 910.

For birth control in the bible:

Brenner, Athalya. *The Intercourse of Knowledge.* Biblical Interpretation Series 26. Leiden:
Brill, 1997, 52–89.

Midrash on Lamech's song:

Genesis Rabbah 23.4; also *Tanḥuma* for Genesis 11.

Women's attractiveness after bearing children:

Genesis Rabbah 45.4; *Song of Songs Rabbah* 2.8; and *Yalkut Shimeoni* for the Torah, 79—
with minimal differences.

Na'amah:

As married and righteous: Ramban, *Genesis Rabbah* 23.

As beautiful: *Tanḥuma,* additions to *Ḥukkot* 1.1; *Yalkut Shimeoni* to the Torah, 161.

As demonic and a seducer: Ramban after *Pirke de'rabi Eliezer* 52, *New Zohar* 1.19.2; Rashi in his commentary to *b. Yoma* 67b.

As idolatrous: *Genesis Rabbah* 23.3, and elsewhere in midrash collections.

Chapter 2/Dinah

On Dinah's going out:

Rashi, following *Genesis Rabbah* to the chapter, and other midrash sources.

Diamant, Anita. *The Red Tent.* New York: St. Martin's, 1997.

Rape or no rape:

Bechtel, Lyn M. "What If Dinah Is Not Raped? (Genesis 34)." *JSOT (Journal for the Study of the Old Testament)* 62 (1994): 19–36.

Tchernichowsky, Shaul. *Collected Poems* [Hebrew]. 2 vols. Tel Aviv: Dvir, 1966. "The Dinah Affair" is 2.736–41 and was written in Tel Aviv in two days: June 24–25, 1937. See http://www.jafi.org.il/education/100/people/BIOS/shaul.html.

van Wolde, Ellen. "Love and Hatred in a Multiracial Society: The Dinah and Shechem Story in Genesis 34 in the Context of Genesis 28–35." In *Reading from Right to Left: Essays on the Hebrew Bible in Honour of David J. A. Clines,* edited by J. Cheryl Exum and H. G. M. Williamson. JSOT Supplement Series 373. Sheffield, UK: Sheffield Academic, 2003.

For Dinah as daughter/sister:

Meyers, Carol. "Dinah." In *Anchor Bible Dictionary* CD-ROM.

For Genesis 34 as polemics against the Samaritans:

Amit, Yairah. "Implicit Reduction and Latent Polemic in the Story of the Rape of Dinah." In *Texts, Temples and Tradition: A Tribute to Menahem Haran,* edited by Michael V. Fox, et al., 11–28. Winona Lake, Ind.: Eisenbrauns, 1996.

On the situation of the British mandate in Palestine/EI (Eretz Israel) in the 1930s:

http://www.multied.com/dates/1936.html
http://cvu.strath.ac.uk/~tomlin_t/pal_history.html
http://www.encyclopedia.com/html/section/Palestin_History.asp

Dinah's domestication:

Genesis Rabbah 57.

For contemporary Shechem/Nablus:

http://www.us-israel.org/jsource/Society_&_Culture/geo/Shechem.html
http://i-cias.com/e.o/nablus.htm
http://www.visit-palestine.com/nablus/nab-main.htm

Chapter 3/Madam Potiphar

Kugel, James. *In Potiphar's House: The Interpretive Life of Biblical Texts.* Cambridge: Harvard Univ. Press, 1994.

Brenner, Athalya, and J. W. van Henten, "Madame Potiphar through a Culture Trip, or, Which Side Are You On?" In *Biblical Studies/Cultural Studies: The Third Sheffield*

Colloquium, edited by J. Cheryl Exum and Stephen D. Moore, 203–19. JSOT
Supplement Series 266, Sheffield, UK: Sheffield Academic Press, 1998.

Josephus:
http://www.ccel.org/j/josephus/JOSEPHUS.HTM
http://members.aol.com/FLJOSEPHUS/home.htm
http://josephus.yorku.ca

Philo of Alexandria:
http://www.torreys.org/bible/philopag.html
http://www.utm.edu/research/iep/p/philo.htm

Testament of Joseph:
http://www.ccel.org/fathers2/ANF-08/anf08-15.htm

Some rabbinic sources dealing with the story:
*Genesis Rabbah, Psalms Rabbah, Midrash Tanḥuma, Midrash Ha-Gadol, Sefer Ha-Yashar,
Sekhel Tov, Yalkut Shimeoni* (search in order for the biblical chapter).

Islamic sources:
Brosh, Na'amah, and Rachel Milstein. *Biblical Stories in Islamic Painting* [Hebrew and
English]. Jerusalem: The Israel Museum, 1991.

Laws for men and women on their own (Heb. *yiḥḥud*):
b. Qiddushin. 81.1; *b. Sanhedrin* 21.2.
Mann, Thomas. *Joseph and His Brothers.* Translated by H. T. Lowe-Porter. New York:
Knopf, 1948.

Paintings of Madam Potiphar and Joseph (a selection):
Tintoretto. *Joseph and Potiphar's Wife.* Oil on canvas. Museo del Prado, Madrid,
c. 1555.
Cigoli. *Joseph and Potiphar's Wife.* Oil on canvas. Galleria Borghese, Rome, 1610.
Gentileschi, Orazio. *Joseph and Potiphar's Wife.* Oil on canvas. Royal Collection,
Windsor, 1626–30.
Gentileschi, Artemisia. *Joseph and Potiphar's Wife.* Oil on canvas. Fogg Art Museum,
Cambridge, Mass., c. 1622–23.
Barbieri, Giovanni Francesco [called Guercino, Bolognese]. *Joseph and Potiphar's Wife.*
Oil on canvas, 1649.
van Rijn, Rembrandt. *Joseph Accused by Potiphar's Wife.* Oil on canvas, National Gallery
of Art, Washington, D.C., 1655.
Cignani, Carlo. *Joseph and Potiphar's Wife.* Oil on canvas, Gemäldegalerie, Dresden,
1678–80.
van Mieris, Willem. *Joseph and Potiphar's Wife.* Oak Panel Wallace Collection, Hertford
House, England, 1691.

Chapter 4/Zipporah

Zipporah in general:
Sarna, Nahum. "Zipporah." In *Encyclopedia Judaica* CD-ROM, Jerusalem: Keter, 1970.

Zipporah in the midrash:
Exodus Rabbah 1.32; *Midrash Psalms* 7.18; *Tanḥuma* Buber, to Exodus 6.

"Zipporah, in the Midrash." *Encyclopedia Judaica* CD-ROM, 1970.

Harpies:
http://www.occultopedia.com/h/harpy.htm
Jong, Erica. *Fear of Flying.* New York: Holt, Rinehart, Winston, 1973.
For Max, the Bird Child:
Patterson, James. *When the Wind Blows.* New York: Warner, 1998).

For a new assessment and English translation of "The Arabian Nights":
Warner, Marina. "A Thousand and One Tales to Tell." *The Financial Times,* July 26,
    2003, W5 (adapted from an introduction to a new edition, published by the Folio
    Society).

For Sheherazade and her literary fate in the nineteenth century:
Poe, Edgar Allan. "The Thousand and Second Tale of Scheharazade." In *Tales of
    Mystery and Imagination,* 332–49. London: Everyman's Library, 1998.
Gautier, T. *La Mille et Deuxième Nuit.* Paris: Le Seuil, 1993. First published 1842.
Mernissi, Fatema. *Sheherazade Goes West: Different Cultures, Different Harems.* New York:
    Washington Square, 2001, 79–95.

For the "Hassan of Basrah" story:
Burton, Richard. *A Thousand and One Nights.* Vol. 8. Benares: Kamashastra Society,
    1885–86, 7–145.
Mernissi, Fatema. *Sheherazade Goes West: Different Cultures, Different Harems.* New York:
    Washington Square, 2001. See esp. chap. 1.
Marzolph, Ulrich, Richard van Leeuwen, and Hassan Wassouf. *The Arabian Nights: An
    Encyclopedia.* Santa Barbara, Calif.: ABC-CLIO, 2004. See "Stories," for the story of
    "Hassan of Basra," its tale-type origins, and [part] equivalents/parallels. The
    discussion in the work focuses on Hassan rather than "his bride," as is done here.

The immaturity of the young Hebrew god:
Miles, Jack. *God: A Biography.* New York: Knopf, 1996, 78–94.

Zipporah's Biography:
Exum, J. Cheryl. *Fragmented Women: Feminist (Sub)versions of Biblical Narratives.* Valley
    Forge, Pa.: Trinity Press International, 1993.
Bal, Mieke. *Narratology: Introduction to the Theory of Narrative.* 2nd ed. Translated by
    Christine van Boheemen. Toronto: Univ. of Toronto Press, 1997.
Pardes, Ilana. *Countertraditions in the Bible: A Feminist Approach.* Cambridge: Harvard
    Univ. Press, 1992.

On the circumcision episode:
Pardes, Ilana. *Countertraditions in the Bible: A Feminist Approach.* Cambridge: Harvard
    Univ. Press, 1992, 79–97.

Rabbinic Sources on Zipporah's "divorce":
Mekhilta Amalek 3; *Aboth deRabbi Nathan* a, addition to 4; *Sifre Lev.* 99.

For Amelia Earhart:
http://www.ameliaearhart.com
http://www.history.navy.mil/faqs/faq3-1.htm

For "Spikkeltje":

Schmidt, Annie M. G. *Heksen en zo: sprookjes* [Witches and Such: Fairy Tales]. Amsterdam: De Arbeiderspers, 1964, 7-14.

Woman poets and singing birds:

Shacham, Chaya. *Women and Masks from Lot's Wife to Cinderella: Representations of Female Images in Women's Hebrew Poetry* [Hebrew]. Tel Aviv: Ha-Kibbutz Ha-Me'uchad, 2001, 226-64.

Andersen, Hans Christian. "The Nightingale." In *Fairy Tales and Stories*. Translated by H. W. Dulcken. New York: Routledge, 1882(?). Original Illustrations by Vilhelm Pedersen and Lorenz Frølich (1844), http://hca.gilead.org.il/#nighting.

Wilde, Oscar. "The Nightingale and the Rose." In *The Happy Prince and Other Stories*. London: Nutt, 1888. A PDF version is available at http://www.planetmonk.com/wilde.

Chapter 5/Rahab

Rabbinic sources for Rahab's story:

Sifre Zuta 10; *Ruth Rabbah* 2; and the *Mekhilta*, among others.

Suppression of female names:

Reinhartz, Adele. "Anonymous Women and the Collapse of the Monarchy: A Study in Narrative Technique." In *A Feminist Companion to Samuel and Kings*, edited by Athalya Brenner, 43-65. Feminist Companion to the Bible 1/5. Sheffield, UK: Sheffield Academic Press, 1994.

Bohmbach, Karla G. "Names and Naming in the Biblical World." In *Women in Scripture*, edited by Carol Meyers, 33-39. Boston: Houghton Mifflin, 2000.

War in ancient Israel:

Rambam (Maimonides), *Mishnah Torah*, Kings, 6.4

Niditch, Susan. *War in the Hebrew Bible: A Study in the Ethics of Violence.* New York: Oxford Univ. Press, 1993.

Jewish commentators on Rahab's prostitute/non-prostitute status:

Josephus Flavius, *Antiquities* 5.1.2; Rashi and Abrabanel to the chapter.

For birth control:

Brenner, Athalya. *The Intercourse of Knowledge: On Gendering Desire and Sexuality in the Hebrew Bible.* Biblical Interpretation Series 26. Leiden: Brill, 1997, 52-89.

For stones as weapons:

Yadin, Yigael. *The Art of Warfare in Biblical Lands: In Light of Archaeological Study*. 2 vols. New York: McGraw-Hill, 1963.

The escape scene and the humor in it:

Zakovitch, Yair. "Humor and Theology or the Successful Failure of Israelite Intelligence: A Literary Folkloristic Approach to Joshua." In *Text and Tradition: The Hebrew Bible and Folklore,* edited by Susan Niditch, 75-98. Atlanta: Scholars, 1993.

Chapter 6/Ruth, Orpah, Naomi

Ruth and Torah:

Irmtraud Fischer, "Das Buch Rut—eine 'feministische' Auslegung der Tora?': in *Hermeneutik—sozialgeschichtlich. Kontextualität in den Bibelwissenschaften aus der Sicht (latein) amerikanischer und europäischer Exegetinnen und Exegeten,* edited by Erhard S. Gerstenberger and Ulrich Schoenborn (Exegese in unserer Zeit 1: Münster 1999), 39–58.

Ruth and Orpah (and their royal origin?) in rabbinic literature:

Ruth Rabbah 4.6

Bronner, Leila Leah. "A Thematic Approach to Ruth in Rabbinic Literature." In *A Feminist Companion to Ruth,* edited by Athalya Brenner, 146–69 (esp. 163–64). Feminist Companion to the Bible 1/3. Sheffield, UK: Sheffield Academic, 1993.

Asenath in post-biblical literature:

Kraemer, Ross Shepard. *When Aseneth Met Joseph: A Late Antique Tale of the Biblical Patriarch and His Egyptian Wife, Reconsidered.* New York: Oxford Univ. Press, 1998.

Orpah's letters:

Dube, Musa W. "The Unpublished Letters of Orpah to Ruth." In *A Feminist Companion to Ruth and Esther,* edited by Athalya Brenner, 145–50. Feminist Companion to the Bible 2/3. Sheffield, UK: Sheffield Academic Press, 1999.

Female love in rabbinic literature:

t. Sotah 5.7,b; *b. Sanhedrin* 69b; *b. Yebamot* 76a; *y. Gittin* 8.10, 49c.

"Triangle of Love" theory:

Sternberg, R. J. "The Triangular Theory of Love." *Psychological Review* 93 (1986): 119–35.

Chapter 7/Rizpah

For Rizpah's initial description:

Edelman, Diana V. "Rizpah." In *Anchor Bible Dictionary* CD-ROM, 1992.

Rizpah after Abner's death:

y. Yebamot 2.3,4; *t.* to *b. Yebamot* 21a; Radak to 2 Samuel 3:5; *Mezudat Zion* to 2 Samuel 12:8.

For Michal's life:

Eskenazi, Tamara C., and David J. A. Clines, eds. *Telling Queen Michal's Story.* JSOT Supplement Series 119. Sheffield, UK: JSOT Press, 1991.
Josephus, *Antiquities* 7.12.1.

The Gibeonites and their demands, Rizpah's praises:

Numbers Rabbah 8.4; *y. Sanhedrin* 6.23,3 and 4; *Midrash Samuel* 28.

Examples of "Rizpah" organizations and their homepages:

"Daughters of Rizpah" (an African American faith community run by a pastor named Jacqueline McCullough: http://www.rizpah.org/home.htm.

Another evangelical organization is Joan A. Carr's "House of Rizpah: A Place of Healing and Refuge":
http://www.forministry.com/USMDNONDETHORI/
An example of a health/community care organization is "Rizpah's Shriners" of Madisonville, Kentucky, claiming an international membership of over half a million in its "fraternity clubs" and supporting the "official philanthropy" of children's orthopedic hospitals in North America: http://www.rizpahtemple.org.

For Hebrew theatre on biblical themes:
Ben Meir, Ofrah. "Biblical Thematics in Stage Design for the Hebrew Theatre." http://www.tau.ac.il/arts/publications/ASSAPHTH11/BEN-MEIR.html.
Elchanan, Haim (Y. H. Ben David). *Rizpah Daughter of Ayah* [Hebrew]. Tel Aviv: Snir, 1941.
Ashman, Aharon. *Michal Daughter of Saul, in Three Plays* [Hebrew]. Vol. 1. Tel Aviv: Yesod, 1973.

Chapter 8/Tamar and Tamar

Magical cooking by Tamar:
Bledstein, Adrien. "Was Habbirya a Healing Ritual Performed by a Woman in King David's House?" *Biblical Research* 38 (1992): 15–31.

Tamar's speech:
Josephus, *Antiquities* 7.169.

Royal sibling marriage in ancient Israel/Judah:
Rambam (Maimonides), *Kings* 8.8.
van Dijk-Hemmes, Fokkelien. "Tamar and the Limits of Patriarchy: Between Rape and Seduction." In *Anti-Covenant: Counter-Reading Women's Lives in the Hebrew Bible*, edited by Mieke Bal, 135–56. Sheffield, UK: Almond, 1989. The lampooning section is in the appendix to the article, p. 156.

For a general analysis of the story:
Bar-Efrat, Shimon. *Narrative Art in the Bible*. JSOT Supplement Series 70. Sheffield, UK: Almond, 1989.

The rape/non-rape issue:
See chapter 2 of this book (Dinah).

Chapter 9/Zeruiah

For the identification of Jesse with Nahash:
b. Shabbat 58b; *b. Baba Batra* 17a; *y. Yebamot* 8.3,9c; and so also Rashi, Radak, Ralbag.

Zeruiah's name:
Edelman, Diana V. "Zeruiah." In *Women in Scripture,* edited by Carol Meyers, 168. Boston: Houghton Mifflin, 2000.

For Rivka Guber on a postal stamp:
http://www-personal.umich.edu/~szwetch/Stamps.of.Israel/24.html
Guber, R. *Village of the Brothers* [Hebrew]. Tel Aviv: Shengold, 1979.

Chapter 10/Huldah

Huldah as an Asherah prophetess?:
Edelman, Diana V. "Hulda the Prophet—Of Yahweh or Asherah?" In *A Feminist Companion to Samuel and Kings,* edited by Athalya Brenner, 231–50. Feminist Companion to the Bible 5. Sheffield, UK: Sheffield Academic, 1994.

Huldah's choice as the prophet to be consulted:
Rashi to 2 Kings 22:14; Radak to 2 Kings 23:2; Rashi to 2 Chronicles 34:22 (so also *Metzudat David*); *Pesikta Rabbati* 26; *Yalkut Shimeoni*; and more. Referred to by Radak to 2 Kings 22:14 and Zephaniah 1:1.

On Huldah's genealogy from Joshua and Rahab:
See chapter 5 of this book (Rahab), and *b. Megillah* 14b.

Seven female prophets in the bible:
b. Megillah 14a-b; cf. *Seder Olam Rabbah*; and more. For an alternative list of nine female prophets: Eisenstein, *Treasure of Midrash* [Hebrew], 474.

For the "Mishneh" and Huldah's gates:
m. Middot 1.3; Rashi to 2 Chronicles 34:22.

Huldah's grave:
t. Baba Batra 1.11; *t. Nega'im* 1.2; and the so-called small tractates of the Mishnah: *Aboth de Rabbi Nathan* 35 [39], *Semitica* 14.10.

Chapter 11/Anonymous Woman from Song of Songs

Bird Woman in the "Hassan of Basrah" story:
See chapter 4 of this book (Zipporah).

Obscenity and pornography in the Song of Songs:
Boer, R. *Knockin' on Heaven's Door: The Bible and Popular Culture.* Biblical Limits. London: Routledge, 1999, 53–70.

Burros, Virginia, and Stephen D. Moore. "Unsafe Sex: Feminism, Pornography and the Song of Songs." *Biblical Interpretation* 11 (2003): 24–52.

Moore, Stephen D. *God's Beauty Parlor: And Other Queer Spaces in and around the Bible.* Contraversions: Jews and Other Differences Series. Stanford, Calif.: Stanford Univ. Press, 2001.

Freud, Sigmund. *Jokes and Their Relation to the Unconscious.* Translated and edited by James Strachey. New York: Norton, 1960.

Shakespeare's sonnets on the Internet:
http://www.shakespeares-sonnets.com

Andrew Marvell (1621–1678), "To His Coy Mistress":
http://www.luminarium.org/sevenlit/marvell/coy.htm
http://eir.library.utoronto.ca/rpo/display/poem1386.html

Landy, Francis. *Paradoxes of Paradise: Identity and Difference in the Song of Songs.* Bible and Literature Series 7. Sheffield, UK: Almond, 1983.

Interpretation of the Song of Songs:
Pope, Marvin H. *The Song of Songs: A New Translation with a Commentary*. Anchor Bible 7C. Garden City, N.Y.: Doubleday, 1977.

Chapter 12/The Convener

Josephus on the medium of Endor:
Josephus, *Antiquities*, 6.327-42 [6.14.2-4].

Examples of associating females with magic:
Exodus 22:17 and Ezekiel 13; see also *b. Sanhedrin* 65a; *y. Sanhedrin* 7.25,3.

For the spirit-recalling scene:
Leviticus Rabbah 16.7; *Tanḥuma* Buber *Emor* 4; *Tanḥuma* Warsaw *Emor* 2; *Midrash Samuel* 24; *Yalkut Shimeoni* to 1 Samuel 28; *m. Sanhedrin* 7.7; Rashi to 1 Samuel 28.14; and similarly other Jewish medieval commentators: Radak to 1 Samuel 28:24; Ibn Ezra to Leviticus 19:31 and 20:27; and more.

For the medium's name:
Pirke de Rabbi Eliezer 33.

A "witch"?:
See reference to Pseudo-Philo, *Encyclopedia Judaica* CD-ROM, 64.3-5.

Abraham's generosity:
Genesis 18; see also Josephus, *Antiquities* 1.196-97 [1.11.2].

Chapter 13

Davis, Natalie Zemon. *The Return of Martin Guerre*. Cambridge: Harvard Univ. Press, 1983.

————. *Women on the Margins: Three Seventeenth-Century Lives*. Cambridge: Harvard Univ. Press, 1995.

Judy Chicago's homepage, including official biography and descriptions of projects (parts of which quoted here), and book editions: http://www.judychicago.com.

...שִׁיר, שִׁיר, עֲלֵה נָא,
בַּפַּטִּישִׁים נַגֵּן ,נַגֵּנָה,
בַּמַּחֲרֵשׁוֹת רַנֵּנָה,
הַשִּׁיר לֹא תַם, הוּא רַק מַתְחִיל...

Arise, arise, Song;
Make, make music with the hammers;
Sing in the ploughs;
The song is not over, it's just beginning

*From "Song of Work," lyrics by Nathan Altermann and tune by
Nahum Nardi (Text © Nathan Altermann)*